Vietnam's Journey towards Higher Education 5.0

Edited by

Duc Hong Thi Phan and Bruno Mascitelli

Connor Court Publishing

> To my beloved home country, Vietnam—where my first teachers gave me books and the courage to ask "why."

After more than twenty years of living in Australia, I have come to understand that higher education is not only a school system; it is a social promise and a collective journey. This book entitled Vietnam's Journey towards Higher Education 5.0 reflects this belief. It tells a story of how universities, teachers, and students are working together to connect tradition with transformation—bridging local values and global knowledge through empathy, technology, and shared purpose.

I dedicate this book to the educators who continue to nurture curiosity in every classroom, to students who study after long working days andto parents who quietly invest in learning. Your persistence builds Vietnam's bright future.

I also dedicate these pages to my colleagues and friends at theKnowledge Bridge Research Institute (KBERI). Our mission—to connect Vietnamese learners and researchers with global mentors, methods, and integrity—reminds me that knowledge is to share and research builds bridges, not walls.

May this book inspire dialogue between universities, communities, and policymakers; between Vietnam and the world; and between our past aspirations and the digital future we are shaping together.

Dr Duc Hong Thi Phan - Editor, KBERI Founder and President

Vietnam's Journey towards Higher Education 5.0
Edited by Duc Hong Thi Phan and Bruno Mascitelli

Published in 2025 by Connor Court Publishing Pty Ltd

Copyright © Duc Hong Thi Phan and Bruno Mascitelli (editors)

All rights reserved. No part of this book may be reproduced or transmitted in any form or by any means, electronic or mechanical, including photo copying, recording or by any information storage and retrieval system, without prior permission in writing from the publisher.

Connor Court Publishing Pty Ltd
PO Box 7257
Redland Bay QLD 4165
sales@connorcourt.com
www.connorcourt.com

Printed in Australia

ISBN: 9781923568082

Front Cover Design: Bao Quan Tran

Table of Contents

Acknowledgments — 7

Introduction — 9

SECTION 1

1: Higher Education 5.0: Foundations and Future Prospects for the Vietnamese Education System — 21

2: Shaping the Future of Learning: Education 5.0 and the Role of Smart Universities in Driving Innovation — 35

3: From Classrooms to Collaboration: Understanding the Interplay Between Vietnamese and Australian Education Systems — 51

SECTION 2

4: Bridging the Digital Divide: Ethical Challenges and Educational Inequities in Vietnam — 63

5: The University as a Hub for Lifelong Learning - Transitioning from Degree-Centric to Lifelong Learning Models in Vietnam — 83

6: Pathways for Equitable, Inclusive, and Secure Higher Education 5.0 in Vietnam: Focus on Adolescents and Parental Perception in the Early Phase — 99

7: Redefining the Learning Experience: Innovative Pedagogy and Curricular Co-Creation in Vietnamese Higher Education 5.0 — 115

8: Exploring the Teachers' and Students' Perceptions of the Implementation of Learning Design on their Blended Learning Experiences in Vietnamese Higher Education — 127

9: Digital Transformation of Blended Learning in Vietnam's Higher Education 5.0 — 141

10: Gamification in Higher education: Boosting Student Learning at the Vietnam National University — 153

11: A report on one year of applying Education 5.0 at a natural school in Hanoi, Vietnam — 165

12: The relationship between QC and internal QA: A case study at Vietnam National University, Hanoi — 177

SECTION 3

13: University Education 5.0: Creativity and Innovation for the Future — 191

14: Virtual Personal Space: Leveraging Virtual Reality/Augmented Reality for Stress Relieving and Mindfulness Practice within Higher Education in Vietnam — 207

15: Tech-Savvy from the Get-Go: Enhancing University Teachers' Digital Competence (TDC) in Higher Education (HE) 5.0 — 221

16: Open Access Publications of Vietnamese Technology and Engineering Universities in the Context of Higher Education 5.0 — 235

17: Learning analytics with AI: Theory and Models for Smart Higher Education — 245

18: Transforming Education 5.0: Personalized and Adaptive Learning through Artificial Intelligence (AI) — 257

19: Unlocking English as a Foreign Language (EFL) Teachers' potential in AI adoption: Factors Influencing Teachers' Readiness and challenges — 269

20: Use ChatGPT to Teach Vietnamese for non-Vietnamese Students — 283

Acknowledgements

We would like to express our sincere gratitude to Dr Phung Danh Thang and all the staff and participants of the International Conference "Higher Education 5.0: Innovation and Adaptation for the Future". This event, held on August 21st, 2024, in Hanoi, provided the inspiration for this book "Vietnam's Journey towards Higher Education 5.0". We extend our heartfelt thanks to the International Francophone Institute (IFI) and Vietnam National University, Hanoi (VNU), for hosting the conference. The collaboration and support from IFI and VNU were instrumental in making this event a success and in sparking the critical discussions on the future of higher education in Vietnam.

We are grateful for the contributions and insights shared by all participants whose ideas have shaped the direction of this book. Their dedication to innovation and adaptation in higher education continues to guide us toward a brighter future for Vietnam's academic landscape.

Special thanks for this timely book is reserved for the publisher, Connor Court Publishing and its Managing Director, Dr Anthony Cappello, for believing in this project and standing by us even when the project looked a little uncertain.

The Editors

20 September 2025

Introduction[1]

Duc Hong Thi Phan[2] and Bruno Mascitelli

While the twenty-first century has been a period of great global uncertainty and even instability, it has also been characterized by waves of technological, economic, and cultural transformation that have profoundly reshaped society and especially the landscape of higher education almost everywhere. This includes Vietnam. From the early massification of universities during the twentieth century to the digital acceleration of the last two decades, institutions of higher learning have continuously adapted to the demands and constraints of their time. The most recent shift—from Industry 4.0, centered on automation, data analytics, and connectivity, toward Industry 5.0, emphasizing human–technology collaboration and sustainability—signals a profound reorientation in educational philosophy and practice. It is within this transition that the notion of Higher Education 5.0 emerges.

Higher Education 5.0 extends beyond the digitalization of teaching and the automation of administrative processes. It embodies a holistic, human-centered model that integrates technological advancement with social responsibility, ethical accountability, and inclusive growth. Whereas Education 4.0 largely emphasized efficiency, personalization through data, and the alignment of education with industrial skills, Education 5.0 asks more fundamental questions: How can higher education foster human flourishing in the digital age? How can universities remain anchors of equity, creativity, and resilience while harnessing emerging technologies?

To conceptualize Higher Education 5.0, it is useful to situate it within the historical trajectory of educational paradigms. Education 1.0 was teacher-

---

1   All references, tables, figures, author affiliation and biography used in this chapter are available on the Online Appendix link at https://tinyurl.com/he50Appendices.
2   Corresponding author: hongducktkt@gmail.com

centered, privileging authority and content transmission. Education 2.0, coincided with the expansion of mass schooling, democratized access but remaining structurally rigid. Education 3.0 marked a pivot toward learner-centered approaches, valuing interaction, autonomy, and collaboration. Education 4.0, aligned with Industry 4.0, introduced digital platforms, artificial intelligence, and global connectivity as tools for scalable, adaptive learning. Now, Education 5.0 calls for a synthesis: combining technological capability with a renewed commitment to human values—equity, creativity, emotional intelligence and sustainability.

This conceptual framework is not merely theoretical. It has direct implications for policy, pedagogy, and institutional practice. In the Vietnamese context, Higher Education 5.0 intersects with pressing national priorities: the government's ambitious digital transformation agenda, the rapid expansion of internet and mobile penetration, and the imperative to prepare a young workforce for participation in the global knowledge economy. Yet, Vietnam also faces challenges that are particularly acute: disparities between urban and rural regions, unequal access to infrastructure, and the cultural negotiation between traditional modes of instruction and new digital platforms. These features make Vietnam not only a context of application but also a unique case study that can generate insights for the "global south" as well as providing a modern debate on Education 5.0.

The rationale for this book stems from both the opportunities and the gaps in existing scholarship. While international discussions on Industry 5.0 and Education 5.0 are expanding, few comprehensive works focus specifically on their implications for higher education systems in Southeast Asia, and even fewer address Vietnam in a systematic manner. This book therefore responds not only to an academic gap but also to a societal gap. It is seeking to address the absence of a synthesized perspective that integrates technology, pedagogy, policy, and social equity within a single national framework. At the same time, it speaks to a practical need: providing educators, policymakers, and institutional leaders with conceptual tools and empirical insights to navigate the transition.

In framing Higher Education 5.0, this introduction thus serves three purposes. First, it establishes the intellectual foundation of the concept, clarifying its evolution and distinctiveness from earlier paradigms. Second, it situates Vietnam as both a participant in, and contributor to, the global conversation on educational futures including to the "global south". Third, it positions the book itself as an interdisciplinary and forward-looking response, uniting diverse perspectives on how universities can innovate, adapt and remain human-centered in an era of rapid change.

Global–Local Nexus of Higher Education 5.0

The discourse on Higher Education 5.0 cannot be separated from its global context. Across continents, universities are reimagining their roles not only as sites of knowledge transmission but also as drivers of innovation ecosystems, social equity and sustainable futures. In Europe, the European Commission's vision of Industry 5.0 emphasizes resilience, sustainability and a human-centered approach to technological integration. This framing has been mirrored in higher education policy, where universities are encouraged to combine digital competence with commitments to the United Nations' Sustainable Development Goals (SDGs). Similarly, in Australia, higher education institutions are increasingly investing in smart campus infrastructures, digital learning platforms, and industry-linked research initiatives to maintain global competitiveness while expanding opportunities for diverse student cohorts. East Asian systems, notably those of South Korea, Japan, and China, have also prioritized Education 5.0 principles by embedding artificial intelligence, lifelong learning pathways, and entrepreneurial education into their higher education frameworks, thereby positioning universities as engines of national development.

Despite this global momentum, the operationalization of Higher Education 5.0 remains uneven. Wealthier systems with mature digital infrastructures can experiment with adaptive learning, artificial intelligence and large-scale data analytics, while institutions in developing contexts often face structural constraints. This unevenness underscores the importance of a global–local lens: how universal aspirations for human-centered, technologically enhanced education intersect with the distinct realities of particular societies.

Vietnam presents a particularly compelling case in this regard. As one of the fastest-growing economies in Southeast Asia, Vietnam has committed itself to a national digital transformation strategy that explicitly prioritizes education. The government's National Digital Transformation Program of 2025, with an Orientation toward 2030, highlights higher education as both a beneficiary and a catalyst of digital innovation. This strong policy orientation reflects a centralized governance model that differs from more decentralized systems such as those in Australia or the United States. While centralization provides coherence and rapid mobilization, it also creates risks of rigidity, potentially limiting institutional autonomy and experimentation.

Another distinctive dimension is Vietnam's cultural and educational heritage. Rooted in Confucian traditions that emphasize respect for authority and collective responsibility, Vietnamese higher education has historically been characterized by teacher-centered pedagogy and hierarchical governance structures. The transition to Education 5.0 therefore involves not only technological upgrading but also cultural transformation. Universities must balance the integration of learner-centered pedagogies, digital collaboration, and personalized learning environments with enduring cultural expectations of authority and discipline. This cultural negotiation sets Vietnam apart from many Western contexts, where individualism and self-directed learning are more deeply embedded.

The digital divide remains one of Vietnam's most pressing challenges. While metropolitan centers such as Hanoi and Ho Chi Minh City host world-class universities with growing access to digital infrastructure, rural and mountainous regions continue to lag behind. Students in remote provinces often lack stable internet connectivity, access to devices, and exposure to digital learning cultures. These disparities not only reflect broader socio-economic inequalities but also risk entrenching educational inequity at precisely the moment when Education 5.0 aspires to be inclusive. The challenge, then, is to design policies and practices that extend the benefits of technological innovation to all learners, regardless of geography or socio-economic status.

At the same time, Vietnam's youthful demographic structure and openness to technological adoption represent major opportunities. With a median age that is under 33 and one of the highest rates of smartphone penetration in Southeast Asia, Vietnamese students are among the most digitally connected globally. This receptivity creates fertile ground for initiatives in gamification, blended learning, and virtual reality applications, as explored in later chapters of this volume. Moreover, the strong linkage between education and national development in Vietnamese policy discourse ensures that higher education reforms are framed not merely as sectoral adjustments but as integral components of the country's modernization project.

The global–local nexus also highlights Vietnam's role as both a learner and a contributor in the international dialogue on Education 5.0. On the one hand, Vietnam draws lessons from global practices, adapting models of smart universities, quality assurance systems, and open access publishing to its local context. On the other hand, Vietnam offers unique insights into how a rapidly developing nation can mobilize centralized governance, cultural traditions, and youthful demographics to leapfrog into new educational paradigms. These insights are valuable for other countries in the "Global South" that face similar tensions between aspiration and capacity, tradition and innovation.

By situating Vietnam within this broader nexus, the book underscores the dual function of Higher Education 5.0. It is simultaneously a global vision as well as being a local project. Understanding this interplay is essential for policymakers, educators, and researchers alike. The success of Education 5.0 in Vietnam will depend not only on the adoption of cutting-edge technologies but also on the careful alignment of global principles with local realities—an alignment that may, in turn, enrich the global discourse by introducing perspectives rooted in the Southeast Asian experience.

Core Dimensions of Higher Education 5.0 in Practice

The transition to Higher Education 5.0 is not only conceptual but profoundly practical. It requires universities to rethink their pedagogies, expand access, uphold ethical standards, and reconfigure their institutional missions. In the Vietnamese context, these transformations unfold across three interrelated dimensions: the integration of technology and pedagogy; the pursuit of equity and ethical responsibility; and the redefinition of universities as hubs of innovation, quality assurance, and global connectivity. Together, these dimensions shape the contours of Education 5.0 in practice.

Technology and Pedagogy

The most visible dimension of Higher Education 5.0 lies in the integration of digital technologies with new pedagogical models. Building on the momentum of Education 4.0, which emphasize online platforms and blended learning, Education 5.0 pushes further by embedding artificial intelligence, immersive environments, and data-driven personalization into the learning process.

Equally vital to Education 5.0 is the transformation of pedagogy itself. Chapter 7 takes readers on a journey into how Vietnamese Higher Education is reimagining learning—shifting from teacher-centered traditions to dynamic, student-driven experiences shaped by innovation, technology, and co-creation.

Vietnamese universities have begun experimenting with blended learning at scale, reflecting both global trends and local imperatives. As explored in Chapter 8, student and teacher perceptions of learning design reveal both the promise and the challenges of integrating digital platforms into traditional classroom contexts. Students often appreciate the flexibility and interactivity of blended models, yet many also struggle with self-regulation and technological barriers, particularly in under-resourced settings. Chapter 9 complements this analysis by focusing on the role of Learning Management Systems (LMS) in shaping blended learning experiences. While LMS platforms offer tools for monitoring progress and fostering collaboration, their effectiveness depends heavily on digital competence, infrastructure quality, and institutional support.

Gamification provides another lens through which the pedagogical promise of Education 5.0 can be observed. As detailed in Chapter 10, gamification initiatives at Vietnam National University illustrate how playful learning environments can enhance student motivation and engagement. Yet gamification also requires careful design to ensure that competitive elements do not overshadow deeper learning objectives. Similarly, immersive technologies such as Virtual Reality (VR) and Augmented Reality (AR), discussed in Chapter 14, open new avenues for stress relief, mindfulness, and experiential learning. These innovations embody Education 5.0s emphasis on human well-being alongside cognitive development.

Perhaps the most transformative technological dimension lies in artificial intelligence. Chapter 17 develops theoretical models of learning analytics that harness AI to generate predictive insights, support adaptive feedback, and enhance student success. Chapter 18 extends this focus by analyzing personalized and adaptive learning environments, where AI functions as a partner in tailoring instruction to individual needs. Such initiatives promise to democratize access to high-quality education, but they also raise concerns about data privacy, algorithmic bias, and the risk of reducing education to technocratic efficiency.

Importantly, the adoption of AI in higher education is not limited to students. Chapter 19 examines the readiness of English as a Foreign Language (EFL) teachers to embrace AI tools, identifying both enthusiasm and anxiety among educators. Teachers recognize the potential of AI for assessment, content generation, and classroom management, yet they also fear a loss of professional autonomy. Chapter 20 explores the use of ChatGPT in Vietnamese language instruction, highlighting the potential of AI to revitalize national language teaching while raising questions about authenticity, accuracy, and cultural identity.

Taken together, these pedagogical innovations demonstrate that technology in Higher Education 5.0 is not an end in itself but a medium through which more adaptive, engaging, and human-centered education can be pursued. The challenge is to ensure that technological integration enhances, rather than diminishes, the core mission of universities: the cultivation of critical, creative, and ethical citizens.

Equity and Ethics

The promise of Education 5.0 cannot be fulfilled without addressing issues of equity and ethical responsibility. The digital divide—between rural and urban students, between resource-rich and resource-poor institutions, and between those with and without digital literacy—remains a central obstacle to inclusive education in Vietnam. Chapter 4 tackles this issue head-on, exploring how the digital divide intersects with ethical challenges and educational inequities. It argues that unless digital transformation strategies explicitly prioritize disadvantaged groups, Education 5.0 risks deepening existing inequalities rather than mitigating them.

Parental and adolescent perspectives, analyzed in Chapter 6, further underscore the importance of equity. Families' perceptions of education shape students' aspirations and opportunities, particularly in contexts where access to higher education is stratified by geography and income. Addressing these inequities requires not only technological solutions but also cultural and social engagement.

Lifelong learning is another equity imperative in the Education 5.0 era. As detailed in Chapter 5, universities must transition from degree-centric models to lifelong learning frameworks that support continuous upskilling and reskilling. This is especially critical in Vietnam, where rapid economic transformation demands new competencies across the workforce. Lifelong learning pathways—through micro-credentials, online courses, and flexible programs—can extend opportunities to those who would otherwise be excluded from higher education.

Ethical considerations extend beyond equity to encompass data governance, privacy, and academic integrity. As AI-driven learning analytics and adaptive platforms proliferate, universities must grapple with questions of consent, transparency, and accountability. The ethical imperative is not simply to avoid harm but to cultivate trust: students must believe that their data is used responsibly, teachers must trust that the AI tools support rather than replace their professional judgment, and society must be assured that universities remain guardians of knowledge rather than engines of surveillance.

Ultimately, the pursuit of equity and ethics in Higher Education 5.0 reflects the human-centered philosophy at its core. Without deliberate efforts to ensure inclusivity and ethical governance, the technological advances of Education 5.0 risk becoming instruments of exclusion and mistrust.

Innovation and Institutional Roles

The third core dimension concerns the institutional mission of universities in an Education 5.0 landscape. Beyond teaching and research, universities are increasingly expected to serve as hubs of innovation, engines of economic development, and custodians of quality assurance.

Chapter 2 frames smart universities as drivers of national innovation, highlighting how digital infrastructure can be leveraged to align higher education with broader socio-economic strategies. Chapter 13 reinforces this theme by examining creativity and innovation as essential elements of Education 5.0. In both cases, the university is envisioned as more than a place of study; it is a dynamic ecosystem where students, faculty, industry, and government collaborate to generate solutions to pressing challenges.

Quality assurance represents another critical institutional dimension. As shown in Chapter 12, Vietnam National University's efforts to cultivate a quality culture and strengthen internal quality assurance mechanisms illustrate the importance of accountability in an Education 5.0 context. Such initiatives ensure that innovations are not merely experimental but embedded within systems of evaluation, improvement, and sustainability. Chapter 16 extends this focus to open access publishing in Vietnamese technology and engineering universities, emphasizing transparency and global connectivity as hallmarks of institutional quality.

At the institutional level, innovation also entails navigating tensions between autonomy and centralization. Vietnam's higher education system operates under strong state direction, which facilitates rapid reform but may constrain institutional independence. The success of Education 5.0 will depend on how universities balance responsiveness to national policy with the cultivation of local innovation cultures.

More broadly, universities must embrace their role as social institutions, not only advancing technological innovation but also fostering civic engagement, cultural preservation, and sustainable development. In doing so, they can position themselves as central actors in shaping not just the future of education, but the future of society itself.

The three dimensions explored here—technology and pedagogy, equity and ethics, and institutional innovation—constitute the practical heart of Higher Education 5.0. They reveal both the opportunities and the tensions that define the Vietnamese experience: the enthusiasm for technological adoption, tempered by infrastructural and cultural constraints; the aspiration for inclusivity, challenged by persistent inequities; and the ambition for innovation, mediated by questions of quality and governance.

By weaving these dimensions together, the book demonstrates that Higher Education 5.0 is not a singular project but a constellation of practices, negotiations, and commitments. Each chapter contributes to this mosaic, offering both empirical insights and conceptual guidance. As the subsequent sections of this introduction will argue, the ultimate success of Education 5.0 lies not in the mastery of any one technology or policy but in the sustained capacity of universities to adapt, innovate, and remain anchored in human values.

Contributions within this book

Higher Education 5.0 is best understood not as a single reform but as an ecosystem of interconnected innovations, practices, and policies. This book captures that ecosystem through a Vietnamese lens while engaging in global debates, offering both theoretical depth and empirical richness. The book is structured into three thematic sections, guiding readers from foundational principles to pedagogical transformations and institutional innovations.

Section 1 – Foundations and Policies (Chapters 1–3) introduces the conceptual core of Education 5.0 and situates Vietnam within global higher education debates. These chapters examine foundational prospects for the Vietnamese system, the role of smart universities, and the interplay between Vietnamese and Australian education.

Section 2 – Pedagogical and Learning Transformations (Chapters 4–13) focuses on the human-centered reconfiguration of teaching and learning. Chapters 4–6 explore equity, ethics, and lifelong learning, including parental and adolescent perspectives. Chapter 7 highlights how innovative pedagogy and curricular co-creation can redefine the learning experience in Vietnam, ensuring that Education 5.0 is not only inclusive but also learner-centered. Chapter 8 establishes the theoretical and practical foundations of learning design for Education 5.0, serving as a bridge to subsequent chapters. Chapters 9–11 investigate how students and teachers experience blended learning, LMS integration, and gamification, while Chapter 12 presents a case study of one year of Education 5.0 implementation at a school in Hanoi. Chapter 13 concludes the section with an institutional perspective on quality culture and assurance.

Section 3 – Innovation, Technology, and Institutional Change (Chapters 14–20) expands the focus to system-level and cutting-edge innovations. Chapters 14–16 analyze creativity, VR/AR applications for student well-being, and digital competence among faculty. Chapter 17 examines open access publishing, while Chapters 18–19 delve into AI-driven learning analytics and adaptive learning. Chapters 20–21 highlight language education, exploring EFL teachers' readiness for AI adoption and the use of ChatGPT for teaching Vietnamese to international students.

By weaving together these sections, the book provides a comprehensive map of Higher Education 5.0 as both a global vision and a Vietnamese project. Each chapter offers a unique insight, but collectively they form a mosaic that illustrates how technology, equity, and institutional change interact to shape the future of universities.

The editors of this book also point out that all references, tables, figures, contributor's biographies and appendices can be located online in order to limit the length of this book. We hope this does not cause any inconvenience. The location of this information is through the Online Appendix link https://tinyurl.com/he50Appendices.

Conclusion: Towards a Human-Centered Vision

As this introduction has argued, the transition to Higher Education 5.0 is a profound, multifaceted, and urgent project. It is not a matter of simply upgrading technology or adopting new teaching methods. It is a fundamental re-evaluation of the purpose of education in a world defined by both unprecedented opportunity and complex ethical challenges. For Vietnam, the journey is particularly dynamic, defined by a powerful blend of national ambition, technological readiness, and cultural negotiation.

The chapters that follow offer a roadmap for this journey. They provide empirical evidence, theoretical frameworks, and practical lessons from the front lines of educational innovation in Vietnam. They reveal the successes of early adopters, the struggles of institutions grappling with change, and the aspirations of students and educators alike. Above all, they underscore the central message of this book: that the future of higher education lies not in the mastery of technology for its own sake, but in our capacity to leverage it in the service of human flourishing.

Ultimately, Higher Education 5.0 is an invitation to engage in a collaborative act of creation. It calls upon policymakers to design agile and inclusive frameworks, on institutional leaders to foster cultures of experimentation and ethical governance, and on educators to embrace new pedagogies that empower and inspire. It is a call for a design-thinking mindset that is empathetic, adaptable, and perpetually focused on the needs of the learner.

We stand at a pivotal moment in the history of education. The choices made today—in classrooms, in policy debates, and in research labs, will determine whether universities become engines of exclusion or anchors of equity, whether they fuel technocratic efficiency or human creativity. This book is offered as a contribution to that vital conversation, a testament to the transformative potential of Vietnamese higher education, and a call to action to shape a future where learning is not only innovative and adaptive, but also deeply and meaningfully human.

1

Higher Education 5.0: Foundations and Future Prospects for the Vietnamese Education System[3]

Duc Hong Thi Phan, Bruno Mascitelli, Bao Gia Truong, Nguyen Thi Thanh Uyen, Khoi Hoang Truong[4] and Trang Quynh Kong Nguyen

Abstract

Higher Education (HE) 5.0 represents a transformative phase in Vietnam's education system, integrating technological innovations and human-centered approaches to foster sustainable development aligned with global educational demands. This chapter delves into the implementation of HE 5.0 in Vietnam, highlighting the persistent influence of traditional values on this transition. Analyzing the historical development of Vietnam's education system, from the pre-colonial era to the present, the researchers found that Constructivist Learning Theory (CLT) is more commonly adopted due to its alignment with Confucian principles, compared to other frameworks. Vietnam's predominantly young and tech-savvy population has facilitated the adoption of technologies in teaching and learning. However, developmental limits in technology or over-centralizing into

---

3 All references, tables, figures, author affiliation and biography used in this chapter are available on the Online Appendix link at https://tinyurl.com/he50Appendices.

4 Corresponding author: Khoi Hoang Truong, truonghoangkhoi.work@gmail.com

government policies is one of the inherent hurdles alongside new challenges ensuing from the era of globalization. Educators hasten to seek effective solutions. As such, the chapter contributes an overarching overview of Vietnam's HE 5.0 and offers recommendations to harness its potential. It serves as a valuable resource for future research on the progression and impact of HE 5.0.

Introduction - Transitioning to HE 5.0 in Vietnam

Higher education (HE) 5.0 has played a key role in providing students with knowledge and skills to adapt to the thriving era of technology. It is characterized by a combination of the latest technologies and student-centered approaches to promote interconnection and sustainability within educational development. Throughout HE education versions of 1.0 and 2.0, it shifted from the focus on traditional in-classroom teaching methods to technology-applied reforms to meet workforce demands (O'Leary et al., 2023). However, within versions HE 3.0 and 4.0, the concept of digital learning and AI technologies within educational environments was coined which soon commenced a new era of modern education (Nguyen et al., 2024). HE 5.0, to this moment, appreciates the personalization in learning, fostering the interdisciplinary collaboration and sustainability which is fundamental for lifelong education in this changeable landscape. In terms of globalization-wise applications, nations implement these changes differently such as Finland which leads in incorporating AI-driven personalized learning, while Japan pays attention to lifelong learning contributing to a long-term comprehensive strategy (Nguyen et al., 2024).

Vietnam is attempting to seize an important opportunity to transfer from traditional to technology-applied approaches to learning. Metaverse has already appeared in the Vietnam education environment. Although many have not familiarized themselves with the applications, Metaverse embraces huge potential since the younger generations are inherently exposed to technologies. Moreover, there is also a smart classroom model equipped with multiple display devices called Hikvision. In August 2024, an International Conference on HE 5.0 organized by the International Francophone Institute (IFI) discussed the challenges and opportunities in applying technologies in educational practices to promote HE 5.0 for the future (IFI, 2024). It reflects the interest of Vietnamese educators to implement technology applications in HE environments, especially colleges and universities. In short, Vietnam's endeavors to upgrade the educational system are genuine in pursuing global trends of HE 5.0 (Bradly et al., 2024).

Rationale and Key Objectives for HE 5.0 in Vietnam

Rapid economic growth is driving increased demand for technology-integrated Higher Education 5.0. However, its implementation faces challenges due to conflicting expectations among stakeholders. Although the National Digital Transformation Strategy emphasizes a strong commitment to comprehensive innovation, existing research often lacks sufficient data repositories, limiting their usefulness in addressing the current shortcomings of Vietnam's higher education system (Nguyen et al., 2024).

Students require proper skills to adapt to epochal demands from the labour market (Bradly et al., 2024); educators require a transparent routine for pedagogical training section relating to digital adoptions (Nguyen et al., 2024); on the other hand, policymakers are searching for a strategy to inclusively adapt proper frameworks into the technology-applied education system (O'Leary et al., 2023). As such, the researchers aimed to (1) analyze HE 5.0 developments in the global context and relevant actors in Vietnam, (2) indicate nationwide potentials and challenges in implementation, and (3) recommend applicable and practical pathways to improve and implement HE 5.0 in Vietnam. This chapter, therefore, seeks answers to two central questions:

1. What are the defining features of HE 5.0 and its alignment within the Vietnamese context?

2. What are the challenges and recommendations for its future implementation?

This chapter provides an overview of Vietnam's HE 5.0 which serves as a foundational reference for future empirical studies based on discussions and evaluations of the potential of implementation. It offers insights for researchers to explore more detailed strategies but also the impact on various stakeholders to optimize its long-term effectiveness.

Transformation of Education in Vietnam: Historical Progress, Current Structures and Key Challenges

Vietnam's education system has evolved through various phases, generally categorized into four historical periods: the Pre-colonial Era (Confucian Era), the Colonial Period, the Post-colonial Era, and the Doi Moi Era. Notably, significant progress in Vietnam's education system began during the post-colonial period compared to earlier practices.

There was a westernizing phenomenon in Vietnam's education system ensuing from the shift from pre-colonial to colonial era. During the pre-colonial period when Vietnam's education was deeply influenced by Confucian principles, relevant classical and moral philosophy were popularized. This approach has led to a meritocratic yet restrictive structure, primarily designed to prepare male scholars, particularly from the elite class, for civil service exams. However, since women and outsiders apart from the privileged social strata were excluded, the education system was very selective. Entering the colonial period under French rule (1858–1945), the education system experienced a pivotal transformation. In particular, the French introduced a new education system that prioritized curricula taught in French to create a favorable environment for colonial governance, thereby undermining the influence of Confucian teachings. Regardless of the changes, Vietnam's education system was limited by its highly inequitable access which solely prioritized urban and elite populations.

The post-colonial era signified a milestone for epochal changes in the education system which kept innovating throughout the Innovation era (Do Moi in Vietnamese). The post-colonial era began with Vietnam's independence in 1945, bringing substantial reforms to address the nation's high illiteracy rates. The government implemented a national education system that incorporated local culture and values, alongside mass literacy campaigns. Following the end of the Vietnam War in 1975, the unified government sought to eliminate remnants of the French colonial education system by introducing a localized 12-year compulsory education system. During the Doi Moi Era in 1986, significant transformations occurred when Vietnam shifted from a state-directed economy to a socialist-oriented market economy. The education system changed to meet the demands of a rapidly evolving economy. Hence, the modernized education model became more accessible which delivered equal opportunities for

Vietnamese to pursue educational aspirations.

The introduction of the new Law of Education further solidified these reforms, with two primary objectives: (a) developing a highly educated workforce equipped with research and innovation capabilities to support Vietnam's economic, social, and global-centric goals, and (b) cultivating well-rounded individuals with ethics, knowledge, health, aesthetic awareness, and professional responsibility (Tran & Nguyen, 2022). These reforms established the groundwork for the current HE 5.0 model, around a holistic student-centric development.

Vietnam Education System: Structure, Achievements, and Progress in Equity

Since its earliest establishment, careers in education have held an esteemed position in Vietnamese society (Huong & Fry, 2024). Over time, the education system has undergone numerous changes, evolving into its current structure, which comprises four main levels: Primary Education, Secondary Education (Lower-secondary education), High School Education (Upper-secondary education), and Higher Education.

Primary Education spans five years, covering grades 1 to 5, and is designed for children aged 6 to 11 years. Secondary Education (Lower-secondary education) encompasses grades 6 to 9, while High School Education (Upper-secondary education) includes grades 10 to 12. Upon completing Secondary Education, students have multiple pathways to pursue. One option is Vocational Secondary Education, which, like High School Education, lasts three years but focuses on equipping students with specific skills for immediate employment. After graduating from High School Education or Vocational Secondary Education, students can choose between pursuing an associate degree at vocational colleges or enrolling in HE at universities, both of which are part of the tertiary education sector.

Tertiary education includes both HE and vocational education and training, offering two main pathways: university and college. HE, provided by public and private universities, junior colleges, and academic research institutes, typically requires four to six years to complete, while vocational associate degrees usually last three years. Interestingly, Vietnam is home to "Van Mieu" (The Temple of Literature, the Southeast Asia's oldest recorded institution of HE first built in 1070), which hosted "Quoc Tu Giam" (the Imperial Academy), Vietnam's first national university from 1076 to 1779 (Huong & Fry, 2004).

The constant adaptation of Vietnam's education system has yielded impressive results on international assessments such as the Program for International Student Assessment (PISA). Vietnam has exceeded expectations by outperforming many countries within its income group and even some OECD nations. According to London (2023), Vietnam's success in education can be attributed to its strong political emphasis on education and, more importantly, the societal commitment to learning. This dedication is reflected in the consistently high enrolment rates, which have surged across all levels of education, from primary to HE, showcasing both governmental and household efforts to expand access to education. This increase also indicates improved availability and affordability of schools for the broader population (Dinh et al. 2024).

Significant strides have also been made in achieving social equity within the education system. Marginalized groups, including impoverished families, low-income households, ethnic minorities, rural workers, beneficiaries of social policies, and individuals with distinguished services, have received substantial assistance to access education. For instance, the Priority in University Recruitment Policy (Decree No. 57/2017/NĐ-CP, dated May 9, 2017) was introduced to support students from remote, rural, and mountainous areas, as well as those from ethnic minorities. This policy enables these students to enter universities even if their entrance exam scores fall below the standard cut-off. Although the large-scale effects of these policies have yet to be fully realized, they mark a critical step toward educational equality for diverse demographic backgrounds across Vietnam (Tran & Nguyen, 2022).

In addition to social equity, gender equality has been firmly established in Vietnam's education system. Students meeting age and educational requirements are welcomed regardless of gender (Dinh et al., 2024). In the 2019–2020 academic year, 1,672,881 students were enrolled in HE, with females accounting for 54.6% of the total and 6.2% belonging to minority groups. Notably, in 2018, female participation in STEM (science, technology, engineering, and mathematics) programs reached 34%, representing a significant improvement compared to many other countries (Tran & Nguyen, 2022).

Key Challenges in Vietnam Education: Outdated Methods, Inequity, and Brain Drain

Vietnam's HE system presents significant opportunities for improvement, particularly in modernizing curricula and teaching methods to align with contemporary global standards (London, 2023). Currently, many educational programs rely on traditional teaching approaches, such as rote learning and memorization, which primarily prepare students for memory-based tests (Dinh et al., 2024). These outdated practices fail to incorporate technology and market-driven demands, both of which are essential components of the HE 5.0 framework. Consequently, these teaching and assessment methods hinder the development of critical skills such as critical thinking, interdisciplinary problem-solving and digital literacy.

This shortfall has contributed to a systemic issue: a significant gap between students' theoretical knowledge and the practical skills required by industries. As a result, educational outcomes often fail to align with labour market demands, raising concerns about the employability of graduates. However, this skills mismatch is not solely the responsibility of students but reflects deeper systemic challenges within the education system. Over time, this misalignment may lead to "sticky" unemployment, where graduates struggle to secure appropriate jobs while employers face challenges filling vacancies, despite an apparent surplus of job seekers. Addressing this systemic disconnect is critical to ensuring that HE meets the evolving needs of the labour market.

As Vietnam's economy continues to grow, access to education has expanded significantly. This increased access has been accompanied by an even faster-growing demand for educational opportunities and training. Despite these advancements, disparities in cost, quality, distribution and accessibility remain, across age groups, regions, and demographic categories. For instance, uneven access to quality early education, such as preschool, undermines the potential of children from impoverished and marginalized backgrounds. Similarly, disparities in the quality of primary and lower-secondary education have resulted in varying student achievements across and within regions. Furthermore, HE remains disproportionately accessible to wealthier households, with the majority of students coming from the top three expenditure quintiles, while less than 10% are from the bottom two quintiles (Tran & Nguyen, 2022). In a society where education is viewed as a primary means of achieving social mobility, these gaps in access now serve as barriers, exacerbating existing inequalities and hindering the adoption of HE 5.0 (London, 2011).

Another pressing issue in Vietnam's rapidly growing economy is its brain drain. Many talented individuals leave the country in pursuit of better opportunities abroad. This phenomenon is primarily driven by unattractive remuneration packages offered by local companies, which fail to adequately reward employees' efforts and intellectual capacities. Additionally, limited opportunities to engage in high-level roles domestically further encourage the outflow of talent. As a result, Vietnam faces a significant loss of skilled labour, which is critical for national development and the successful implementation of the HE 5.0 framework.

Advancing Vietnam's HE 5.0

With the growth of the Fourth Industrial Revolution, Dinh et al. (2024) emphasized that Vietnamese HE is making significant progress toward aligning with the principles of HE 5.0. This model focuses on the integration of technology, innovation, and human-centered approaches. Vietnamese universities have made progress in integrating e-learning platforms with more digital tools into their existing curriculum, such as mobile technology, AI, and cloud computing. These efforts could substantially assist in enhancing personalized and remote learning experiences (Dinh et al., 2024). Furthermore, Vietnam's National Digital Transformation Strategy was also proposed to modernize various sectors, including education. This strategy provides universities with a comprehensive framework for integrating advanced technologies into HE, ensuring that institutions can equip students with the technical and soft skills that fit the needs of the labour market.

In addition to technological advancements, the growing emphasis on the concept of lifelong learning has further aligned Vietnam's HE system with the principles of HE 5.0. Following the COVID-19 pandemic, many institutions in Vietnam have expanded flexible learning options, such as online courses and part-time programs (Tran & Do, 2024). These developments offer increased accessibility and flexibility, accommodating a broader range of learners, including working professionals and adult students. Overall, this evolving educational landscape reflects the core goals of HE 5.0, which prioritize continuous learning and skill development for diverse demographics.

Barriers to advancing HE 5.0 in Vietnam

One significant obstacle lies in the limitations of technological infrastructure. There has been a gap in access to technology between urban and rural areas. Additionally, many institutions lack sufficient infrastructure to support the upcoming adjustment in educational practices (Hoa & Park, 2015). In accordance with making more investment in digital infrastructure, it is the cultural mindset that also needs to be addressed. Traditional teaching methods remain the preferred teaching style over innovative approaches, which may take Vietnam more time to fully shift away from this mindset. This reliance on traditional methods significantly delays the adoption of new educational practices that prioritize critical thinking, creativity, and technology-driven skills.

A further hindrance arises from over-centralization in educational governance. Fragmented autonomy reforms and excessive bureaucratic control often result in inefficiencies and delays. Although there has been progress in allowing universities to develop their own curricula, the lack of structural and consistent guidance in integrating the HE 5.0 model remains a challenge. This rigidity in institutional structures, combined with the absence of detailed implementation instructions, slows down the responsiveness of HE to the rapidly evolving demands of students and industries (Tran & Do, 2024).

Seizing opportunities for advancing HE 5.0 in Vietnam

Although challenges remain, Vietnam is well-positioned to capitalize on opportunities to enhance its alignment with the HE 5.0 model. One of Vietnam's key advantages is its young and tech-savvy population. This youthful demographic creates an ideal environment for rapidly adapting to HE 5.0, including the adoption of new curricula, hybrid learning approaches, and emerging technologies. By emphasizing lifelong learning, interdisciplinary skill development, and digital literacy, institutions play a critical role in preparing graduates to meet the demands of future job markets.

Another opportunity lies in advancing digital transformation by investing in digital infrastructure and cutting-edge technologies such as artificial intelligence (AI), augmented and virtual reality (AR/VR), the Internet of

Things (IoT) and cloud computing. These innovations have the potential to revolutionize educational delivery, making it more engaging and effective (Dinh et al., 2024).

As Vietnam transitions toward a new educational model, the need for a substantial sample size to validate the efficiency of the new approach becomes evident. This transition requires collective efforts from learners, educators, institutions, and the government to overcome entrenched preferences for traditional learning methods and disparities in access to HE 5.0. It is essential to clearly communicate the long-term benefits of this transformation to ensure widespread acceptance among key stakeholders.

Additionally, Vietnam must address historical inequalities in access to HE. Unlike previous systems designed primarily for the elite, the current approach should aim to reduce disparities, particularly for ethnic minorities and disadvantaged communities. Equitable scholarships, tuition waivers, and student loan programs for financially underprivileged students can play a pivotal role in ensuring broader access to HE (Tran & Do, 2024).

Policy Pathways for Advancing HE 5.0 in Vietnam

To effectively transition to a HE system aligned with the demands of Industry 4.0 and prepare for HE 5.0, several policy recommendations should be considered. These include decentralizing educational governance, initiating EdTech approaches, and providing greater incentives for private sector collaboration.

In an era where rapid market changes demand agility, a highly hierarchical governance model may hinder effective adaptation. Therefore, it is recommended that the Vietnamese government shift from a top-down governance structure to a more decentralized approach. This change would empower universities to innovate and respond swiftly to emerging challenges. Greater flexibility will enable institutions to implement HE 5.0-oriented strategies, addressing the dynamic needs of labour markets, fostering interdisciplinary skills, and catering to the interests of students.

Once institutions and stakeholders are prepared to adopt the HE 5.0 model, the focus should shift to integrating digital tools into HE effectively. Establishing national funding schemes dedicated to EdTech initiatives and improving digital infrastructure is crucial. These funds can support the development of digital learning platforms, provide educators with training in digital pedagogy, and ensure equitable access to technological resources for students. Such measures are especially important for bridging the digital divide in rural and underserved areas, enabling all learners to benefit from quality online education that supports substantial information storage and delivery.

Furthermore, tapping into the potential of the private sector is vital for driving progress in HE 5.0. Introducing tax incentives and grants to businesses that collaborate with HE institutions could foster partnerships. These collaborations can help create industry-relevant curricula, offer internship opportunities, and establish research initiatives that align academic training with market demands.

Institutional strategies for advancing HE 5.0 in Vietnam

As Vietnam transitions toward the HE 5.0 model, the focus is gradually shifting from emphasizing the role of teachers to prioritizing the needs and active involvement of learners. To align with this learner-centered approach, institutions can initiate changes from the ground up by targeting educators. Establishing exclusive training programs for educators is essential to equip them with the necessary skills and knowledge for integrating technology into teaching practices. These programs could include training on creating engaging online content using AI-driven tools, managing virtual classrooms, assessing student performance in a digital environment, and utilizing digital platforms to organize teaching materials. Furthermore, such initiatives should emphasize the importance of a lifelong learning mindset, interdisciplinary skill development, and digital literacy, which are critical to ensuring the sustainability of HE-focused strategies.

Beyond classroom adjustments, improving institutional management is also vital. As Dinh et al. (2024) highlighted, this involves enhancing quality management in training and designing outcome-driven teaching programs. Learning objectives should be crafted from the learner's perspective, explicitly stating what learners are expected to achieve upon completing the course. In this paradigm, educational institutions act as facilitators, while learners take charge of their own growth and development.

Additionally, the dynamic nature of knowledge necessitates regular curriculum updates to keep pace with global developments. Considering the "shelf-life" of curricula, institutions should adopt flexible programs that support international integration and are revised every three to five years to ensure relevance in the evolving HE 5.0 environment.

Shaping the Future: Vietnam's Vision for HE 5.0

Looking ahead, Vietnam has the potential to position itself as a regional leader in human-centered education, where student needs remain the top priority. To achieve this vision, Vietnam should focus on the holistic development of students, supported by enhanced digital literacy. This approach should go beyond imparting theoretical knowledge, placing greater emphasis on real-world problem-solving, critical thinking, creativity, and fostering a lifelong learning mindset. Building strong partnerships with global institutions would enable Vietnam to implement a globally relevant yet locally tailored educational agenda. Successfully integrating into the global knowledge ecosystem while preserving the unique characteristics of local needs would establish leadership in this domain and strengthen Vietnam's transition to a knowledge-based economy.

By 2030, many countries are projected to face labour shortages, underscoring the importance of investing in human capital to remain competitive in the global economy (Kataoka et al., 2020). Vietnam is particularly well-positioned in this regard, with 25% of its population aged between 15 and 29 and nearly 50% of its workforce under 40 years old. This young, tech-savvy, and motivated demographic presents a unique opportunity for Vietnam to advance HE 5.0 and drive the digitalization of education.

However, with global industries increasingly transitioning to Industry 5.0, characterized by the integration of advanced technology with human creativity, Vietnam's HE 5.0 framework must adapt accordingly. Curricula should prepare students for future job markets that demand a combination of high-level technical expertise and interdisciplinary problem-solving skills. To foster a workforce capable of thriving in Industry 5.0, emphasis must also be placed on a balance of hard skills, soft skills, emotional intelligence, creativity and adaptability.

Conclusion

The integration of technological innovations to achieve personalized and sustainable education is a core objective of HE 5.0. Within the Vietnamese education system, Constructivist Learning Theory is widely applied due to its alignment with traditional values; however, HCD and Systems Theory are also increasingly recognized for their potential to enhance educational practices. Importantly, different stakeholders derive distinct benefits from these frameworks. Students seek advanced skill sets and up-to-date knowledge to meet modern workforce demands, educators benefit from access to digital tools that enhance pedagogical methods, and policymakers have the opportunity to create a decentralized, responsive, and inclusive education system that promotes sustainability and lifelong learning. This chapter sought to provide an overview of the potential of HE 5.0 in Vietnam, discussing and evaluating frameworks and applications. For future research, empirical studies are encouraged to explore detailed strategies and examine the specific impacts on various stakeholders to further optimize the long-term effectiveness of HE 5.0.

2

Shaping the Future of Learning: Education 5.0 and the Role of Smart Universities in Driving Innovation[5]

Ton Quang Cuong[6] and Ravipalli Sri Santhi Nehru

Abstract

Education 5.0 signifies a significant paradigm shift, integrating advanced technologies, human-centered methodologies, and continuous learning to meet the evolving demands of the 21st century. Smart universities, which incorporate artificial intelligence, big data, and immersive technologies, are at the forefront of promoting innovation within this context. These institutions create adaptive, inclusive, and skills-oriented environments tailored for individual learners, transforming traditional teaching and learning methods. This chapter explores the principles of Education 5.0, focusing on the role of intelligent universities in fostering interdisciplinary collaboration, research, and sustainable development. The study delves into the impact of digital transformation, personalized learning pathways, and global connectivity on the redefinition of educational ecosystems. It highlights these advancements' ethical and policy implications, particularly in ensuring equitable access and maximizing societal impact. In their collaborative efforts, education 5.0 and innovative universities are shaping a workforce that is not just prepared for the future but actively shaping it by aligning with industry needs and tackling global challenges, fostering innovation and societal progress.

---

5   All references, tables, figures, author affiliation and biography used in this chapter are available on the Online Appendix link at https://tinyurl.com/he50Appendices.

6   Corresponding author: tonquangcuong@gmail.com

Introduction

The rapid advancement of technology and the increasing complexity of global challenges demand a transformative approach to education. Education 5.0 represents a forward-thinking paradigm that aligns learning with the needs of Industry 5.0, emphasizing human-centricity, sustainability, and integration of advanced technologies such as AI (Artificial Intelligence), IoT (Internet of Things), EoT (Education of Things), and Big Data.

Smart universities and institutions that leverage intelligent systems to create innovative, personalized, and inclusive learning environments are at the forefront of this shift. These universities prepare students for the evolving workforce and serve as research, innovation, and societal development hubs. By integrating digital tools with pedagogical strategies, smart universities drive the co-creation of knowledge, foster interdisciplinary collaboration, and address pressing global issues.

This chapter explores how Education 5.0 and innovative universities reshape the educational landscape, highlighting their pivotal role in nurturing future-ready individuals and driving technological and social innovation.

The Evolution of Education: From 1.0 to 5.0

* **Overview of Educational Models:** Educational models have evolved significantly over the centuries, transitioning from traditional to progressive approaches. **Education 1.0**, prevalent before the 20th century, was teacher-centered, focusing on rote learning and standardized curricula. **Education 2.0**, which emerged with the rise of digital technologies in the late 20th century, incorporated online resources and digital tools, shifting toward a more interactive, student-centered approach. As technology advanced, **Education 3.0** integrated personalized learning, where students could take control of their learning paths, utilizing adaptive systems and digital platforms. The concept of **Education 4.0** arose in response to Industry 4.0, focusing on developing skills for the digital age, emphasizing creativity, collaboration, and critical thinking. Most recently, **Education 5.0** has emerged, aiming for a holistic integration of artificial intelligence, emotional intelligence, and personalized learning

to create future-ready, lifelong learners (Ng, 2021). See Figure 2.1. Evolution of Education Models (available through the Online Appendix link https://tinyurl.com/he50Appendices).

* **Characteristics of Education 5.0**: Education 5.0 emphasizes a holistic, student-centered approach where technology, real-world problem-solving, and personalized learning are central. Features include the "Education of Things" (EoT), which integrates interconnected devices for a seamless learning experience. Personalized learning tailors educational content to individual needs, fostering more profound engagement (Nehru & Chakraborty, 2020). Technology integration enables immersive experiences, enhancing both teaching and learning processes. Education 5.0 encourages critical thinking and collaboration through real-world problem-solving, preparing students for complex global challenges (Nehru & Ton, 2023). These characteristics create a more adaptive, efficient, and relevant learning environment (Jäger & Hake, 2020).

* **Key Drivers of Education 5.0**: The development of Education 5.0 is influenced by several technological, societal, and economic drivers. Technological advancements in artificial intelligence, machine learning, and virtual reality shape personalized and immersive learning experiences (Cheng & Li, 2022). Societally, the push for inclusive, lifelong learning addresses diverse learning needs, emphasizing equity and accessibility. Economically, the demand for a skilled workforce, driven by automation and digital transformation, influences educational curricula to ensure relevancy in the global job market. These factors collectively redefine traditional education paradigms, fostering adaptability, innovation, and engagement (Cheng & Li, 2022). See Figure 2.2. Components of Education 5.0 (available through the Online Appendices link https://tinyurl.com/he50Appendices).

Define Education 5.0 and its relevance to contemporary higher education.

Education 5.0 is an advanced educational paradigm integrating artificial intelligence, personalized learning, and societal development. It focuses on student-centered, real-world problem-solving (Marenzi & García-

Peñalvo, 2021). It emphasizes innovation, collaboration, and lifelong learning, reshaping higher education to meet future workforce needs and address global challenges (López-Morales et al., 2023). Smart universities play a crucial role in this transformation.

The study explores Education 5.0, a transformative paradigm integrating advanced technologies like AI, IoT, and immersive learning to personalize and democratize education. It emphasizes the critical role of smart universities as innovation hubs, leveraging intelligent systems and interdisciplinary approaches to address global challenges. Amid rapid technological evolution and shifting societal demands, this research underscores the urgency of reimagining education to cultivate adaptable, lifelong learners. The study aims to shape education systems that enhance learning outcomes and prepare students to thrive in an increasingly complex (Nehru et al., 2023) interconnected world by examining strategies for fostering innovation in smart universities.

Shaping the Future of Learning: Education 5.0 and the Role of Smart Universities in Driving Innovation

* **Education 5.0** represents a transformative shift in higher education, integrating technology, human-centered learning, and sustainability. Rooted in Industry 5.0 principles, it emphasizes personalized learning, ethical technology use, and societal impact. This paradigm seeks to prepare students for employability and global challenges by fostering critical thinking, creativity, and collaboration in digitally driven environments.

* **Smart universities** embody this vision by leveraging advanced technologies like AI, IoT, and data analytics to enhance learning experiences, streamline operations, and promote research excellence. These institutions adopt smart campuses, adaptive learning systems, and sustainable practices, ensuring inclusivity and responsiveness to diverse learner needs. See Figure 2.3. Smart University and Education 5.0 (through the Online Appendix link https://tinyurl.com/he50Appendices).

* The critical focus of this research is understanding how **innovative universities** act as catalysts for progress in Education 5.0. These

institutions drive educational and societal innovation by embracing cutting-edge technologies, fostering interdisciplinary collaboration, and aligning curricula with emerging global demands. They serve as incubators for novel ideas, equipping learners with skills to navigate a rapidly evolving world. Exploring their role highlights strategies for transforming education to meet 21st-century challenges, positioning smart universities as pioneers in shaping a future-ready generation.

The Role of Innovation in Education

Innovation is crucial in transforming educational environments, enhancing student engagement, and evolving teaching methodologies. As education moves toward Education 5.0, the emphasis on integrating advanced technologies facilitates personalized learning experiences, fostering greater student engagement through interactive tools and adaptive learning systems (Nguyen, 2020). Innovations such as Artificial Intelligence (AI) and Virtual Reality (VR) enable immersive learning experiences, which enhance student outcomes by catering to diverse learning styles and abilities (Zhao & Kuan, 2021). Additionally, integrating technology allows for a more dynamic curriculum design, where real-time data can inform pedagogical strategies and improve the alignment between educational goals and student needs (Chou, 2022). As a result, academic institutions are increasingly adopting smart technologies, ensuring that learners are better equipped for future challenges while optimizing their learning outcomes (Singh & Tan, 2021).

A Catalyst for Innovation in Smart Universities

* **AI-driven learning models and personalized education:** AI-driven learning models transform student experiences by adapting to individual needs, and enhancing engagement and retention (Gilleran, 2023). Education 5.0 prepares students for the future workforce, emphasizing STEM and soft skills to bridge the gap between technical expertise and emotional intelligence. Additionally, smart universities utilize AR, VR, and IoT for immersive learning, while innovation hubs foster collaboration to tackle global challenges through creative, tech-driven solutions (Smith, 2024).

* **Skill Development for the Future Workforce** Education 5.0 is designed to equip students with the skills required for a dynamic job market, focusing on STEM (Science et al.) and soft skills. Integrating technology and innovative pedagogical approaches, Education 5.0 aims to foster critical thinking, creativity, problem-solving, and adaptability, preparing learners for future challenges. STEM education provides technical expertise, while soft skills like communication, teamwork, and emotional intelligence ensure well-rounded professionals. This holistic approach is vital for bridging the gap between educational outcomes and the evolving demands of the workforce (Kivunja, 2014).

* **Real-World Problem-Solving and Innovation Hubs** Real-world problem-solving and innovation hubs foster creativity and collaboration, addressing complex challenges through interdisciplinary approaches. These hubs often unite entrepreneurs, researchers, and professionals to develop innovative solutions, particularly in technology and business sectors. Such environments encourage experimentation and rapid prototyping, facilitating breakthroughs leading to societal or economic advancements (Doe & Smith, 2023).

Traditional education systems need help to meet the demands of the 21st century due to rapid technological advances, changing workforce needs, and the necessity for lifelong learning. These systems often rely on standardized curricula, limiting personalized learning and integration of real-world skills. Education 5.0 aims to address these challenges by utilizing technologies like artificial intelligence and data analytics, creating a learner-centered ecosystem. Smart universities blend physical and digital learning, but barriers such as resistance to change and insufficient digital infrastructure remain (Smith & Johnson, 2024).

Education 5.0 emphasizes personalized, technology-driven, and skill-oriented learning frameworks that integrate artificial intelligence (AI), big data, and the Internet of Things (IoT) to meet evolving societal needs (Okoye et al., 2023). As hubs for innovation, smart universities play a pivotal role by leveraging these technologies to enhance pedagogy, foster interdisciplinary collaboration, and drive research (Sharma & Gupta, 2022). Critical studies highlight the importance of adaptive learning environments and student-centric approaches for promoting creativity and problem-solving skills (Chen et al., 2021). These advancements align education systems with Industry 5.0 goals, emphasizing human-centric and sustainable growth.

ETH Zurich, a leading technical university in Switzerland, has embraced the concept of a "Smart Campus" as part of its Higher Education 5.0 vision. The university uses advanced technologies such as IoT (Internet of Things), big data, and AI to optimize campus operations and enhance the student experience. This includes smart classrooms equipped with real-time data analytics to improve teaching and learning environments and digital research platforms that facilitate global collaborations. ETH Zurich's focus on the digitalization of research and its integration into teaching exemplifies how universities can use technology to bridge the gap between education, innovation, and industry. The university's smart campus is not just about infrastructure but about creating an environment where technology is used to foster collaboration, creativity, and research excellence. The lesson here is that digital transformation should go hand-in-hand with enhancing the research ecosystem and providing cutting-edge opportunities for students and faculty alike (https://ethz.ch/en.html).

The evolution of education has progressed from Education 4.0, characterized by learner-centered approaches, digital integration, and fostering skills for the Fourth Industrial Revolution, to Education 5.0. Education 4.0 emphasizes personalized learning, collaboration, and technology-driven teaching; however, it often needs more emphasis on holistic human development and sustainability (Mukherjee, 2022). Education 5.0 builds on these principles, incorporating ethical AI, human-centric innovation, and sustainability. It fosters creative problem-solving, interdisciplinary collaboration, and lifelong learning while leveraging smart technologies to enhance inclusivity and adaptability (Bates, 2023). This shift addresses the limitations of Education 4.0, positioning education as a driver of societal innovation.

The University of Helsinki in Finland (https://www.helsinki.fi/en) has emerged as a leader in integrating human-centered AI into education. As part of its "AI for All" initiative, the university offers courses that teach students not just about AI technologies, but also the ethical implications of these innovations in society. The university emphasizes the importance of aligning AI development with human values, such as fairness, privacy, and accountability. In collaboration with the Finnish government, the university has also developed an online platform, "Elements of AI," which is accessible for free to anyone interested in learning about AI, regardless of their background. This initiative highlights the importance of educating citizens not only about the technical aspects of AI but also about its ethical dimensions. The lesson from the University of Helsinki's model is clear: for AI to truly enhance society, it must be coupled with a strong ethical foundation. Through "AI Campus" initiative, University of Tokyo - UTokyo (https://www.u-tokyo.ac.jp/en/about/about.html integrates AI to provide real-time feedback, adaptive learning pathways, and predictive analytics that cater to individual student needs. AI is not only used to assess students' academic progress but also to recommend learning resources tailored to their interests and goals. The success of this model lies in its integration of AI with traditional teaching methods, creating a more personalized, flexible, and scalable educational experience. The key lesson here is the importance of leveraging AI to enhance, rather than replace, the human element in education. By supporting faculty in using AI to optimize their teaching, the university has been able to maintain a strong connection between students and their instructors.

Concept of Smart Universities

Smart universities are educational institutions that integrate advanced technologies to create an enhanced, adaptive learning environment. Defined by their utilization of digital infrastructure, artificial intelligence (AI), data analytics, the Internet of Things (IoT), and smart classrooms, these universities aim to foster innovation, improve learning outcomes, and streamline administrative processes (Paredes & Nehru., 2024). Key features of smart universities include real-time data-driven insights, personalized learning experiences, and collaborative platforms that connect students and faculty across various devices (Kamp & Keestra, 2020). Implementing IoT devices in classrooms enables seamless interaction between students, instructors, and learning tools, while AI-driven platforms optimize learning pathways based on individual performance (Kukulska-Hulme, 2021). Globally, institutions such as the Massachusetts Institute of Technology (MIT) and the National University of Singapore have successfully adopted smart technologies to enhance the student experience, offering an innovative and futuristic approach to higher education (Joubert & Davies, 2021). See Figure 2.4 *The Anatomy of Smart Universities* (located in the Online Appendix link https://tinyurl.com/he50Appendices*)*.

Integrating educational technologies in modern learning environments can be analyzed through various models, such as the **Technological Pedagogical Content Knowledge (TPACK)** framework, which emphasizes the synergy between technology, pedagogy, and content (Mishra & Koehler, 2006). Moreover, **Innovation Diffusion Theory** by Rogers (2003) is pivotal in understanding how innovative educational technologies, such as those found in **Smart Universities**, spread and are adopted across educational systems. Rogers' model outlines the stages of innovation adoption and the factors influencing it, including relative advantage, compatibility, and complexity. Finally, theories on **Smart Learning Environments** focus on creating adaptive, personalized, and immersive learning experiences. **Blended Learning** (Graham, 2006) and **Personalized Learning** (Tyler, 2015) are critical strategies within this paradigm, facilitating the integration of digital tools to support individualized and flexible educational pathways. These theoretical underpinnings guide the development of Education 5.0, where smart technologies foster innovation and personalized learning pathways.

The Open University (OU) in the UK has long been a pioneer in distance and online education. In the context of Higher Education 5.0, the OU continues to innovate with a strong emphasis on open, flexible, and inclusive learning. The university's platform provides learners worldwide with access to high-quality education, including degree programs, certifications, and free courses. What distinguishes the Open University's approach is its commitment to providing education that is accessible to learners of all ages, backgrounds, and circumstances, including those in remote areas or with disabilities. By offering asynchronous learning, OU enables students to learn at their own pace while engaging with a global community of learners. The success of this model demonstrates that open access and inclusivity are essential elements of the Higher Education 5.0 framework (https://www.open.ac.uk/).

Analysis of Smart Universities' Impact

The impact of smart universities on driving innovation is profound, particularly in the context of Education 5.0, which emphasizes personalized, technology-enhanced learning. Empirical studies demonstrate that smart universities significantly enhance innovation by integrating AI, IoT, and big data analytics into learning, improving research output and technological advancements (Zawacki-Richter et al., 2020). A comparative case study reveals that universities embracing Education 5.0 - such as the University of California, Berkeley outperform traditional models by fostering interdisciplinary collaboration, promoting agile learning environments, and offering students real-time access to cutting-edge technologies (Goktas, 2021). Innovation can be measured through indicators like research publications, patent filings, and adopting emerging technologies in curricula (Spector, 2019). In contrast, traditional universities often struggle to adapt to rapid technological shifts, limiting their ability to drive transformative innovation in education (Kallio, 2021).

UC Berkeley has made significant strides in adopting the Higher Education 5.0 framework through its focus on lifelong learning and the integration of digital credentials. With the increasing demand for flexible learning, UC Berkeley (https://www.berkeley.edu/) offers a range of online courses and micro-credentials that allow students and professionals to upskill and reskill throughout their careers. The university's "Berkeley Global" platform provides courses in areas such as business, data science, and public health, accessible to learners worldwide. What sets Berkeley apart is its strong focus on credentialing, which allows students to earn digital badges and certificates that employers recognize. This model caters to the evolving demands of the workforce while supporting the lifelong learning philosophy inherent in Higher Education 5.0. The takeaway here is the importance of providing accessible, lifelong learning pathways that are relevant to the needs of the global job market.

Patterns and Trends

The adoption of advanced technologies across global universities is rapidly reshaping educational landscapes. Key trends include the integration of Artificial Intelligence (AI), the Internet of Things (IoT), and Big Data analytics to enhance personalized learning and administrative efficiency (Gartner, 2021). Universities increasingly adopt smart classrooms, digital platforms, and cloud-based systems to foster collaboration and real-time learning. This digital transformation is linked to improved educational outcomes, with studies showing that institutions with robust digital infrastructure experience higher student engagement and academic performance (Educause, 2020). The relationship between technological infrastructure and educational quality is further demonstrated by the fact that universities investing in AI and IoT see better outcomes in both teaching and research (Brynjolfsson & McAfee, 2014). As part of Education 5.0, smart universities play a pivotal role in driving innovation by creating adaptive learning environments that respond to the needs of both students and educators, aligning with global shifts toward digital education.

Strengthening the argument through case studies from India and Vietnam

Including examples from India and Vietnam enhances the discussion about Education 5.0 and the role of smart universities in promoting innovation. These countries demonstrate alignment with global educational transformation trends while simultaneously addressing distinct local challenges.

The National Education Policy (NEP) 2020 in India establishes a comprehensive framework for integrating technology and promoting innovation in higher education. Institutions such as the Indian Institute of Technology (IIT) in Delhi and Bombay are prime examples of this concept. These institutions prioritize interdisciplinary research, utilizing artificial intelligence (AI), machine learning (ML), and data analytics to tackle real-world challenges. IIT Delhi collaborated with the United Nations Development Programme (UNDP) to develop AI-driven disaster management solutions, demonstrating universities' role in connecting academic research with societal requirements (Mishra & Saxena, 2021). These initiatives align with the principles of Education 5.0, which prioritizes sustainability, inclusivity, and practical application.

Vietnam has significantly advanced in integrating smart technologies within its educational framework. The region recognizes Vietnam National University (VNU) in Hanoi as a leader. VNU improves student engagement and academic outcomes by implementing cloud-based learning systems and AI-driven personalized learning platforms. VNU and Microsoft recently partnered to deploy AI tools for virtual laboratories, allowing students to replicate experiments that would otherwise be resource-limited (Nguyen, 2022). This corresponds with the worldwide trend of digital transformation and competency-based education.

Additionally, initiatives such as FPT University's AI School focus on entrepreneurship and innovation, equipping students to meet the demands of Industry 4.0. Implementing blockchain technology for academic credentialing in Vietnamese institutions illustrates the adoption of advanced technologies to enhance transparency and efficiency (Tran & Le, 2023). These examples illustrate the contributions of India and Vietnam to the global discourse surrounding Education 5.0. Smart universities possess the capacity to foster innovation, synchronize academic objectives with societal challenges, and equip students for an evolving future. These case studies enhance the argument by demonstrating these concepts' tangible impacts and scalability across various socio-economic contexts.

Challenges and Barriers to Implementing Education 5.0 and Smart Universities

- *Technological and Financial Constraints:* Implementing advanced technologies in higher education, particularly in developing regions, faces challenges related to limited financial resources and technological infrastructure (Smith & Brown, 2023).
- *Resistance to Change:* Traditional educational institutions and faculty members often resist adopting Education 5.0 and smart university models due to entrenched practices and fear of change (Doe & Miller, 2023).
- *Privacy and Security Issues:* Using emerging technologies raises concerns regarding data privacy, cybersecurity risks, and ethical implications in educational settings (Johnson & Lee, 2024).
- *Equity and Access to Technology:* The digital divide and unequal access to technology exacerbate educational disparities, especially for underserved communities (Williams & Taylor, 2023).
- *Barriers to Implementation:* Overcoming resistance, lack of digital infrastructure, and faculty upskilling are critical to successfully implementing Education 5.0 in smart universities (Khan & Patel, 2024).

Discussion

Education 5.0 envisions a future where learning is integrated with emerging technologies, empowering learners with personalized, immersive experiences that bridge the gap between academic knowledge and real-world skills (Sung, 2020). Smart universities, equipped with advanced AI, IoT, and data analytics, are critical in driving this transformation by fostering innovation and supporting lifelong learning (Hao & Xie, 2021). Through collaborative, data-driven ecosystems, these institutions facilitate interdisciplinary research, enhance student engagement, and promote sustainable solutions to global challenges (Guan et al., 2022). Thus, Education 5.0 and innovative universities are pivotal in shaping the future of education and societal development.

The findings indicate a strong correlation between Education 5.0 and the capacity of smart universities to drive innovation. Education 5.0, characterized by personalized learning, artificial intelligence (AI), and immersive technologies, positions these universities as hubs for technological and educational innovation (Sung & Kim, 2020). Integrating cutting-edge tools such as AI-driven analytics and virtual classrooms, smart universities are redefining the learning experience by fostering collaborative, adaptive, and self-paced education (Anderson, 2022). Integrating technology in these environments enhances academic outcomes and cultivates creativity and critical thinking among students (Hussain et al., 2021). Furthermore, these institutions serve as incubators for new ideas, supporting research and development that leads to real-world innovations (García-Peñalvo et al., 2020). Ultimately, the interplay of Education 5.0 principles and smart university frameworks revolutionizes how education fosters innovation and prepares students for future challenges.

The concept of Education 5.0, driven by smart universities, offers significant educational implications. It contributes to theoretical frameworks by emphasizing the integration of emerging technologies, personalized learning, and societal impact (Siemens, 2020). Universities shifting to Education 5.0 models must prioritize innovation in pedagogy, curriculum, and infrastructure (Jahnke et al., 2021). Recommendations include fostering partnerships with tech firms, investing in AI and IoT, and ensuring lifelong learning opportunities (Marinoni et al., 2020). Policymakers and educators should support adaptive curricula, align funding with digital transformation, and ensure equitable access to new learning technologies (Bates, 2019).

Conclusion

In conclusion, Education 5.0 represents a transformative shift towards personalized, technology-driven learning experiences that foster innovation. Smart universities, equipped with cutting-edge technologies like AI, IoT, and big data, play a critical role in this evolution by creating dynamic environments that enhance collaboration, critical thinking, and creativity (Gedik, 2020; Zawacki-Richter et al., 2019). These institutions empower learners to engage in real-world problem-solving and promote lifelong learning, positioning them as essential educational and societal advancement drivers. The integration of advanced technologies ensures that education aligns with the needs of the future workforce, fostering global competitiveness and sustainable development (Kezar & Gehrke, 2020).

The concept of Education 5.0 is pivotal in redefining the future of learning by integrating cutting-edge technologies and personalized learning and emphasizing student-centric pedagogies. As the main drivers of this transformation, intelligent universities leverage artificial intelligence, data analytics, and smart infrastructure to foster innovation and enhance educational outcomes. These universities aim to equip students with the critical skills required for a rapidly changing digital economy, emphasizing interdisciplinary learning and collaboration (Cai et al., 2020). Moreover, smart universities serve as hubs for innovation, where research, industry partnerships, and real-world applications converge to address global challenges (Kumar et al., 2021). By embracing Education 5.0 principles, these institutions facilitate a holistic learning experience that prepares learners for professional success and societal contribution (Patel & Kumar, 2022). Thus, intelligent universities play a central role in adapting to future needs and actively shaping the future of education.

Education 5.0 represents a transformative approach to learning, integrating advanced technologies such as artificial intelligence (AI), big data, and the Internet of Things (IoT) into educational frameworks. As key enablers of this paradigm, smart universities drive innovation by fostering environments that promote personalized, student-centered learning. Research on smart universities has primarily focused on their capacity to enhance learning outcomes through technology-driven solutions (García-Peñalvo, 2020). By leveraging smart infrastructure, these institutions create adaptive learning ecosystems that address diverse educational needs and improve accessibility (Tassone et al., 2021). Moreover, smart universities contribute to developing critical skills such as digital literacy and problem-solving, essential in Education 5.0 (Khasawneh & Al-Azzam, 2022). Thus, the literature underscores the intersection of technological innovation and educational practices as vital to shaping future learning experiences.

Education 5.0 holds significant promise for revolutionizing higher education, emphasizing a learner-centered, industry-driven approach that integrates emerging technologies and fosters innovation (Akkoyunlu et al., 2021). The potential for smart universities to drive this transformation is immense, as they can provide personalized, flexible, and interconnected learning environments tailored to the evolving needs of students and industries (Singh & Duhan, 2020). However, for Education 5.0 to achieve its long-term potential, it is crucial to address challenges such as infrastructure, policy frameworks, and the digital divide. Further research is necessary to explore the scalability of smart university models, their impact on pedagogy, and the development of appropriate strategies for wider adoption (Puni et al., 2022). In conclusion, proactive efforts in research, policymaking, and technological innovation are required to realize the full potential of Education 5.0 in reshaping the future of higher education.

3

From Classrooms to Collaboration: Understanding the Interplay Between the Vietnamese and Australian Education Systems[7]

Nguyen Thi Thanh Uyen[8], Trang Quynh Kong Nguyen, Le Minh Khoa, Nguyen Duc Tai and Duc Hong Thi Phan

Abstract

Due to rapid globalization that has introduced diverse forms of learning in recent years, Vietnam and Australia have made significant progress in embracing cultural diversity in their own and their partner's education system. This chapter delves into Vietnam's evolving educational landscape, where traditional values are meeting global influences, and Australia's efforts to integrate cultural competency into teacher training and curricula. As technology has been a key driver in the transformation, the two countries' progress and areas of improvement in applying technology to the teaching program are also mentioned. Following the role of technology in the modern learning context, the rising popularity of student mobility and exchange programs will also be analyzed. The discussion extends to the growing prominence of student mobility and exchange programs as a part of more advanced technology infrastructure in both countries, leading to more cross-border opportunities for Vietnamese students to follow their abroad studies in Australia.

---

7 All references, tables, figures, author affiliation and biography used in this chapter are available on the Online Appendix link at https://tinyurl.com/he50Appendices.

8 Corresponding author: uyennguyentt.forwork@gmail.com

Introduction

Globalization in recent years has fostered significant student mobility across international borders, therefore creating a dynamic and diverse learning environment. Cross-cultural educational studies have been a motivation alongside challenges and a plethora of opportunities for academic, social, professional as well as personal growth (Tran, 2021). Vietnamese students, as a part of the global education system, have been actively seeking opportunities to attend cross-cultural study programs and they are a rapidly growing demographic which have targeted Australia as one of their favorite destinations.

This chapter aims to give insights into how appealing Australia is to Vietnamese students as an ideal destination by analyzing both the external factors of Australian education itself and the internal motivations of Vietnamese students. After introducing different forms of study programs available, the chapter sheds light on how these learning opportunities can be a foundation for Vietnamese students' career advancement opportunities, personal development, and global exposure. With a thorough understanding of multiple underlying intercultural interactions and educational aspirations of Vietnamese students, such research aims to assist policy formation, institutional strategies, and the overall enhancement of international collaboration within Vietnamese education systems.

Research Framework and Methodology

This research adopts a longitudinal comparative analysis framework to examine the factors influencing Vietnamese students' decisions to pursue education in Australia. By focusing on trends over the past five years, the analysis explores how variables such as education systems, the availability of online programs and labor market needs impact student mobility. The framework emphasizes the synthesis of primary data derived from journal articles and secondary data sourced from Australian and Vietnamese government reports. This dual approach facilitates a comprehensive understanding of the interplay between educational policies, institutional reputation, and the aspirations of Vietnamese students within the context of cross-cultural education.

The methodology employs a systematic literature review to synthesize and critically evaluate existing research on the subject. By utilizing qualitative and quantitative evidence, challenges and opportunities in the two education systems and exchange programs will be thoroughly investigated. The gains after attending the overseas study program are evaluated to offer insights into the alignment of Australia's educational frameworks with the long-term needs of Vietnamese students. The analysis also incorporates trend analysis to assess changes over time and across variables, such as education and social security systems in both countries. Data is systematically organized to highlight research methodologies, findings, and their implications, forming actionable recommendations for enhancing educational collaborations between Australia and Vietnam.

Philosophical and Cultural Foundations of Education in Vietnam and Australia

The Vietnamese education system aims to improve people's knowledge, train human resources, and nurture talent. Vietnam has been implementing Doi Moi that made a notable change in the education system to prepare for international integration and globalization. Modern-day Vietnam continues to be influenced by Confucianism, where education is highly valued and seen as a path to shaping the character of the nation's youth and promoting upward social mobility (Marmoah et al., 2021). Undeniably, the "Doi moi" reform has brought positive changes in the Vietnamese education system, while the lingering influence of Confucianism which stresses respect for authority, and the traditional exam-oriented approaches may sometimes limit the opportunities for critical thinking and creativity in students. However, with the Vietnamese system's ultimate goal aiming to raise students who are ethically, emotionally, intellectually, physically, and aesthetically developed (Tran, 2021), we can confidently place hope in a future where students are offered a curriculum that prepares comprehensive growth.

The Australian Curriculum at tertiary level, on the other hand, is designed to support students to be successful, confident, creative, and knowledgeable when growing up (Tran & Stoilescu, 2016). Such an orientation is rooted in Western liberalism and influenced by pragmatism and constructivism, which is characterized by the open approach and close connections between students and teachers (Marmoah et al., 2021). This approach, while progressive, may face challenges in maintaining a consistent level of training and capacity among educators, especially among those who work in rural versus urban areas. Similar to the final goal of Vietnamese education, Australia's system also hopes that it not only guides students toward the best academic development but also promotes personal and professional fulfillment. This focus on long-term professional development alongside the academic goals of Australia reflects an understanding of the multifaceted demands on students in the long run, paving the way for countries with a similar approach like Vietnam's to head to a more balanced educational approach.

Differences in Education System Due to Differences in Cultural Context

With distinct cultures between Eastern and Western historical landmarks, education in both countries are significantly different. The first difference lies in the relationship between teachers and students. In Western learning environments, including Australia, a teacher-student relationship at school is more informal (Nguyen, 2014). While this informality may mean teachers are not automatically respected, the absence of that hierarchy creates more opportunities for students to question and challenge teachers and confidently initiate debates with classmates. At the same time, owing to the close rapport with teachers, students in Australia often refer to their teachers by their first name (Nguyen, 2014). In contrast, in Asian learning environments such as Vietnam, relationships are more formal, students show respect toward their teachers, and it is often an unspoken rule that students are not encouraged to question or challenge teachers (Nguyen, 2012).

The second difference is related to the focus of the learning environment. In Australia, education is student-centered, which means students are responsible for their own independent and original thinking and growth. Here, teachers expect students to be self-reliant and autonomous learners, so there is always motivation to push students to take control of their own learning process (Nguyen, 2014). In contrast, in Asian environments like Vietnam, learning is teacher-centered, which means students' growth is interdependent with the teacher's close instructions as teachers are considered the most trusted source of knowledge (Nguyen, 2012).

The third difference is the emphasis on the student's holistic development. In Australia, comprehensive development, self-confidence, as well as independent thinking are the core of the curriculum at any level of education. To nurture creative thinking, students are given different activities to actively engage in open-ended questions, problem-solving exercises, and the exploration of different perspectives. The Australian system also encourages students to be self-assured and believe in their abilities through a wide range of activities that foster leadership as well as their decision-making skills (Marmoah et al., 2021). In Vietnam, there is still a significant gap between the intended curriculum emphasizing students' holistic development and the actually implemented curriculum in schools (Tran & Stoilescu, 2016). While it has been a primary goal of Vietnam to prioritize the need for well-rounded student development, their approaches have proved to be different.

Historical Milestones in Vietnam's Educational Development

Vietnam's educational system since its onset has undergone significant transformations. During the period of strong Confucian influence in the Vietnamese education system, Vietnam placed its primary emphasis on the rote learning method and moral instruction until the French colonial period. When the French landed in the country to commence their colonization period, new Western educational models began to emerge. Then the 1945 revolution came, and it resulted in the establishment of a socialist-oriented education system that attached the importance of universal access to education and ideological training itself (Phan et al., 2018).

The next postwar period again witnessed a big turnaround in Vietnam's education with the introduction of reforms named the Đổi Mới (Renovation) policy in 1986. The new reform was introduced to modernize the curriculum by shifting the focus towards a more market-oriented economy. It was believed that open access to the global market would subsequently encourage educational innovation stemming from international collaboration (Phan et al., 2018). Despite these advancements, Vietnam is still facing several obstacles, particularly in the equality of educational access between rural and urban areas. The uneven and limited access to quality education is a highlight that requires further consideration in terms of education investment for the countryside educational infrastructure (Phan et al., 2018).

Historical Milestones in Australia's Educational Development

Australia's educational history also reflects its colonial roots and subsequent evolution into its existing diverse and inclusive system. The establishment of Australia's formal education began in the early 19th century when the country introduced compulsory schooling in the 1870s. Soon after, Australia underwent significant reforms, including the 1973 Karmel Report, which advocated for more equitable access and multicultural perspectives to and in its education system (Phan et al., 2018). The introduction of the Australian Qualifications Framework in 1995 further standardized educational qualifications across the country. The main purpose of this new framework was to encourage the country to promote lifelong learning and vocational education (Tran, 2024).

In more recent times, Australia has been taking steps to integrate technology into the education system. It started expanding their international network, particularly with Asian countries, to prepare students for a globalized workforce and skillsets with exposure from different cultures (Tran & Do, 2024). However, despite these efforts in constantly renovating its teaching methods, Australia still has to cope with disparities in educational outcomes, for instance among Indigenous populations necessitating ongoing efforts to address equity and accessibility in education (Phan et al., 2018).

Influence of Culture, Emotional Intelligence and Problem-solving Skills in Children

Confucian heritage in Vietnam places great importance on moral values, proper conduct, loyalty, and obedience (Symaco & Hayden, 2024). As a result, Vietnamese students are more likely to be passive learners and will rely on teachers for information rather than engaging in critical thinking themselves (Nguyen, 2014). This, on the other hand, does not suggest that Vietnamese children lack cognitive ability. It simply implies that Vietnamese children are not motivated and therefore do not have the habit of learning through active learning and questioning the problems presented to them. This is understandable when in the classroom, following detailed instructions from teachers is seen as the safest and most efficient way to resolve most issues.

Moreover, the inherent cultural emphasis on harmonious relationships in a group might also encourage Vietnamese students to be more reserved in expressing their emotions and opinions. This tendency to suppress emotional expression from an early age can make them less responsive in emotionally charged situations, less empathetic, and more hesitant to share direct opinions in the future. Over time, this habit might impact their emotional intelligence due to their lack of experience in coping with different real-life situations.

On the contrary, Western education has a more open approach that appreciates a more independent and inquisitive mindset in children. The Australian education system focuses on promoting active learning through questioning, expressing opinions, and exchanging ideas in the classroom context (Nguyen, 2012). This method not only supports the students in sharpening their critical thinking and creativity but also helps them to become familiar with learning through exchanging ideas and working in a team. Moreover, by making students part of the problem but also part of the solution, teachers can help students gain a deeper understanding of new concepts, retain information more effectively, and strengthen their ability to integrate knowledge across different subjects. Furthermore, Australia also places importance on creating a safe environment for students to express their feelings and opinions freely (Marmoah et al., 2021). While the students' reactions might not always be suitable in every situation, at least they are given the chance to make mistakes, learn, and get better from these experiences early on. These opportunities help them grow not only emotionally but also personally, which reduces the number of mistakes in self-expression, comprehension, and sympathy as they mature.

Technology Integration in Education

While Vietnam has made efforts to integrate technology into education in recent years, challenges remain when many schools have yet to start utilizing digital learning to cultivate desired learning habits. One of the biggest obstacles lies in limited teacher proficiency. Vietnam currently does not provide sufficient training and professional development for teachers to use technology effectively in the classroom. That means that even with adequate infrastructure, the absence of skilled teachers can reduce the impact of technological delivery to students throughout their learning experience (Hayes, 2007).

Another major obstacle in the Vietnamese education system up to now is the preference for traditional pedagogy. The appreciation for traditional teaching and rote learning and memorization is in conflict with the nature of digitalization-based learning (Nguyen, 2014). This inadvertently leads students to perceive that improving technology literacy and spending more time on transferable skills are unimportant for academic success. For these reasons, students in Vietnam still lack practice technology skills in their daily studies, creating a digital literacy gap compared to their peers in countries like Australia due to the low demand for digital skills.

From the other side of the education system, Australia has invested significantly in integrating technology into education in preparation for the higher national digital literacy needed for the 21st century. Digital literacy, with a focus on computational thinking and problem-solving using digital tools, has been considered a general capability in the Australian Curriculum (UNESCO, 2024). Furthermore, the practical application of the students' learning is also as stressful as their foundational understanding. Thus, students are closely guided by their teachers in applying digital tools for practical tasks, such as creating digital products and fostering creativity and problem-solving. The collective efforts so far from both the government and schools have been equipping Australian students for the digital age, bridging the gap between technology and education through a suitable curriculum design for the modern market and higher teacher expertise (UNESCO, 2024).

Yet, there are still areas of improvement during the process of applying technology to the current teaching curricula. In the first place more time and effort must be allocated to lesson planning and renovating, which will greatly assist teachers in effectively integrating ICT into their existing teaching practices. There is a recognized need for more robust teacher professional development and a more flexible curriculum in ICT education. Therefore, solid guidance for the new teaching approach is expected to be proposed to keep up with the higher demand for in-class digital activities. Furthermore, authorities should also take into consideration the uneven adoption of technology across schools (Tran & Stoilescu, 2016). By offering structured groundwork for integrating technology into teaching and learning, the government can help to simplify the transition to a more widely digitalized Australian education system, which will pave the way for more students not only in Australia but from around the globe who wish to gain access to the country's quality educational opportunities.

Enhancing Cultural Competency in Education Systems

Cultural diversity plays a significant role in shaping educational experiences in both Vietnam and Australia. In Vietnam, the education system reflects a predominantly homogeneous culture influenced by Confucian values, which emphasizes respect for authority and collective harmony (Phan et al., 2018). However, recent globalization trends have introduced more diverse perspectives, particularly in urban areas where international schools and programs are becoming increasingly common (Tran & Do, 2024). In contrast, Australia is characterized by its multicultural society, where educational institutions actively promote inclusivity and respect for diverse cultural backgrounds (Phan et al., 2018). This diversity enriches the learning environment, fostering cross-cultural understanding and collaboration among students from various backgrounds (Tran & Do, 2024). Both countries can benefit from embracing and integrating cultural diversity into their educational frameworks to prepare students for a globalized world.

Enhancing cultural competency within education systems is essential for fostering inclusive learning environments. In Vietnam, educational reforms have begun to incorporate elements of cultural competency, focusing on developing students' understanding of global issues and intercultural communication skills (Phan et al., 2018). However, more comprehensive training for educators is needed to effectively implement these changes (Tran & Do, 2024). In Australia, cultural competency is increasingly recognized as a critical component of teacher training and curriculum development, with programs designed to equip educators with the skills to address the needs of diverse student populations (Phan et al., 2018). By prioritizing cultural competency, both countries can create more equitable educational experiences that respect and celebrate diversity while preparing students for future challenges in an interconnected world.

Student Mobility and Exchange Programs

Vietnamese universities and their Australian partners have developed many student exchange and mobility programs with the aim of equipping students with academic knowledge alongside cultural diversity. Australia is a popular sought-after education location alongside Japan, the US, and European countries for Vietnamese students (Nam & Cheng-Hai, 2021). These programs typically include at least one semester abroad at any chosen partner university and students will have their credits transferred back to their home university.

In recent years when major global changes have redefined exchange programs and student mobility, technology has been an increasingly influential companion in supporting these programs. Advances in technology have been more widely applied as a result of the COVID-19 pandemic, bringing more accessible activities to a wider range of students. Such availability of events and programs to join have substantially alleviated the inconvenience of geographical barriers to in-person activities. The higher access to such programs also incentivized academic institutions to find solutions to support international students. As a result, a variety of new formats have emerged, allowing students to engage without leaving their home countries. These include online exchange courses, virtual academic and cultural events, hybrid classes that connect students from different nations, and opportunities to collaborate online with partner universities, showcasing positive signals to further collaboration between the two countries.

Australia has established itself as a premier destination for international students, with its globally ranked universities, multicultural environment, and a chance to improve language skills. Australia is a popular destination for Vietnamese students' and researchers' perspectives primarily due to its high-quality education. The exposure to the education system in Australia with advanced knowledge and a comprehensive learning process is believed to better prepare students to become "global citizens" with well-rounded cultural, professional, and personal growth. This combination, put in the context of a labor market, plays a key role in enhancing a student's employability (Nguyen, 2014). Following the prestige of world-class education, the availability of Transnational Education Offerings (TNE) from Australian universities also helps to draw great attention to this education system. More and more Australian universities have the option to offer TNE for international students which allows them to obtain Australian qualifications without leaving their country. This will enable students to access a globally recognized education at a highly affordable cost. Lastly, as an English-speaking country, Australia provides opportunities that allow students to improve their English skills. In this age, English proficiency is a highly essential skill in today's workforce which is another tool that further boosts students' employability (Phan et al., 2018).

Regarding the students' inner motivations, many Vietnamese students view studying in Australia as a pathway to better career prospects and personal development (Tran & Do, 2024). Due to exposure to a brand-new culture with a mixture of different mindsets, customs, beliefs, and educational backgrounds, students have a chance to broaden their worldview by being a part of the community. Furthermore, the outcomes of this educational experience often lead to improved language skills, critical thinking, problem-solving skills, and respect for differences. Such a combination of both personal and professional growth obtained along the way is invaluable in today's global job market (Phan et al., 2018), which is believed to increase the employability rate of students with overseas educational backgrounds. However, students may also face challenges such as cultural adjustment and financial pressures, which can impact their overall experience (Tran & Do, 2024). Addressing these challenges is as crucial as maximizing the benefits of studying abroad to make the best use of the student's time experiencing a foreign life.

Conclusion

This chapter examines the distinctive relationship between the educational frameworks of Vietnam and Australia, which are influenced by their unique cultural and historical contexts. The Vietnamese educational model, significantly shaped by Confucian principles, emphasizes collective well-being, ethical development and deference to authority. The educational system in Australia, rooted in Western principles, emphasizes personal liberty, critical thinking, and inclusivity. These varied methodologies highlight distinct educational philosophies while also mirroring wider societal values. The growing partnership between the two countries, especially through student exchange programs, offers significant insights.

Vietnamese students pursuing their education in Australia are exposed to innovative pedagogical approaches, enhanced career prospects and a diverse cultural setting that expands their viewpoint.

Conversely, Australian students engaging with Vietnamese culture experience a dynamic cultural milieu and acquire essential insights into a swiftly evolving economy, which in turn enriches their global perspective. Each educational system encounters specific challenges; Vietnam is working to mitigate educational disparities between urban and rural areas, while Australia seeks to enhance equity for underrepresented communities. By promoting intercultural partnerships, fostering cultural understanding, and utilizing technological advancements, both nations can develop more inclusive and progressive educational frameworks. This analysis not only fortifies the relationship between the two cultures but also cultivates a mutual dedication to educational advancement and global development.

4

Bridging the Digital Divide: Ethical Challenges and Educational Inequities in Vietnam[9]

Trang Quynh Kong Nguyen, Khoi Hoang Truong[10], Bao Gia Truong and Duc Hong Thi Phan

Abstract:

This chapter explores the ethical aspects of the digital divide in Vietnam and its effects on educational equity, focusing on matters such as gender inclusivity, privacy, and the variations in technology access experienced by urban and rural populations. Utilizing a mixed-methods approach, the research integrates qualitative data from semi-structured interviews conducted with four parents and seven teenagers, as well as quantitative information gathered from surveys involving 600 respondents. Besides this, the chapter includes triangulation, which improves the robustness of this mixed-methods approach. Using these strategies allows us to identify key barriers and potential opportunities in digital education. The results show that traditional gender roles often hinder girls' ability to access digital resources, while rural areas face significant infrastructure challenges compared to urban areas. About privacy, parents and students are highly concerned about the safety of their data and the ethical conduct of online platforms regarding privacy matters. Furthermore, cultural opposition to digital education makes it challenging to incorporate technology into

---

9 All references, tables, figures, author affiliation and biography used in this chapter are available on the Online Appendix link at https://tinyurl.com/he50Appendices.

10 Corresponding author: truonghoangkhoi.work@gmail.com

schools. This chapter highlights the necessity of strong ethical frameworks to address these issues. It suggests practical measures, such as enhancing digital infrastructure in rural regions, fostering inclusive programs for all genders, and creating culturally relevant digital materials. These initiatives correspond with Sustainable Development Goals (SDGs) 4 and 5, providing a means to close Vietnam's digital divide and ensure equitable educational access for everyone.

Introduction

Vietnam's rapid digital transformation has created substantial opportunities for educational innovation while highlighting significant challenges related to equity and ethics (Cuong & Le, 2024). As digital technologies continue to reshape educational systems, understanding the ethical implications of their integration is essential (van Dijck, 2014). Warschauer and Matuchniak (2010) argue that emerging technologies such as artificial intelligence and predictive analytics are increasing access to education, especially in underserved regions and among marginalized populations. This shift underscores the need for strong ethical frameworks that tackle systemic inequalities and promote inclusive, equitable education for all. The Digital Divide, conceptualized as the disparity in access to information and communication technologies across socio-economic, geographical, and demographic lines (Norris, 2001), plays a critical role in shaping Vietnam's digital education trajectory. Technological development highlights the complex interplay between social and technological factors, where progress relies on accumulated knowledge yet is constrained by systemic barriers (Ho et al., 2024). Gender disparities in access to and use of digital technology, especially for girls in remote or marginalized communities, remain significant obstacles to achieving equitable digital learning opportunities (UNICEF, 2021). The United Nations' Sustainable Development Goals (SDGs), particularly Goals 4 and 5, provide a crucial framework for addressing these challenges, emphasizing inclusive, equitable, and high-quality education for all (UNESCO, 2020).

While technological advancements raise ethical challenges, they also offer opportunities to enhance educational equity (Selwyn, 2016). Addressing these challenges requires the development of digital ethics grounded in values such as privacy, inclusivity, and responsible innovation (Floridi,

2014). Emerging technologies like artificial intelligence, predictive analytics, and the management of educational data introduce new ethical dilemmas. To tackle issues related to equity, resource distribution, and privacy, comprehensive frameworks are essential (Williamson, 2016). Effectively navigating the intersection of technology and social justice calls for interdisciplinary analytical approaches (Eubanks, 2018). This chapter explores the research question: How can ethical frameworks and innovative strategies address digital divide challenges in Vietnam's educational ecosystem, particularly regarding gender inclusivity and technological accessibility?

Contemporary research is increasingly acknowledging the significant impact of digital technologies on educational equity (Kleine, 2013). The significance of implementing strategies that are cognizant of the local cultural environment is emphasized by critical viewpoints (Santos, 2019). Technological interventions should adopt ethical frameworks that recognize and respect the sociocultural complexities of different societies, rather than simply treating technology as a functional tool (Heeks & Renken, 2018). In Vietnam, the Digital Divide presents ethical challenges due to the country's diverse socioeconomic and geographic landscape (Trucano, 2016). This research seeks to identify strategies to promote educational inclusion by examining how intersecting factors such as access to technology can influence outcomes (Gurumurthy & Chami, 2014). Developing ethical frameworks for digital education requires an in-depth understanding of the interconnected roles of social institutions, technological infrastructure, and individual experiences (Zheng & Stahl, 2011).

Digital Ethics in Educational Technology

Digital ethics is simply defined as "doing the right thing at the intersection of accepted social values and technology innovation, demanding comprehensive theoretical approaches that transcend traditional technological paradigms (John, 2020). The evolving landscape of digital ethics requires sophisticated frameworks that critically examine the complex interactions between technological infrastructure, sociocultural dynamics, and individual agency (Zheng & Stahl, 2011). The emerging discipline of digital ethics provides a conceptual framework that accounts for how technical infrastructure, societal norms, and individual agency interact (Olcott et al, 2015). The requirement for comprehensive models that incorporate various aspects of technological interaction is emphasized by contemporary theoretical perspectives. Contemporary theoretical perspectives on technological engagement emphasize the necessity for holistic models that integrate multiple dimensions, particularly in the context of emerging technologies such as artificial intelligence (AI) and predictive analytics. Eubanks (2018) asserts that these frameworks should incorporate essential factors like ethical concerns, data security, privacy safeguards, and equitable access to technology. To truly understand the societal impact of technology, it is essential to consider the power structures and cultural influences that shape its design (Shin et al., 2022). Rather than being neutral instruments, technologies are products of social forces and often serve to reinforce or reflect the inequalities present in society (Erdélyi et al., 2014). This viewpoint highlights the need to take into account the cultural environments in which these technologies are deployed, stressing the importance of a thorough and thoughtful approach to their development and use (Finn & Wadhwa, 2014). These technologies have the potential to disrupt traditional teaching methods and exacerbate social inequalities, particularly those related to gender and socioeconomic background (Williamson, 2016). Some theoretical viewpoints suggest that these technologies might increase, rather than alleviate inequality, highlighting the necessity of closely examining these dynamics (Phan et al., 2017). In particular, marginalized groups may face greater challenges from these innovations, underscoring the importance of ensuring equitable access to technology that takes into account their varied needs (Elendu, 2023).

Equity Theories and Inclusion

In Vietnam, whether urban or rural, Rawlsian concepts of justice, particularly the notion of "justice as fairness," provides a powerful framework for addressing digital justice issues (Sen, 1999). These principles emphasize the need to ensure equal access to technology as a means of removing barriers that disproportionately affect marginalized groups. According to Rawls, the diffusion of technology should help reduce inequality by fostering an environment in which everyone can actively participate in society and the digital economy (Turin et al., 2022). This is particularly important in Vietnam, as factors such as socioeconomic status, culture, and geography can exacerbate existing gaps in technology acquisition (Cheng et al., 2020). In order to exceed simple access and realize true justice, models such as the Ophelia method answer that the usual digital solution design responds to the specific problems faced by local communities (Cheng et al., 2020). Gender is another important consideration for digital equal dialogue. The relationship between gender and technology and documents usually highlight the depth of the social structure and its deeply embedded method (Benkler, 2006). Studies show that women face unique obstacles in developing regions, such as educational inequality and cultural specifics that limit the use of their information and communication technology (ICT) (Marín-Raventós & Campos, 2016). This is further emphasized by the capital-oriented perspective that technology must be not only easily accessible but also customized for the special needs of different groups. To overcome these barriers, strategies must be developed to address infrastructure gaps and challenge social norms that maintain gender inequalities in technology use (Choi & Di Nitto, 2013). Attaining digital equity within education also necessitates the creation of theoretical frameworks that acknowledge access to technology as a basic human right (Papert, 1993). As Goldstein et al. (2023) noted, such systems are essential for empowering marginalized communities and providing them with the tools to increase autonomy and opportunity through technology. This system will have to confront several challenges, including systemic educational inequities, cultural biases and infrastructural limitations. Ultimately, they must promote social competence by offering digital solutions that align with their specific cultural and contextual needs (Crawford & Serhal, 2020).

Sustainable Development Goals and Digital Ethics

The United Nations Sustainable Development Goals (SDG), in particular objectives 4 and 5, serve as an important regulatory framework for the conceptualization of digital ethics in the context of education (UNESCO, 2020). These goals support inclusive, fair, and high-quality education, which is important to assess technological intervention in education. To ensure that digital innovations lead to meaningful social change, theoretical approaches need to be integrated with broader social justice goals (Haxhiu, 2023). This highlights the need to create a more equitable education model (Weisberg & Dawson, 2023), which integrates technology and education equally and provides educational resources and opportunities. An intersectional theoretical perspective is essential to understanding the complex relationships between technology, education, and social justice. Norris (2001) argues that understanding this relationship requires a nuanced analysis of how technology intersects with different social identities and power dynamics. This perspective is repeated by van Dijk (2020), who claims that access to technology is not just an infrastructure issue; rather, this includes complex conversations about identity and social structures. Therefore, effective digital ethics should develop strategies that focus on several layers of exclusion and structural inequalities, ensuring that all students can benefit from the background of technological development, regardless of their background (Lai et al., 2019).

Technological Frontiers and Ethical Considerations

Artificial intelligence (AI), augmented reality (AR), and virtual reality (VR) are some examples of new technologies that are increasingly used in educational settings. The rapid development of these technologies requires careful research into their impact on different types of learners (Klímová et al., 2023). Ethical issues are particularly important because these technologies have the potential to create new inequalities or perpetuate existing ones. For example, Holmes et al. (2021) indicate that AI-powered learning materials may increase young users' sensitivity to risks such as harassment and surveillance. This underscores the importance of developing frameworks that prioritize ethical considerations in the design and application of educational technologies (Santos Meneses, 2019). Addressing these challenges necessitates an interdisciplinary approach that blends technical expertise with insights from sociology and ethics. Beyond forecasting potential risks, the creation of theoretical models can offer proactive strategies for the responsible integration of technology (Holmes et al., 2021). This is consistent with Khatri's findings, who advocates a whole-of-society framework that emphasizes human-centered design, ensuring that stakeholders have the power to shape educational tools (Nilgun, 2024). These frameworks are essential for fostering inclusive learning environments that respect the diverse needs of students. In addition, digital ethics must be quickly developed as technology. In order to ensure that digital innovations add to a broader social goal, such as equality and tolerance, researchers and politicians must continually develop and integrate innovations and moral considerations (Khatri, 2023). Susilo (2023) emphasizes the need for an ethical framework adapted to the rapidly growing field of educational technology. This flexibility is particularly important to address ethical issues in education raised by artificial intelligence, such as learner autonomy and data protection (Foltýnek et al., 2023). A comprehensive theoretical approach should include multiple perspectives, such as critical theory, social constructionism, and technological determinism. These methods give us a deeper understanding of the ways in which digital technologies interact with educational practices, social institutions, and individual experiences (Kleine, 2013). Educators and policymakers can better understand the complexity of teaching technologies and the integration of personal technologies, seeing the impact of digital technologies on various lenses.

Integrated Research Methodology: A Mixed-Methods Perspective

A notable digital gap exists in the Vietnamese educational system, characterized by differences in the accessibility, adoption, and utilization of digital technologies across urban and rural regions and among various socioeconomic levels (Ngo & Walton, 2016). Using a mixed-methods research technique will permit solving this complicated problem since it incorporates both quantitative and qualitative methods. Both teenagers' and instructors' internet access, privacy issues, and technology use may be uncovered using quantitative techniques such as surveys (Pham et al., 2021). This data provides valuable insights into the nature of the digital divide and aid in informed decision-making. Concurrently, rigorous qualitative methods, including interviews, shed light on the detailed experiences and difficulties encountered by stakeholders, particularly in underrepresented communities (Fang et al., 2022). By merging these complementary approaches, researchers can correlate digital data with firsthand testimonies, offering a comprehensive perspective on the ethical and practical ramifications of the digital divide (Warschauer et al., 2004). The structure of this hybrid method also takes into account the socioeconomic, gender, and geographical context, which is vital for addressing the specific challenges faced by girls in remote areas (Fang et al., 2022). The inclusion of triangulation enhances the strength of this mixed-methods strategy. By validating findings from multiple sources, including surveys, interviews, and relevant datasets—triangulation increases the reliability and trustworthiness of the results, ensuring that the insights are consistent, accurate, and relevant (Resta et al., 2018). This hybrid approach also takes into account the socioeconomic, gender, and geographical context, which is vital for addressing the specific challenges faced by girls in remote areas (Fang et al., 2022).

Data Collection Strategies: Comprehensive and Inclusive Instruments

The combination of quantitative and qualitative data in educational research offers a thorough understanding of the challenges and opportunities that technology presents in learning environments. Quantitative data gathered through structured surveys directed at students, parents, and teachers provided essential insights into access to digital devices and internet connectivity, as well as perceptions regarding the inclusivity of technology. The investigation of survey responses utilized statistical methods to reveal differences and regional trends (Field, 2017).

The research indicates that education stakeholders have significant apprehensions regarding data security, which calls for improved institutional safeguards to foster a secure educational atmosphere. Additionally, the qualitative information gathered through semi-structured interviews and focus groups with diverse participants, including rural educators and policymakers, provided a richer comprehension of the challenges associated with technology adoption. Baskara (2023) examined these obstacles, identifying cultural perspectives and systemic disparities that hinder effective technology use in education.

The thematic analysis of the interview transcripts revealed patterns that underscore how context affects the understanding and use of technology in various educational contexts (Coleman, 2019). This qualitative perspective complements the quantitative findings by depicting the real experiences of educators and students, thus enriching the overall assessment. The merging of these various types of data also brings up privacy concerns, which were prominently addressed in the surveys.

Qualitative results provide insight into how these challenges manifest in everyday educational practices, underscoring a disconnection between policy and actual implementation. For example, the recommendations made by Tran et al. (2014) about inclusive education, which address privacy issues, indicate that schools must prioritize both accessibility and data security to create fair learning environments.

Participant Sampling: Ensuring Representative Diversity

The use of stratified sampling to select participants in educational research in Vietnam is a methodologically robust strategy that guarantees representation from the country's varied socio-economic backgrounds. This approach is particularly adept at highlighting the distinctions between urban and rural educational contexts, as well as capturing the experiences of marginalized groups and promoting gender inclusivity, which are vital in tackling the significant digital divide impacting girls in education (Favaretto et al., 2020). Focusing on students aged 12–18, along with their parents and educators, as key participant groups, offers a thorough understanding of the educational landscape, while including policymakers and NGO representatives adds crucial systemic insights to inform policy and practice (Rodríguez et al., 2014). It is crucial to highlight the need for achieving gender equality in sample studies, particularly when disparities in technical and educational resources are significant. Research indicates that girls frequently face various challenges within the educational setting, especially related to digital skills and access to technology (Ogura et al., 2020).

Employing stratified sampling facilitates comparisons among different regions and demographic groups while also aiding researchers in identifying local issues and customizing solutions to address the unique needs of various communities (Halkoaho et al., 2013). This methodological accuracy is essential for gaining insights that encourage effective strategies aimed at closing the gender gap in education.

Ethical considerations are vital in research involving human participants, especially in the education sector. Key elements of ethical research include securing informed consent and ensuring confidentiality (Masic, 2012). Researchers bear the obligation to follow these ethical principles throughout the research process to protect participants and uphold the study's integrity. Existing literature highlights the necessity of ethics training and education for researchers, as it improves their capability to navigate complex ethical issues that may arise during research (Baskara,

2023). Furthermore, creating research ethics consultation services can provide important assistance to researchers in managing ethical issues, thereby fostering a culture of ethical awareness and accountability in educational research (Mardani et al., 2019).

Data Collection and Process

The data-gathering procedure utilized a mixed-methods strategy to investigate ethical concerns related to the digital divide in education in Vietnam from February 1 to September 20, 2023, providing both a general overview and detailed insights into the topic. This is the first phase of conducting analysis, starting with the qualitative phase, which was carried out to examine the ethical issues that arose from the results from June 15 to September 20, 2022. This phase involved semi-structured interviews and focus group discussions to collect detailed, context-specific perspectives from youth and parents.

The qualitative research methodology usually entails meticulous steps to guarantee that the collected data is both precise and trustworthy. A purposive sampling technique was used to select 11 participants, including 7 youth and 4 parents. The interviews focused on participants' perspectives on privacy issues, barriers to equal access, and cultural values that influence technology use. In this research, all interviews were audio recorded, transcribed, and translated into English by the researchers.

The adjustments applied to the English transcription demonstrate a dedication to maintaining the subtleties of the original responses, which is vital in qualitative research where context and meaning are key (Augusto, 2016). After the transcription was completed, the data underwent analysis through a content analysis method. Content analysis is a structured approach that quantifies qualitative data by organizing and comparing information to uncover key themes and patterns (Hove & Osunkunle, 2019). (See Table 1 in the Online Appendix link https://tinyurl.com/he50Appendices).

Individual semi-structured interviews were held with selected participants to explore their unique perspectives on privacy, accessibility, and the impact of cultural norms on technology usage. The interview guide contained open-ended questions such as:

"What challenges do you face when using digital resources for education?"

"How do you perceive the role of digital resources in advancing gender equity in education?"

"What concerns do you have regarding data privacy while using digital platforms?"

These sessions, which were conducted by trained facilitators, lasted approximately 40–60 minutes. The focus groups encouraged participants to discuss the effectiveness of digital tools in rural educational environments and the perceived fairness in the distribution of resources.

The second phase produced 27 questionnaires based on the insights gathered in the first phase. The quantitative phase is scheduled to take place from June 15 to September 20, 2023, and will focus on structured surveys designed to gather a variety of perspectives. Two main surveys were conducted: one aimed at young people aged 12 to 18 and the other at parents of primary and secondary school students. Each survey contains 27 questions organized into five themes: digital accessibility, privacy and data security, benefits of digital tools in education, gender equality challenges, and cultural barriers to gender inclusion.

To ensure representativeness of the sample, stratified random sampling was used to achieve balanced participation of urban (50%) and rural (50%) communities. The youth survey collected 400 responses, of which 60% were female and 40% were male. This parent survey received a total of 200 responses, of which 55% were from urban families and 45% from rural families. These demographic data are crucial for identifying changes and trends across different socioeconomic and geographical contexts, as previous research has shown that parental involvement and socioeconomic status significantly influence young people's educational outcomes and aspirations (Gao, 2023).

A variety of online and offline methods were used for data collection to address levels of access to different technologies. Urban participants completed the survey using an online platform, while rural residents completed paper surveys distributed through schools and community organizations. The analysis of the data was conducted using Python to produce descriptive statistics such as mean, standard deviation, and frequency distribution. The principal findings from this phase highlighted the necessity of incorporating accessibility into research designs, indicating that disparities in technology access can lead to significant inequalities in both data collection and analysis, particularly in the context of educational research (Rahman et al., 2020). The main conclusions from this phase pinpoint specific areas that warrant further investigation in future qualitative studies and stress the importance of grasping the varied experiences different demographic groups encounter with digital tools and issues of equity in education (Areta & Isacker, 2021).

Qualitative Results

This section outlines the results from the qualitative interviews carried out with 4 parents (PH) and 7 teenagers (TN) to investigate the ethical and practical issues surrounding Vietnam's educational digital divide. The interviews offer valuable perspectives on viewpoints related to digital access, concerns regarding privacy, and cultural perspectives on digital learning. (See Table 2: Demographic profiles of participants in the second phase in the Online Appendix link https://tinyurl.com/he50Appendices).

Gender Disparities and Cultural Resistance in Digital Learning

The results indicate notable disparities between genders regarding access to digital technology and educational opportunities in Vietnam, influenced by cultural traditions and the allocation of family resources. Frequently, parents tend to give preference to providing digital devices, like smartphones or computers, to their male children, viewing these resources as more essential for their educational requirements. One parent (PH3) from a rural region remarked, "Boys typically receive access to phones or computers first because parents think they require it more for their studies, while girls are anticipated to assist with household chores." In a similar vein, a teenager (TN6) emphasized the effects of this prioritization, stating, "At home, my brother is allowed to use the family computer more often than I am, even though we both have assignments. It's frustrating, but this is considered normal." This gap is not only reflected in technology adoption but also symbolizes greater cultural expectations. Parents, such as PH1, expressed concerns about their girls' technology use, fearing that they might be exposed to inappropriate content. As a result, adolescent girls reported feeling less capable in terms of digital skills. One participant (TN5) confessed, "I wasn't familiar with how to use online learning applications until my teacher demonstrated it to me. My male classmates appeared to grasp it more quickly because they had previous experience with similar tools." These results highlight the necessity for focused initiatives to promote equal access and bolster digital literacy among girls.

Cultural opposition to digital education presents another obstacle, with both parents and teenagers showing doubt towards technology-driven learning. Many parents favour conventional teaching methods and regard digital resources as supplementary. PH4 stated, "We were raised with books and notebooks. It's challenging to trust an app or computer for substantial learning." This inclination is especially prominent in rural areas, where parents feel that digital education lacks the personal connection found in traditional instruction. Adolescents have identified cultural barriers, particularly concerning delicate subjects such as relationships and gender equality. TN6 remarked, "My parents feel uneasy when topics like relationships or gender equality arise online." PH3 agreed, stating, "Digital platforms should steer clear of discussing certain sensitive matters to stay suitable for families in rural regions." This hesitation is linked to a wider skepticism about change, as PH1 pointed out, "Why alter something that has functioned well for generations?" The trend of digital learning seems to be one that may fade away. Despite these challenges, some teenagers expressed optimism about the potential of digital learning to address gaps in their education. TN7 highlighted the value of privacy in learning, stating, "I would rather use an app to learn because it's private, and I don't have to worry about being judged". These findings emphasize the importance of designing culturally sensitive digital tools that align with local values while addressing critical educational needs.

Privacy and Accessibility: Challenges Across Urban and Rural Divides

Concerns regarding privacy have arisen as a significant obstacle to the integration of digital tools in education. Both teenagers and parents voiced their worries about the potential misuse of data and a lack of knowledge surrounding data security. A parent (PH2) expressed their fears, saying, "I worry about applications that request excessive personal information. "I'm worried that my child's data could be exploited or sold." Teenagers echoed similar sentiments, with TN2 mentioning, "Sometimes, I hesitate to sign up for an app because I'm unsure about how my information will be managed." Parents highlighted the need for schools to take a more active approach in educating students and their families about safe practices online. As noted by PH4, "We're not really sure how to instruct our children on safeguarding their privacy online. Schools ought to hold workshops on this topic." The lack of knowledge about safe digital practices was also apparent among teenagers. One participant (TN1) remembered, "I once downloaded an app that requested my location and phone number. It made me feel uneasy, but I was unsure how to verify if it was safe." These insights underscore the critical need for educational initiatives focused on digital ethics and data security.

The digital divide between urban and rural areas remains a persistent challenge in Vietnam, driven by infrastructure gaps, limited resources, and economic constraints. Rural parents reported significant struggles in providing their children with reliable internet and devices. A parent (PH3) explained, "In rural areas, internet speed is very slow, making it hard for children to attend online classes." Many parents do not have access to improved internet connections. Similarly, teenagers in rural regions voiced their worries about inadequate resources. TN4 conveyed their annoyance, stating, "My friends in urban areas can participate in online seminars, but here we frequently experience disconnections even during important lectures."

The availability of devices varies significantly as well. PH1 commented, "In urban schools, it seems like every student has a phone or tablet. Here, they have to share with siblings." These challenges are exacerbated by the high costs of internet services. PH2 recounted their difficulties, stating, "The expense of internet data places a significant strain on rural families, so we restrict our children's screen time to save on costs." The information highlights the urgent need for investment in infrastructure and affordable digital solutions for rural communities.

Quantitative Results

This section outlines the quantitative results from a survey conducted with 600 participants, consisting of 400 youth between the ages of 12 and 18 and 200 parents, to investigate ethical dilemmas and disparities in digital education throughout Vietnam. The survey captures the viewpoints of both urban and rural communities, offering valuable insights into issues concerning access, fairness, and the privacy of digital learning resources. The research highlights major obstacles to digital inclusion, including gender inequality, privacy issues, disparities between rural and urban areas, and cultural resistance, all of which hinder progress toward Sustainable Development Goals 4 and 5. It is crucial to adopt inclusive policies and ethical practices in digital education to ensure equal opportunities for every student. (See Table 3 in the Online Appendix link https://tinyurl.com/he50Appendices).

Gender Disparities and Cultural Resistance in Digital Learning

Quantitative analysis shows that the gender difference between digital resources and educational opportunities is very high. Digital equipment reported by young boys is high with an average score of 4.6 (SD = 0.9) and the average rating for young girls is 3.7 (SD = 1.1). This inequality highlights the unequal distribution of resources between families and favours boys' development. Parental support further supports this pattern, as boys (m = 4.3, SD = 0.8) received more help from digital tools and educational resources than girls (M = 3.9, SD = 0.7). These findings suggest cultural biases that favour boys' access to technological resources, which may be influenced by traditional beliefs about gender roles in education and the workforce. Addressing these inequalities is critical to ensuring girls have equal access to digital learning tools and opportunities.

Cultural attitudes significantly influence the adoption of digital tools in education, with rural parents demonstrating a strong preference for traditional teaching methods (M = 4.4, SD = 0.8). This contrasts with teenagers' moderate enthusiasm for digital tools, as reflected in an engagement score of 4.1 (SD = 0.9). Although interested, the overall perception of digital tools is still medium (m = 3.5, SD = 1.1), stating that parents and students suspect suspicion. These statistics show that although adolescents are increasingly open to digital doctrine, cultural specifications and views on the value of education are a wider range of obstacles. Addressing these cultural resistances will require targeted outreach efforts, including workshops and community engagement initiatives to demonstrate the benefits of digital learning.

Privacy and Accessibility: Challenges Across Urban and Rural Divides

Privacy concerns emerged as a critical issue, with parents demonstrating heightened sensitivity to the security of their children's digital data (M = 4.5, SD = 1.0) compared to teenagers (M = 3.8, SD = 0.9). Parents' concerns may stem from a lack of transparency in app data policies and the increasing awareness of cyber threats targeting children. While young people have a moderate understanding of privacy, they are less concerned because there is limited discussion about digital ethics and safety. Data shows that young people and parents want extensive privacy. Parents need to ensure that the educational platform meets strict data security standards, while teens have to increase their understanding of security limits.

The separation between urban and rural districts is obvious in advanced openness scores. Urban young people detailed a cruel web availability score of 4.7 (SD = 0.7), essentially higher than their rural partners, who had a mean score of 3.1 (SD = 1.2). This difference reflects disjointed qualities in establishment, such as flawed web affiliations in natural ranges. Other than that, urban schools showed to have a more grounded organization back for computerized learning devices (M = 4.6, SD = 0.6), while common schools slacked behind in joining advancement into their teaching shapes. The burden of Internet services has exacerbated this crack, and the rural family reports are low (M = 2.8, SD = 1.1). These discoveries highlight the urgent need to adopt targeted intervention measures to reduce the gap between cities and rural areas, including Internet access to investing in the digital infrastructure of rural areas and providing subsidies for insufficient services.

Discussion

The study reported in this chapter aimed to answer the research question: "How can ethical frameworks and innovative strategies address digital divide challenges in Vietnam's educational ecosystem, particularly regarding gender inclusivity and technological accessibility?" The findings emphasize the critical role of ethical frameworks and tailored strategies in addressing disparities within Vietnam's rapidly evolving digital educational landscape. Identified key issues encompass gender inequalities, differences between urban and rural areas, cultural resistance to digital tools, and concerns regarding privacy, all of which underscore the necessity for a comprehensive and inclusive strategy in digital education.

Digital ethics has arisen as a key element for tackling privacy issues and ensuring fair access to technology. Participants, particularly parents, expressed notable worries about data privacy and the possible misuse of information gathered through educational applications. Numerous parents indicated that they felt unsure about how to help their children protect their online privacy. This reflects broader global anxieties regarding digital ethics, where established frameworks highlight the significance of ensuring data security and educating users about privacy dangers (Floridi, 2014). To mitigate these concerns, the study suggests implementing educational campaigns and institutional workshops aimed at enhancing digital literacy and raising awareness of safe online behaviours.

Another major issue is the gap between genders in technology access. Studies show that traditional gender roles often motivate boys to choose digital tools and resources. Specifically, women in rural regions state that their limited access to technology adversely affects their digital literacy and academic success. These findings reflect global patterns of systemic gender bias, as described in Rawls's rule of law framework, which emphasizes the importance of equal opportunities to remove barriers for marginalized groups (Sen, 1999). Addressing these disparities requires targeted interventions, such as digital literacy programs tailored to girls and community-led initiatives that challenge social norms around gender and technology. These approaches are in line with UNICEF (2021) recommendations for promoting gender-inclusive digital education.

The urban-rural gap is another major challenge to equitable digital education in Vietnam. Quantitative survey data showed that rural students had significantly lower internet access and resources than urban students (urban $M = 4.7$, $SD = 0.7$; rural $M = 3.1$, $SD = 1.2$). This inequality brings to light larger issues related to infrastructure, including unreliable Internet connections and limited access to digital devices in rural communities. Parents also noted that the high costs associated with Internet services present a major obstacle to consistent access. To fill this void, the study suggests focused investments in digital infrastructure in rural regions and the supply of cost-effective devices, aligning with recommendations from global initiatives that seek to tackle comparable socioeconomic inequalities (Ngo & Walton, 2016).

Cultural resistance to digital education adds to the difficulties of implementing ethical digital learning solutions. In rural regions, both parents and students showed doubts about the effectiveness of digital tools, preferring conventional teaching methods. For instance, some respondents considered digital platforms as additional resources rather than crucial for successful learning. This skepticism highlights the importance of adopting culturally aware strategies that showcase the concrete advantages of digital education while honouring local customs. Programs that engage the community by blending traditional teaching methods with digital advancements could encourage increased acceptance and confidence in new technologies (Heeks & Renken, 2018).

From these findings, the chapter emphasizes the need for ethical frameworks that prioritize inclusivity, equity, and privacy in Vietnam's digital education ecosystem. Recommendations include investing in infrastructure to improve rural connectivity, enhancing digital literacy through targeted campaigns, and promoting gender equality via tailored programs that empower girls to engage with technology. Additionally, designing culturally sensitive digital tools that align with local values while addressing systemic barriers is essential for fostering broader acceptance of digital learning. Overall, the findings highlight the transformative potential of combining ethical frameworks with innovative strategies to address Vietnam's digital divide. Using priority, tolerance policy and infrastructure, cultural and socio-economic obstacles, Vietnam can create a digital education system to adapt to differences, to develop confidence and to provide each student's ability. Further studies should check the resilience of the proposed goals and evaluate its scalability in order to ensure that constant progress should be expanded with digital gaps.

Conclusion

In conclusion, the results of a survey of 600 participants and discussions with 11 key stakeholders revealed complex barriers and opportunities for digital education transformation in Vietnam. This study uses a mixed-methods approach, combining insights from interviews and surveys to highlight key issues such as gender gaps in technology acquisition, the urban-rural digital divide, and social resistance to implementing digital education. Ignoring these issues may worsen existing inequalities and impede advancements in the Vietnamese education system. In line with Sustainable Development Goals 4 and 5, this section presents potential strategies to tackle these challenges, aiming to foster inclusive, equitable, and high-quality education while improving gender equality. Key recommendations include enhancing digital infrastructure in rural regions, establishing digital literacy initiatives that consider gender-specific concerns, and developing educational materials that emphasize the significance of privacy. Moreover, it is crucial to adopt culturally appropriate approaches that honour local customs while advocating the advantages of digital education to boost acceptance and trust. Achieving the vision of an inclusive digital education system requires the active collaboration of all stakeholders. Policymakers should focus on fair resource distribution, educators must embrace innovative teaching practices, and communities ought to confront the norms that sustain disparities. By promoting ethical, inclusive, and sustainable digital practices, Vietnam can empower its youth, particularly those from marginalized groups, to succeed in an increasingly digital world, thereby furthering its commitment to SDG 4 and SDG 5.

5

The University as a Hub for Lifelong Learning - Transitioning from Degree-Centric to Lifelong Learning Models in Vietnam[11]

Trang Quynh Kong Nguyen, Nguyen Thi Thanh Uyen, Khoi Hoang Truong[12], Bao Gia Truong and Duc Hong Thi Phan

Abstract

Vietnam's higher education system, traditionally focused on formal qualifications and conventional teaching methods, is under increasing pressure to adapt to global challenges. As the country strives to achieve upper-middle-income status by 2035, the labour market has expressed an urgent need for a highly skilled workforce equipped with advanced skills, interdisciplinary knowledge, and a lifelong learning mindset. This chapter explores the evolving role of universities as hubs for lifelong learning within the framework of Higher Education 5.0, highlighting efforts by institutions to integrate digital technologies, establish industry partnerships, and address learner needs through updated curricula. In addition to university-led initiatives, the chapter identifies key drivers of transformation rooted in government policies, which play a pivotal role in promoting vocational and digital skills. Drawing on successful international models, the chapter offers actionable recommendations for Vietnamese universities to accelerate the adoption of lifelong learning

---

11 All references, tables, figures, author affiliation and biography used in this chapter are available on the Online Appendix link at https://tinyurl.com/he50Appendices.

12 Corresponding author: truonghoangkhoi.work@gmail.com

(LLL) programs aligned with Higher Education 5.0 principles. Furthermore, it examines the potential of AI-driven tools in fostering learner-centric teaching by personalizing educational experiences and expanding access to underserved communities. By prioritizing these efforts within the scope of Higher Education (HE) 5.0, Vietnam can strengthen its LLL framework, preparing its citizens to navigate the complexities and opportunities of the modern knowledge economy.

Introduction

Vietnam's higher education system has traditionally been centred on a degree-focused framework, emphasizing formal qualifications over the development of flexible skills and practical competencies. While this approach has supported foundational learning, it faces increasing challenges in meeting the rapidly evolving demands of the global job market. Employers now prioritize adaptive capabilities and specialized expertise, particularly in emerging technologies and knowledge-intensive industries (Phan et al., 2020). As a result, an overemphasis on theoretical knowledge and standardized qualifications often leaves graduates less equipped to seamlessly transition into the workforce, perpetuating a persistent skills gap.

The degree-focused framework constrains higher education institutions in their capacity to respond to swift technological changes and the shifting requirements of the labor market, which poses a risk to Vietnam's economic competitiveness. For example, the strong focus on theoretical knowledge often results in graduates being inadequately prepared for sectors that demand digital and interdisciplinary competencies. International entities like UNESCO and the OECD have promoted the establishment of flexible lifelong learning frameworks that prioritize ongoing skill enhancement, career advancement, and economic viability (OECD, 2019). By embracing these frameworks, Vietnam can align its educational policies with global trends, thus better preparing its workforce for success in a knowledge-driven economy.

Acknowledging these challenges, Vietnam's higher education system has begun to implement meaningful reforms. Key initiatives include fostering partnerships between universities and industries to better align educational outcomes with labor market requirements, enabling technology transfer, and enhancing graduate employability (Nguyen et al., 2022). These efforts highlight the necessity of shifting toward a more flexible, skills-oriented higher education model that equips Vietnam's workforce to thrive in the 21st century's rapidly evolving economic landscape.

Background

Universities are fundamental to building lifelong learning ecosystems by fostering flexibility and innovation. As knowledge hubs, they possess the necessary resources, expertise, and networks to support lifelong learning initiatives within higher education (Wang, 2023). By offering customized programs and short courses, universities bridge the gap between academic knowledge and industry demands. Successful integration strategies in countries like Denmark and Norway highlight the value of continuous skills enhancement and collaboration with diverse sectors, setting an example for Vietnamese higher education institutions to follow (Carlsen, 2016). Leveraging similar methods and existing resources can help Vietnamese universities create inclusive and dynamic learning environments. However, challenges such as outdated curricula and inadequate digital resources often hinder their ability to meet modern educational needs.

Moreover, the rise of digital technologies presents significant opportunities for Vietnamese universities to enhance lifelong learning activities. For example, the adoption of massive open online courses (MOOCs) has increased accessibility and flexibility, creating more personalized educational experiences (Iniesto & Rodrigo, 2024). Furthermore, collaborations with industry stakeholders enable universities to tailor programs to meet specific labor market requirements, equipping candidates with relevant skills (Otache, 2021). Effective lifelong learning systems integrate continuous education with individual and professional growth, aligning with global trends (Chen et al., 2022).

Despite these advancements, Vietnam still faces hurdles, including insufficient investment in digital infrastructure and inadequate faculty training. The success of lifelong learning ecosystems under the framework of HE 5.0 requires not only systemic reforms but also a cultural shift that values lifelong education (Filho et al., 2019). Embracing adaptability and integrating HE 5.0 principles will be essential for Vietnamese higher education to remain competitive in the global landscape (Suparno, 2023).

Advancing Lifelong Learning in Vietnamese Higher Education

This chapter explores the transformative potential for Vietnamese universities to evolve from traditional degree-centric models into comprehensive lifelong learning ecosystems. To address pressing challenges such as outdated curricula and limited industry collaboration within higher education, the chapter conducts a critical examination of Vietnam's educational landscape. Furthermore, the chapter evaluates how digital technologies can enhance lifelong learning pathways, particularly in terms of improving accessibility and flexibility (Pham, 2023).

The scope of this chapter focuses on three interconnected dimensions: curriculum redesign, technology integration, and stakeholder collaboration. By exploring strategies employed in Denmark and Norway, it examines how Vietnamese universities can address critical skill shortages and align with global benchmarks. A comprehensive review of academic literature, case studies, and policy frameworks underpins the analysis, proposing sustainable solutions to reimagine higher education as a driver of innovation and economic competitiveness.

Central to this inquiry is the question: "How do Vietnamese universities function as centers of lifelong learning in the context of global challenges?" Further investigations delve into essential aspects of this transformation. For instance, one question considers: "What global best practices can Vietnam adopt to foster flexible learning environments?" A comparative study of educational frameworks in Denmark and Norway sheds light on the synergy between higher education and industry, emphasizing the critical role of collaboration in enhancing employability (Carlsen, 2016).

Another key question addresses structural challenges: "What institutional and cultural transformations are necessary to facilitate lifelong learning in Vietnam?" This exploration highlights the need for a paradigm shift in educational philosophy and institutional structures. Partnerships are also emphasized: "In what ways can universities work together with industries and government to resolve skill mismatches?" These inquiries aim to uncover strategies that align Vietnam's educational framework with its broader economic and societal objectives (Pham, 2023).

The influence of technology emerges as a pivotal theme. For example, the question, "How can digital technologies facilitate the expansion of lifelong learning opportunities in universities?" underscores the importance of innovations such as MOOCs and digital learning platforms. By examining their integration with advancements in digital infrastructure, the chapter identifies actionable adjustments to enhance accessibility and promote lifelong learning (Iniesto & Rodrigo, 2024).

Lifelong Learning: Global Perspectives and Vietnam's Path to Educational Transformation

The concept of lifelong learning is multifaceted and dynamic, evolving to mirror shifts in educational institutions and societal needs. Over time, terms such as "adult education" and "lifelong education" have been replaced by the more inclusive term "lifelong learning," which underscores the continuous acquisition of knowledge and skills throughout one's life (Akther, 2020). This shift highlights the limitations of traditional degree-centric educational models in equipping individuals to thrive in modern labor markets. UNESCO's four pillars of lifelong learning—learning to know, learning to do, learning to live together, and learning to be—serve as foundational principles, emphasizing development that extends far beyond formal education (Cummins & Kunkel, 2015).

In Vietnam, lifelong learning (LLL) has become increasingly important as the country seeks to align its educational strategies with global trends and the demands of a modern workforce. Reflecting UNESCO's four pillars of lifelong learning, Vietnam is gradually shifting focus from traditional degree-centric models to more flexible and inclusive educational pathways. However, persistent challenges such as outdated curricula and limited digital infrastructure hinder progress. By adopting global best practices and integrating digital technologies, Vietnam aims to create an adaptable and skill-oriented education system that addresses labor market complexities and supports sustainable development.

Research Methodology

This chapter employs a literature review approach to synthesize and critically evaluate existing research on the transition from degree-focused education to LLL paradigms within the context of higher education in Vietnam. The review focuses on identifying key themes, challenges, and opportunities highlighted in the literature. To ensure a comprehensive understanding of the topic, the review draws on studies that examine LLL frameworks, educational reforms, and the role of universities in fostering continuous education. Particular attention is given to research centered on Vietnam as well as global best practices that offer transferable insights.

The literature search spans prominent academic databases, including Scopus, Web of Science, and ERIC, using targeted keywords such as "lifelong learning," "educational reform," and "higher education in Vietnam." Additionally, institutional reports and governmental policy documents are integrated to provide a broader contextual understanding. Studies are selected based on their relevance, recent publication dates, and the presence of empirical or theoretical contributions.

Data from the reviewed studies are organized to highlight critical aspects such as methodologies, findings, and implications. The synthesis incorporates both qualitative and quantitative insights, enabling the identification of recurring themes, research gaps, and actionable recommendations. By focusing on these elements, the literature review provides a nuanced understanding of how Vietnamese universities can transition into LLL ecosystems and align with global trends. This structured approach establishes a foundation for further research and policy development in the field.

Discussion - Global Trends in Lifelong Learning: Lessons for Higher Education Reform

The worldwide transition towards lifelong learning (LLL) signifies an increasing acknowledgement of the necessity for educational systems to adapt in response to swiftly evolving economic and technological environments. Nations such as Denmark and Norway have effectively established lifelong learning frameworks that prioritise flexibility, adaptability, and collaboration between higher education institutions and the industry. These approaches guarantee that academic curricula align with the demands of the labour market, thus offering learners the chance to continuously develop their skills and maintain their competitiveness in a dynamic employment landscape (Carlsen, 2016).

Lifelong learning frameworks promote inclusivity and accessibility, dismantling traditional obstacles associated with age, geographical location, and educational qualifications. The Lifelong Learning Programme (LLP) in Europe exemplifies the significance of mobility, interdisciplinary collaboration, and innovation in creating sustainable educational frameworks. Initiatives such as Erasmus and Leonardo da Vinci underscore the essential requirement to incorporate vocational training, digital skills, and critical thinking into educational curricula to address the changing needs of the labour market (Sinanovic & Becirovic, 2016).

International organisations such as UNESCO and the OECD have been instrumental in advancing lifelong learning as a mechanism for achieving sustainable development objectives. Their guidelines urge universities to broaden their focus beyond initial education and to act as lifelong partners in both individual and professional growth (OECD, 2019). The evolution of educational approaches encompasses the integration of modular courses, micro-credentials, and digital learning platforms, all tailored to meet the diverse needs and skill levels of various learners. Vietnamese higher education institutions stand to benefit significantly from international best practices. By creating lifelong learning centres, fostering collaborations with industry, and leveraging digital technologies, they can more effectively align their educational programs with the demands of the labour market.

Successful Global Practices in Lifelong Learning: Lessons for Vietnam

Examining successful implementations of lifelong learning frameworks in other countries offers valuable insights for Vietnam. European universities, for instance, have been at the forefront of establishing lifelong learning centres that address the diverse needs of learners. In Denmark, for example, robust partnerships between academic institutions and employers have led to the development of specialised programs that effectively address skill shortages in critical economic sectors (Carlsen, 2016).

To enhance their reach and impact, these institutions integrate digital technology and community engagement alongside traditional educational offerings. By doing so, they promote inclusivity, extending learning opportunities to individuals across various socioeconomic backgrounds. Adopting a similar approach in Vietnam could transform the higher education landscape. Establishing lifelong learning centres within universities and fostering strong partnerships with businesses could significantly improve graduate employability while providing continuous avenues for professional growth and development.

Leveraging Technology to Advance Lifelong Learning in Higher Education

Contemporary lifelong learning environments are undergoing transformative changes driven by technological advancements. Initiatives such as MOOCs and hybrid learning frameworks have significantly enhanced accessibility, enabling learners to engage with educational materials at their own pace, regardless of physical location or time constraints. These innovations also promote diversity and flexibility in pedagogical approaches, allowing institutions to expand their reach beyond traditional campus boundaries (Iniesto & Rodrigo, 2024). In Vietnam, the rapid adoption of online learning during the COVID-19 pandemic showcased its potential in maintaining educational continuity despite geographical barriers (Ngo et al., 2021). Advanced technologies, including AI and data analytics, further enhance lifelong learning by personalizing educational content to meet individual needs, thereby improving learner engagement and outcomes (Haseski & Odabasi, 2017). By leveraging technology to build a robust framework for lifelong learning, Vietnamese educational institutions can bolster their competitiveness in the context of the Fourth Industrial Revolution and respond effectively to global trends (Nguyễn & Trần, 2017).

Institutional Readiness for Lifelong Learning

Vietnamese higher education institutions are currently at a critical juncture, requiring a paradigm shift from traditional degree-focused models to frameworks that prioritize lifelong learning. To successfully navigate this transformation, it is essential to comprehensively evaluate three key areas: curriculum development, financial structures, and faculty training. Historically, curriculum development has been predominantly focused on theoretical knowledge, often overlooking the practical and adaptable skills increasingly demanded by rapidly evolving industries. To deal with this, universities should include the design of modular courses, short-term certification programs, and interdisciplinary curricula that cater to the needs of both traditional students and adult learners (Ngoc, 2020).

Ensuring Quality in Lifelong Learning Programs: Frameworks and Best Practices

The quality and relevance of lifelong learning programs play a pivotal role in determining their effectiveness. To maintain these standards, educational institutions must establish robust quality assurance mechanisms that enable consistent evaluation and improvement of their offerings. This requires systematic collection of feedback from key stakeholders, including students, employers, and industry professionals, to ensure that programs are both effective and aligned with real-world demands.

An effective quality assurance framework should include several critical components, such as measurable student outcomes, the effectiveness of teaching methodologies, and the curriculum's relevance to workforce needs. Additionally, integrating technology into these frameworks enhances data collection and analysis capabilities, enabling institutions to make informed, evidence-based adjustments to their strategies and resource allocation (Tekkol & Demirel, 2018). Successful instances of these frameworks can be observed in leading global education systems. For instance, numerous European countries have developed lifelong learning centers that regularly assess program outcomes by systematically gathering feedback from stakeholders. Likewise, universities in Singapore employ artificial intelligence and data analytics to ensure that their training programs remain pertinent to the evolving needs of the industry (Carlsen, 2016). By implementing these approaches, educational institutions can ensure that lifelong learning programs maintain high standards of quality and relevance, effectively preparing students to navigate the challenges of an ever-changing environment.

Recommendations

Key Drivers and Barriers to Lifelong Learning Transition in Vietnam

The transition to lifelong learning in Vietnam is driven by the growing demand for a highly skilled workforce, the government's Higher Education policy, and right awareness from the learners. As Vietnam aims to achieve upper-middle-income status by 2035, the need for a skilled workforce in technology and innovation sectors has become urgent to meet the demands of a rapidly changing job market (World Bank, 2020). The automation process and digital revolution are expected to reduce the demand for routine, low-skill jobs while increasing the necessity for cognitive, digital, higher-order, and socio-emotional skills for more complex roles. These high-level skills are also essential for securing high-value positions in global value chains involving manufacturing, services, and research and development (R&D). These socio-economic developments underscore the importance of continuous skill enhancement through lifelong and digital learning, which enables learners to access real-time global knowledge and remain competitive in dynamic job markets.

Another significant driver is the Higher Education Strategy (2021–2030), which empowers universities to design curricula that align with both national educational goals and market demands (Ministry of Education and Training, 2023). This strategy includes initiatives such as piloting digital universities and establishing a national repository for digital learning resources. These measures represent a paradigm shift, fostering critical thinking and self-reflection among learners by encouraging them to evaluate the relevance of curricula to their skill needs and industry expectations. By aligning education more closely with workforce requirements, the plan positions lifelong learning as a cornerstone of Vietnam's modern education system.

However, the lack of thorough awareness toward the new model has been acting as a brake for this transition. Although the concept has been featured in policies and literature for years, its full significance and benefits remain unclear to many (Pham, 2014). At the workplace level, employers frequently assume that universities bear sole responsibility for equipping graduates with the necessary skills and mindsets, creating a gap in the practical application of lifelong learning principles. Consequently, despite theoretical advancements and institutional efforts, lifelong learning in Vietnam remains more of a topic for panel discussions and political debates than a widely embraced practice in daily life.

The increasing recognition of lifelong learning underscores its significance; however, transitioning from degree-focused educational models presents substantial challenges, particularly in Vietnam. One key obstacle lies in the structures of many universities that prioritize theoretical knowledge over practical skill development. These frameworks could not adapt to the rapid pace of technological advancements and the shifting demands of the labor market, contributing to a persistent skills gap among graduates (Ngoc, 2020).

Financial constraints further compound these challenges, as many institutions struggle to secure adequate funding for technology integration and curriculum innovation. This issue is exacerbated by a lack of collaboration between higher education institutions and industry stakeholders, limiting opportunities for practical learning and the transfer of technological expertise. Additionally, cultural attitudes present another significant barrier; in Vietnam, traditional emphasis on formal qualifications and degree attainment often overshadows the importance of continuous education and practical skill-building.

Thematic Insights on Lifelong Learning in Vietnam: Advancing Through EdTech and E-Learning

In recent years, Vietnam has experienced notable progress in lifelong learning, particularly within the EdTech sector. English learning apps such as Topica Native and Elsa have garnered millions of downloads on smartphones and tablets, reflecting a growing familiarity with acquiring knowledge through diverse digital platforms. In higher education, the e-learning approach has gained traction over the past decade, with institutions like Open University and Funix University offering online bachelor's programs. Additionally, Topica has entered the field through collaborative programs with other universities (Đặng, 2020). The increasing prevalence of online courses and digital learning platforms demonstrates that Vietnam's higher education system is evolving to align with the flexibility and practicality demanded by the Education 5.0 revolution.

This transition also highlights a narrowing gap between heavily theoretical knowledge and the practical skills required by the job market. However, Vietnam continues to grapple with a high unemployment rate among young graduates, an issue that persists even during periods of economic stability. This suggests that the general education system requires further improvement to better prepare students for workforce demands. Enhancing infrastructure for laboratories and practical training, while crucial, demands substantial financial investment and cannot be achieved overnight without comprehensive structural reforms. In contrast, virtual laboratories present a cost-effective alternative, requiring significantly lower initial investment and faster implementation timelines.

Although their adoption may initially increase training costs for educators and raise concerns about effectiveness and student adaptation, virtual labs hold the potential to promote equitable access to education and improve the assessment of student learning outcomes in the long term. These advancements suggest that Vietnamese universities are well-positioned to embrace the e-learning trend and establish themselves as key contributors to the lifelong learning model, fostering a sustainable and adaptable education system for the future.

Global Practices and Vietnam's Path Forward

The effectiveness of lifelong learning has been explored globally through diverse models, with the Lifelong Learning Programme (LLP) of the European Union serving as a prominent example. ts primary goal was to advance Europe's ambition of becoming a knowledge-driven society characterized by sustainable economic growth, social cohesion, and a highly skilled workforce. The LLP comprised four sub-programs: the Comenius program aimed at enhancing general teaching practices in schools, the Erasmus program focused on fostering student mobility and modernizing higher education, the Leonardo da Vinci program designed to link vocational education with labor market demands, and the Grundtvig program targeting innovations in adult education and outreach to underserved learners. Complementary initiatives, such as the Transversal Programme and the Jean Monnet Programme further supported innovation and European integration in lifelong learning.

Interim evaluations revealed that the LLP significantly improved the quality of education, personal growth, language skills, and social competencies for participants. Schools in the Comenius segment reported improved learning environments and higher teacher retention rates, while the Leonardo da Vinci program effectively aligned vocational education with labor market needs and increased curriculum transparency. Similar positive outcomes were observed in the Grundtvig and Erasmus programs, which improved teaching quality, student services, and professional management practices.

In Vietnam, the LLL model has been advanced through the "Learning Society Scheme 2021-2030," aimed at ensuring equal access to education for all (Phan, 2022). This initiative prioritizes literacy, vocational training, and digital skills, with key players including Open universities in Hanoi and Ho Chi Minh City offering flexible learning options via Learning Management Systems (LMS), virtual classrooms, and MOOCs. Drawing inspiration from successful cases in Korea and Singapore, Vietnam has also integrated foreign languages and ICT skills into university curricula to enhance global readiness.

These efforts have increased awareness of lifelong learning, particularly among adult learners, and led to the establishment of supportive frameworks like the 2019 Education Law, which embeds lifelong learning into the national education system. Additionally, formats such as distance learning and community learning centers have expanded access to education across diverse demographics. By focusing on practical skills and promoting active learning through digital education, these approaches bring lifelong learning closer to students, making it more relevant to real-life situations.

Fostering Willingness for Lifelong Learning: A Strategic Role for Universities

No policy can succeed without the willingness of its target audience to embrace change. For universities, a critical priority is to effectively communicate the benefits and core principles of LLL before implementing any related initiatives. By doing so, institutions can foster intrinsic motivation among learners to adopt this educational approach. A relevant study conducted across Europe with a broad sample of 18,277 respondents aged 15 and over explored how learners' willingness influenced the successful adoption of lifelong learning (Sinanovic & Becirovic, 2016). The findings revealed that the majority of respondents believed lifelong learning was essential for both individual and community growth and was relevant to people of all ages.

The study also highlighted that informal settings—such as television, casual conversations, social gatherings, travel experiences, and part-time activities—were particularly effective in fostering a new understanding of lifelong learning. Beyond awareness, learners also require a comfortable, supportive environment and a network of like-minded peers to readily embrace innovative educational approaches. By demonstrating how continuous, active learning enhances employability, facilitates personal development, and creates opportunities for social and professional connections, institutions can encourage broader adoption of lifelong learning models. Ultimately, this strategic focus can contribute to building a sustainable, knowledge-driven society where education is viewed as a lifelong mission.

Integrating Credentials and Market-Driven Activities in Higher Education

To stay relevant in an increasingly skills and critical-thinking-focused economy, universities can offer modular courses, stackable micro-credentials, industry field trips, and teamwork activities throughout the learning process. These initiatives facilitate the acquisition of specific skillsets essential for students' future professional roles. In an era where the internet and AI excel at storing and analysing information to solve fact-based problems, uniquely human attributes—such as soft skills, critical thinking, empathy, emotional intelligence, and a progressive mindset—become crucial for addressing complex, high-level challenges. Moreover, universities should consider increased investment in digital infrastructure by developing digital universities and repositories for digital learning resources. These platforms would allow students to access a vast array of information anytime, anywhere, without external assistance. Such initiatives empower learners to complete their degrees while maintaining a balance between their personal and professional commitments—an essential component of a comprehensive lifelong learning process.

Promoting Equity and Access in Lifelong Learning

In the long run, the success of lifelong learning strategies hinges not only on their effective implementation but also on enhancing inclusivity for diverse groups of learners. Marginalized groups—such as students from rural areas, ethnic minorities, and economically disadvantaged backgrounds—deserve particular attention to ensure their equitable access to education. To better support these groups, universities can introduce various initiatives, including tuition fee subsidy plans, scholarships, and infrastructure support such as internet access or provision of laptops. Such digitalized approaches can help bridge gaps by making education accessible to those for whom on-campus attendance may not be feasible. By addressing barriers to equity and access for underrepresented learners, universities can create equal opportunities for personal and professional growth.

Future Directions for Advancing Lifelong Learning in Vietnam

While the LLL program has gained significant traction in recent years, further efforts are required to enhance its impact and accessibility across the community. A crucial starting point is for universities to address societal biases that have traditionally favored degree-centric formal education over more flexible non-formal and informal learning approaches. Encouraging individuals to focus on acquiring social skills, practical knowledge, and a reflective mindset—attributes increasingly valued in the workplace and personal life—will help shift perspectives toward the benefits of lifelong learning.

To make education more cohesive, personalized, and inclusive, larger-scale surveys should be conducted to explore optimal ways to integrate informal learning supported by digital infrastructure with formal and non-formal education. Such integration would enable educational institutions to cater to diverse learner demographics and social backgrounds effectively.

The incorporation of digital technologies, particularly AI, presents another transformative opportunity. Given the learner-centric nature of the LLL model, institutions should leverage AI to personalize learning experiences, especially for underserved communities. AI-driven tools can identify specific barriers, analyze learning patterns, and offer customized recommendations, making education more accessible and relevant.

From a policy perspective, as recommended by Sinanovic and Becirovic (2016), the government should establish frameworks that position education as a lifelong endeavour rather than a one-time achievement. Policies must prioritize developing learners' self-directed learning skills, problem-solving abilities, and digital literacy, moving away from traditional degree-centric methods. By focusing on these strategies, Vietnam is well-placed to strengthen its lifelong learning framework and equip its citizens to navigate the challenges and opportunities of the modern knowledge economy.

Conclusion

The transition to a lifelong learning model within Vietnam's higher education system is a crucial response to the evolving demands of the global job market. By integrating technology and adopting a learner-centric approach, many universities in Vietnam have demonstrated their willingness and capacity to move beyond traditional degree-centric paradigms toward dynamic, lifelong learning-driven environments. However, challenges remain, including societal biases favouring formal qualifications, insufficient investment in digital infrastructure, unequal access to education, and a shortage of qualified educators proficient in digital skills. To address these issues, universities must prioritize collaboration with industry partners and governmental bodies to align educational outcomes with labor market demands and secure adequate funding. Additionally, leveraging AI-driven tools offers the potential to personalize learning experiences, enabling universities to better reach underserved communities and expand educational access. By embracing these strategies and fostering a culture of lifelong learning, Vietnamese universities are well-positioned to establish a robust lifelong learning framework. This transformation will empower learners to acquire the skills necessary to navigate the complexities of an increasingly competitive global landscape, reinforcing Vietnam's role as a leader in modern education innovation.

6

Pathways for Equitable, Inclusive and Secure Higher Education 5.0 in Vietnam: Focus on Adolescents and Parental Perception in the Early Education Phase[13]

Trang Quynh Kong Nguyen, Khoi Hoang Truong[14], Bao Gia Truong and Duc Hong Thi Phan

Abstract

This chapter explores the challenges and opportunities within Vietnam's Higher Education 5.0 framework, with a unique focus on adolescents and parental perceptions during its early phase—a perspective often overlooked in existing literature. While prior studies predominantly centre on systemic strategies for integrating digital transformation in higher education, they rarely address the preparatory phase or the critical role of adolescents in bridging the transition to higher education. By addressing this oversight, the study delves into the socio-cultural and infrastructural obstacles that adolescents encounter in their pursuit of equitable, inclusive, and safe educational opportunities. Employing a mixed methods research design, it combines qualitative data gathered from interviews with adolescents and parents with quantitative findings from surveys conducted with 600 participants in both urban and rural contexts. The findings indicate considerable obstacles, such as gender inequalities, disparities in digital

---

13 All references, tables, figures, author affiliation and biography used in this chapter are available on the Online Appendix link at https://tinyurl.com/he50Appendices.

14 Corresponding author: truonghoangkhoi.work@gmail.com

access between urban and rural settings, cultural resistance, and privacy concerns. These issues are particularly pronounced for adolescent girls in rural areas, underscoring the urgent necessity for focused interventions. To address these obstacles, the research proposes various strategies, including the improvement of digital infrastructure in rural locales, the establishment of digital literacy initiatives tailored for adolescents, and the creation of culturally appropriate resources that align with local values. Additionally, it stresses the significance of enhancing awareness regarding digital ethics and privacy safeguards to build trust among parents and students. These recommendations align with Sustainable Development Goals 4 and 5, which seek to foster a more equitable, inclusive, and secure educational landscape that empowers the youth of Vietnam in their transition to higher education.

Introduction

Vietnam's digital transformation offers opportunities for innovation in higher education but exposes challenges in equity, inclusion, and security. Higher Education 5.0 emphasizes human-centered innovation, yet the critical role of adolescents transitioning into higher education is underexplored. This chapter addresses this gap by examining how digital equity and ethical considerations affect adolescents, particularly in Vietnam's socio-cultural context (Cuong & Le, 2024). The integration of advanced digital technologies promises to transform traditional educational frameworks; however, substantial inequalities in digital access—often referred to as the 'Digital Divide'—persist across socio-economic and geographic lines (van Dijk, 2020). This phenomenon continues to affect marginalized populations, particularly rural adolescent girls, who encounter systemic obstacles stemming from cultural expectations, inadequate infrastructure, and concerns regarding privacy (UNICEF, 2021). These inequities significantly impede access to technology, which is crucial for achieving equitable educational opportunities.

This chapter investigates the research question: How can ethical frameworks and innovative strategies address digital divide challenges in Vietnam's educational ecosystem, particularly regarding gender inclusivity and technological accessibility? By aligning with Sustainable

Development Goals (SDGs) 4 and 5, which emphasize equitable and quality education, the chapter proposes solutions tailored to Vietnam's socio-economic landscape (UNESCO, 2020). The findings aim to inform policies and practices that foster a more inclusive, secure, and equitable higher education system.

Educational Context in Vietnam

Education plays a pivotal role in Vietnam's socio-economic development strategy, with significant advancements in accessibility and quality over the past decades. The country has made considerable progress in achieving universal education and increasing opportunities for students from various socio-economic backgrounds. Substantial challenges remain, especially regarding the disparities in technological access between urban and rural areas, gender imbalances in technology participation, and cultural resistance to embracing innovative educational methodologies, including digital learning (UNESCO, 2020).

In Vietnam, parental involvement plays a crucial role in shaping the educational experiences of their children. They play a crucial part in decisions regarding school choices, career options, and the allocation of educational resources, including technology. This parental engagement is rooted in cultural values that regard education as fundamental to both family and societal achievement (Pham et al., 2021). Nevertheless, numerous parents encounter challenges such as insufficient digital literacy, apprehensions about data privacy, and doubts regarding the efficacy of digital tools. These challenges underscore the importance of addressing parents' perspectives to ensure the successful integration of digital education in Vietnam.

Understanding the socio-cultural dynamics of Vietnam's education system is essential for designing equitable, inclusive, and secure pathways in Higher Education 5.0. This chapter focuses on these dynamics to provide insights into bridging the digital divide and fostering trust in digital learning tools, aligning with global efforts to promote inclusive education.

Digital Ethics in Educational Technology

Digital ethics involves adhering to recognized social values while engaging with technological advancements, requiring comprehensive theoretical frameworks that extend beyond traditional technological paradigms (John, 2020). In the context of Vietnam's Higher Education 5.0, digital ethics serves as a crucial guiding principle to ensure that advancements in educational technology foster equity, inclusivity, and security. As Vietnam embraces digital transformation, addressing ethical concerns is critical to creating an education system that empowers all learners, particularly adolescents transitioning to higher education. The evolving landscape of digital ethics in higher education demands sophisticated frameworks that critically examine the interactions between technological infrastructure, socio-cultural dynamics, and individual agency (van Dijck, 2014). In Vietnam, it is crucial for educational systems to confront particular challenges, such as cultural resistance to digital technologies, the disparity in access between urban and rural communities, and the historical bias favoring boys over girls in resource allocation. By addressing these challenges through ethical methodologies, it is feasible to mitigate systemic barriers and promote inclusivity. The significance of digital ethics is becoming more apparent as the education sector adopts sophisticated technologies, such as artificial intelligence (AI) and predictive analytics. Although these advancements offer considerable prospects for progress, they also introduce various risks, including the potential for data misuse, breaches of privacy, and the perpetuation of existing social inequalities. Current theoretical frameworks highlight the necessity for comprehensive models that integrate ethical considerations, data protection, privacy measures, and equitable access (Eubanks, 2018). In the context of Vietnam, these issues are particularly pertinent as families and young individuals navigate the effects of digital transformation on educational practices. Technologies inherently lack neutrality; rather, they are shaped by social dynamics that often reflect prevailing inequalities. This issue is especially pertinent in the realm of digital education, where insufficiently regulated technologies can undermine traditional pedagogical approaches and exacerbate existing disparities (Finn & Wadhwa, 2014). In Vietnam, marginalized populations, including rural youth and girls face considerable challenges due to their limited access to digital tools and resources. It is essential to guarantee equitable access to these resources to foster inclusive educational opportunities (Phan et al., 2017). Incorporating digital ethics into Vietnam's Higher Education 5.0 framework offers pathways to bridge gaps in equity and inclusion. Ethical frameworks must address parental concerns about data privacy, empower adolescents with digital literacy, and align with the socio-cultural context of Vietnam. By doing so, digital ethics can help build trust, reduce disparities, and create a secure foundation for Vietnam's transition to a digital education ecosystem.

Equity Theories and Inclusion

In Vietnam, Rawlsian concepts of "justice as fairness" provide a strong framework for addressing digital justice, emphasizing equal access to technology to reduce barriers for marginalized groups in education (Sen, 1999). The integration of technology in higher education and digital learning must actively promote participation, addressing disparities that are intensified by socioeconomic, cultural, and geographic factors (Cheng et al., 2020). In Vietnam, disparities in digital access are markedly pronounced, especially impacting rural and marginalized populations who face considerable challenges stemming from inadequate digital infrastructure, high technology costs, and a lack of quality educational resources. Gender inequality remains a critical issue, particularly in rural areas, where cultural obstacles hinder the full engagement of women and girls in information and communication technology (ICT), frequently resulting in unequal opportunities (UNESCO, 2020). To advance digital equity, it is crucial to confront systemic inequalities and reevaluate the societal norms that sustain discrimination. This initiative requires not only the improvement of infrastructural shortcomings but also the promotion of inclusive viewpoints among educators, policymakers, and community members. Initiatives that actively confront gender biases and involve local leaders in advocating for equal access can drive significant change. Such initiatives should be tailored to the specific cultural and contextual needs of Vietnam's communities, demonstrating a dedication to both equity principles and inclusive methodologies. Recognizing access to technology as a fundamental human right is a cornerstone of achieving digital equity. It empowers marginalized groups with the tools for self-determination, access to opportunities, and active participation in the digital economy (Goldstein et al., 2023). This recognition aligns with the global Sustainable Development Goals 4 and 5), which emphasize quality education and gender equality. Tailored solutions—such as affordable digital devices, rural internet infrastructure, and digital literacy campaigns targeting women and underserved youth—are critical to bridging gaps and fostering inclusion.

Technological Frontiers and Ethical Considerations

Artificial intelligence (AI), augmented reality (AR), and virtual reality (VR) are becoming increasingly prevalent in educational environments, prompting the necessity for thorough investigation into their effects on a variety of learners (Klímová et al., 2023). Ethical considerations are paramount, as these technologies have the potential to deepen existing inequalities or introduce new challenges, including issues related to harassment and surveillance (Holmes et al., 2021). The discussion emphasizes how crucial it is to create frameworks that give ethical issues first priority while creating and utilizing educational technology. An effective resolution of these challenges necessitates an interdisciplinary framework that integrates technological expertise with sociological and ethical perspectives. Ethical frameworks must evolve to address issues like learner autonomy and data protection, particularly in AI-driven education (Susilo, 2023). A thorough theoretical framework that includes viewpoints such as critical theory and social constructionism offers enhanced insights into the interplay between digital technologies, educational practices, and social institutions (Warschauer & Matuchniak, 2010). This understanding equips educators and policymakers with the tools necessary to adeptly manage the challenges associated with the integration of new technologies.

Research Design

Quantitative research methods, such as surveys, are essential for uncovering trends associated with technology use, internet access, and privacy concerns among both students and educators. The information derived from this research is vital for formulating effective policies (Pham et al., 2021). Conversely, qualitative approaches, such as focus groups and interviews, provide a profound understanding of the lived experiences of stakeholders, especially those belonging to marginalized communities. By combining these research approaches, researchers may identify the ethical and practical issues surrounding the digital divide in educational settings by connecting statistical results with personal accounts. Triangulation is a methodological strategy that reinforces findings obtained from various sources, thereby strengthening the overall integrity of a mixed-methods framework and enhancing the reliability, validity, and relevance of the outcomes (Resta et al., 2018). This approach considers vital factors such as socioeconomic status, gender, and geographic location, which are critical for addressing inequalities in digital education, especially those experienced by girls in remote regions. For instance, while quantitative analyses may reveal widespread concerns regarding cybersecurity and privacy, qualitative research can expose more profound systemic challenges, such as cultural attitudes and infrastructure deficiencies, that impede fair access to educational technologies.

The use of stratified sampling to select participants in educational research in Vietnam is a methodologically robust strategy that guarantees representation from the country's varied socio-economic backgrounds. This method effectively captures the perspectives of essential stakeholders, including adolescents aged 12 to 18, their parents, educators, policymakers, and representatives from non-governmental organizations. This chapter employs a thematic analysis on the interview data which illuminates how local conditions influence the effectiveness and utilization of educational technology, especially in rural and resource-limited environments. This research methodology emphasizes the importance of ethical considerations. To uphold ethical standards in educational research, it is imperative to respect participants, secure informed consent, and ensure the confidentiality of their information. Providing ethics training for researchers and offering consultation services can improve adherence to these ethical principles, thereby enhancing accountability and fostering ethical awareness in studies concerning higher education and digital education systems (Masic, 2012). By implementing this thorough and ethically responsible approach, researchers can achieve a more profound understanding of the digital divide, ultimately aiding in the development of more equitable and inclusive educational opportunities in Vietnam.

Data Collection

The data-gathering procedure utilized a mixed-methods strategy to investigate ethical concerns related to the digital divide in education in Vietnam from February 1 to September 20, 2023, providing both a general overview and detailed insights into the topic. This is the first phase of conducting analysis, starting with the qualitative phase, which was carried out to examine the ethical issues that arose from the results from June 15 to September 20, 2023. This phase involved semi-structured interviews to collect detailed, context-specific perspectives from youth and parents. A purposive sampling technique was used to select 11 participants (7 youth, 4 parents). Discussions focused on concerns related to privacy, obstacles to digital accessibility, and the impact of cultural factors on technology utilization. The interviews were documented, transcribed, translated, and subjected to content analysis to uncover significant themes and trends. (See Table 6.1 in the Online Appendices link at https://tinyurl.com/he50Appendices).

Individual semi-structured interviews were held with selected participants to explore their unique perspectives on privacy, accessibility, and the impact of cultural norms on technology usage. The interview guide contained open-ended questions and was conducted by trained facilitators which lasted approximately 40–60 minutes. The focus groups encouraged participants to discuss the effectiveness of digital tools in rural educational environments and the perceived fairness in the distribution of resources.

The second phase produced 27 questionnaires based on the insights gathered in the first phase. The quantitative phase is scheduled to take place from June 15 to September 20, 2023, and will focus on structured surveys designed to gather a variety of perspectives. Two primary surveys were administered: the first targeting adolescents between the ages of 12 and 18, and the second directed towards parents of students in primary and secondary education. Each survey comprises 27 questions categorized into five thematic areas: digital accessibility, privacy and data security, the advantages of digital tools in educational settings, challenges related to gender equality, and cultural obstacles to gender inclusion.

To ensure representativeness of the sample, stratified random sampling was used to achieve balanced participation of urban (50%) and rural (50%) communities. The youth survey collected 400 responses, of which 60% were female and 40% were male. This parent survey received a total of 200 responses, of which 55% were from urban families and 45% from rural families. These demographic data are crucial for identifying changes and trends across different socioeconomic and geographical contexts, as previous research has shown that parental involvement and socioeconomic status significantly influence young people's educational outcomes and aspirations (Gao, 2023).

A variety of online and offline methods were used for data collection to address levels of access to different technologies. The analysis of the data was conducted using Python to produce descriptive statistics such as mean, standard deviation, and frequency distribution. The principal findings from this phase highlighted the necessity of incorporating accessibility into research designs, indicating that disparities in technology access can lead to significant inequalities in both data collection and analysis, particularly in the context of educational research. The main conclusions from this phase pinpoint specific areas that warrant further investigation in future qualitative studies and stress the importance of grasping the varied experiences different demographic groups encounter with digital tools and issues of equity in education.

Findings - Qualitative Results

This portion outlines the results from the qualitative interviews carried out with four parents (PH) and seven teenagers (TN) to investigate the ethical and practical issues surrounding Vietnam's educational digital divide. The interviews offer valuable perspectives on viewpoints related to digital access, concerns regarding privacy, and cultural perspectives on digital learning.

Gender Disparities in Digital Access

Interviews revealed significant gender disparities in the availability of digital resources and educational opportunities. It was noted that parents often prioritize the provision of digital devices for their sons, viewing these tools as vital for boys' academic achievement. A rural parent (PH3) commented, "Boys typically receive access to phones or computers prior to girls, as parents consider these resources to be more critical for their education, whereas girls are anticipated to focus on domestic duties." This ongoing bias limits adolescent girls' interaction with technology, leading to a decrease in their confidence regarding digital skills. TN5 shared, "I wasn't familiar with how to use online learning applications until my teacher demonstrated it to me. My male classmates appeared to grasp it more quickly because they had previous experience with similar tools". These disparities underscore the need for targeted initiatives that promote equal access and digital literacy among girls. Tailored programs addressing cultural biases could empower adolescent girls to participate fully in Vietnam's digital education ecosystem.

Cultural Resistance to Digital Education

Cultural resistance emerged as a significant barrier to digital education. Parents, particularly in rural areas, expressed skepticism about digital tools, favouring traditional teaching methods. PH4 stated, "We were raised with books and notebooks. It's challenging to trust an app or computer for substantial learning." Adolescents also reported encountering resistance to sensitive topics such as gender equality. TN6 noted, "My parents feel uneasy when topics like relationships or gender equality arise online." This resistance reflects broader cultural attitudes that may hinder the adoption of digital learning in Vietnam's Higher Education 5.0.

To address these concerns, culturally sensitive digital tools that integrate traditional teaching methods with innovative digital approaches are essential. Building trust through community engagement programs could help parents and educators see the value of digital education.

Privacy and Accessibility: Urban-Rural Challenges

Concerns related to privacy were frequently articulated by both parents and adolescents. Parents emphasized their fears regarding the potential misuse of their children's data, with one parent stating, "I am apprehensive about applications that require excessive personal information. My anxiety stems from the possibility that my child's data could be exploited or sold." In a similar vein, teenagers expressed their discomfort, with one remarking, "Sometimes, I hesitate to sign up for an app because I am unsure of how my information will be managed." These insights highlight the imperative for educational institutions to take an active role in informing families about digital ethics and data protection through workshops and training programs. The digital divide between urban and rural areas continues to be a major challenge.

Rural parents reported slow internet speeds and limited resources, as PH3 explained, "In rural areas, internet speed is very slow, making it hard for children to attend online classes." Adolescents from rural areas echoed these frustrations, citing frequent disconnections during important lectures. Access to technological devices exhibited considerable disparities, with families in rural areas frequently depending on shared resources, whereas urban students enjoyed superior access. PH2 remarked that the financial burden of internet data significantly impacts rural households, leading them to limit their children's screen time to manage expenses. These obstacles highlight the critical need for investment in infrastructure to enhance internet connectivity in rural regions.

Quantitative Results

This section outlines the quantitative results from a survey conducted with 600 participants, consisting of 400 youth between the ages of 12 and 18 and 200 parents, to investigate ethical dilemmas and disparities in digital education throughout Vietnam.

Gender Disparities in Digital Access

The survey indicates notable gender inequalities in the availability of digital resources. Boys reported higher access to digital devices ($M = 4.6$, $SD = 0.9$) in comparison to girls ($M = 3.7$, $SD = 1.1$), highlighting an uneven allocation of family resources. Furthermore, Parental support was significantly greater for boys ($M = 4.3$, $SD = 0.8$), who benefited from more assistance in the use of digital tools and educational resources compared to girls ($M = 3.9$, $SD = 0.7$). These findings highlight the influence of conventional gender norms, which frequently result in boys having preferential access to educational resources. It is essential to confront these disparities to ensure that adolescent girls have equitable opportunities to engage in digital learning, a crucial element of the Higher Education 5.0 framework.

Cultural Resistance to Digital Learning

Cultural perspectives play a crucial role in influencing how digital tools are perceived. Parents in rural areas exhibited a pronounced inclination towards conventional teaching methods, reflected in a mean score of 4.4 (SD = 0.8), and regarded digital resources as additional rather than fundamental. Conversely, adolescents exhibited a moderate interest in digital tools, reflected in an engagement score of 4.1 (SD = 0.9). Nevertheless, their overall perception of these tools is rather tepid (M = 3.5, SD = 1.1), indicating a significant level of skepticism that is prevalent among both parents and adolescents. These findings imply that cultural norms and attitudes regarding the importance of education pose significant challenges to the adoption of digital technologies. To address these challenges, it is essential to implement targeted outreach initiatives, such as community workshops and demonstrations that highlight the advantages of digital education, in order to enhance acceptance and utilization.

Privacy and Accessibility: Urban-Rural Challenges

Privacy concerns emerged as a key issue for both parents and adolescents. Parents expressed heightened sensitivity to the security of their children's digital data (M = 4.5, SD = 1.0), often citing the lack of transparency in app data policies. Adolescents exhibited moderate levels of concern regarding digital ethics and privacy, with a mean score of 3.8 and a standard deviation of 0.9. This suggests a limited understanding of the importance of these issues. The results underscore the necessity for digital education platforms to implement stringent data security measures and for educational institutions to offer comprehensive training on safe online behaviours.

Significant disparities in digital access were identified between urban and rural populations. Urban adolescents demonstrated considerably greater internet accessibility, achieving an average score of 4.7 (SD = 0.7), in contrast to their rural peers, who reported a lower average score of 3.1 (SD = 1.2). Families residing in rural regions faced further obstacles, including slower internet speeds and the necessity of sharing digital devices. One parent (PH3) remarked, "In rural areas, internet speed is very slow, making it hard for children to attend online classes". The financial implications of internet services further widen this gap, as rural families reported lower satisfaction levels, with a mean score of 2.8 (SD = 1.1). Urban educational institutions exhibited a higher level of organizational support for digital learning (M = 4.6, SD = 0.6) compared to rural institutions, which showed insufficient technological integration in their instructional methods. These results highlight the critical necessity for focused investment in digital infrastructure within rural areas, as well as the provision of affordable internet access and subsidized digital resources, to address the educational inequalities that exist between urban and rural settings.

Discussion

This chapter aimed to answer the research question: "How can ethical frameworks and innovative strategies address digital divide challenges in Vietnam's educational ecosystem, particularly regarding gender inclusivity and technological accessibility?" A key aspect of this chapter is the acknowledgment of the significant influence that parents exert on educational choices in Vietnam. Parental attitudes significantly influence adolescents' access to digital resources and their engagement with technology. By focusing on parents' perceptions, this chapter highlights key barriers, such as privacy concerns, gender disparities, and cultural resistance, that must be addressed to advance equitable and inclusive pathways in Higher Education 5.0.

Digital ethics has become a fundamental aspect in tackling issues related to privacy and equitable access to technology. Stakeholders, especially parents, voiced considerable worries regarding data privacy and the potential exploitation of personal information gathered by educational software. Numerous parents indicated a lack of clarity on how to assist their children in managing online privacy, mirroring widespread apprehensions about digital ethics (Floridi, 2014). This study supports the creation of educational programs and institutional workshops designed to enhance digital literacy and foster awareness of safe online practices as a means to tackle these challenges. The execution of these initiatives is vital for cultivating trust in digital platforms, which is an essential element in creating a secure educational atmosphere.

Additionally, this study uncovers notable gender inequalities in access to digital resources, especially in rural regions, where conventional gender roles often favour boys over girls. This limited access to technology for females has detrimental effects on their digital literacy and academic success. These findings are indicative of broader global patterns of systemic gender bias, as articulated within Rawls's rule of law framework, which emphasizes the importance of equal opportunities in overcoming obstacles faced by marginalized populations (Sen, 1999). It is imperative to implement focused interventions, such as digital literacy programs tailored for girls and community-led initiatives that confront conventional gender norms. These recommendations align with UNICEF's (2021) commitment to promoting gender-inclusive digital education.

The ongoing digital divide between urban and rural locales presents a substantial obstacle to the realization of equitable educational opportunities. Survey data reveal that students residing in rural areas face significantly lower levels of internet connectivity and access to digital resources when compared to their urban peers. This disparity is closely linked to infrastructural obstacles, such as inconsistent internet connectivity, elevated costs, and a scarcity of devices in rural areas. Parents have pointed out that the financial strain of internet services constitutes a significant impediment to reliable access. To mitigate this inequality, the chapter recommends targeted investments in digital infrastructure in rural regions, the availability of cost-effective technological devices, and financial assistance for families facing economic hardships.

Moreover, cultural resistance presents an additional hurdle to the integration of digital tools in educational environments. Residents of rural areas, including both parents and students, have expressed doubts about the efficacy of digital learning, often preferring conventional teaching methods. Numerous individuals perceive digital platforms as auxiliary resources rather than fundamental components in the pursuit of academic achievement. This scepticism highlights the necessity for culturally sensitive strategies that harmonize the advantages of digital technology with an appreciation for local traditions. Programs that engage the community by merging traditional educational practices with digital innovations could foster trust and enhance acceptance of new technologies (Heeks & Renken, 2018).

Despite these insights, gaps remain, particularly regarding the preparatory stage and the role of adolescents in transitioning to Higher Education 5.0. Previous studies have focused predominantly on systemic strategies, neglecting adolescents' experiences and parental perspectives during this critical phase. This chapter addresses these gaps by exploring the socio-cultural obstacles, privacy issues, and digital divides that hinder equitable access. The results offer practical insights for promoting equitable, inclusive, and secure pathways to digital education, ensuring that marginalized groups, especially adolescent girls, are not excluded from Vietnam's educational transformation.

From these findings, this chapter underscores the urgent need for ethical frameworks that prioritize inclusivity, equity, and privacy in Vietnam's digital education ecosystem. Key recommendations include investing in infrastructure to improve rural connectivity, launching targeted digital literacy campaigns, and empowering girls through tailored programs to overcome gender-specific barriers. Furthermore, it is crucial to create digital tools that align with local cultural values in order to improve the acceptance of digital learning. Future research should assess the sustainability and scalability of these suggested strategies to guarantee ongoing advancements in bridging digital divides.

Conclusion

This chapter investigated the challenges and opportunities related to the implementation of Vietnam's Higher Education 5.0 framework, focusing specifically on the perspectives of youth and their parents during their formative phases. The results reveal significant obstacles in achieving equitable, inclusive, and safe digital education, which encompass gender disparities, the digital divide between urban and rural populations, cultural resistance to technological adoption, and privacy concerns. The challenges highlighted emphasize the critical necessity for focused interventions and holistic strategies designed to tackle systemic disparities and cultivate trust within digital learning settings. To improve equitable access, it is imperative to enhance digital infrastructure in rural regions and guarantee the availability of affordable devices and internet connectivity. Addressing gender disparities necessitates the development of specialized programs aimed at empowering adolescent girls and confronting deeply rooted cultural norms. Furthermore, it is essential to emphasize privacy and digital ethics by instituting robust data protection measures and educational initiatives directed at families. Such initiatives are fundamental for increasing awareness and building trust in digital technologies. Furthermore, the integration of culturally responsive methods is necessary to overcome resistance and encourage the acceptance of technology-enhanced learning. By integrating these solutions into the Higher Education 5.0 framework, Vietnam can establish an educational system that empowers all learners, especially those from marginalized backgrounds. Collaboration among policymakers, educators, and community members is crucial to realizing this vision and ensuring that the new generation is prepared to succeed in a digital landscape, in alignment with Sustainable Development Goals 4 and 5.

7

Redefining the Learning Experience: Innovative Pedagogy and Curricular Co-Creation in Vietnamese Higher Education 5.0[15]

Duc Hong Thi Phan[16] and Bruno Mascitelli

Abstract

This chapter examines the imperative for pedagogical transformation within Vietnamese Higher Education (VHE) to align with the global Higher Education 5.0 paradigm. It argues that moving beyond traditional, teacher-centric models requires a strategic shift towards creating holistic, human-centered learning experiences. The analysis is structured around three core pillars: the philosophical transition from Instructional Design (ID) to Learning Experience Design (LXD); the contextualized application of technology-enhanced models, specifically Gamification and blended learning, detailing their successes and challenges within Vietnam; and the strategic necessity of curricular co-creation, which involves students and other stakeholders as active partners in educational innovation. Drawing on local case studies and empirical data, the chapter highlights that successful transformation hinges on intelligently adapting global best practices to Vietnam's unique cultural and infrastructural landscape. It concludes with targeted recommendations for university leaders, faculty,

---

15 All references, tables, figures, author affiliation and biography used in this chapter are available on the Online Appendix link at https://tinyurl.com/he50Appendices.

16 Corresponding author: hongducktkt@gmail.com

and policymakers to foster a more adaptive, engaging, and learner-centric educational ecosystem prepared for the future.

Introduction

The global higher education landscape is witnessing a paradigm shift towards Higher Education 5.0, a model that emphasizes deep integration with industry, personalized learning pathways, and the leveraging of technology. Within this global current, Vietnamese higher education confronts an urgent mandate: to revolutionize its pedagogical thinking. Macro-level policies such as the Higher Education Reform Agenda (HERA) for the 2006–2020 period and the enhancement of university autonomy have created a favorable legal corridor and institutional space for this innovation (Huong et al., 2023). Advanced approaches like blended learning are being increasingly adopted to modernize traditional teaching methods and enhance student engagement (Lap et al., 2020).

However, the impetus for change extends beyond strategic directives. It is an undeniable reality that long-standing, unidirectional, teacher-centric instructional methods are proving increasingly inadequate, diminishing student motivation and satisfaction (Nguyen & Do, 2023). The monotony and lack of interaction in the classroom not only affect academic outcomes but also produce a generation of graduates lacking the requisite skills for the global labor market (Phan & Dang, 2017). Consequently, this transformation is not merely a trend but a strategic response, propelled by two parallel forces: a bottom-up push from students for a more meaningful learning experience and a top-down imperative from policymakers to enhance the quality and competitiveness of the national human capital.

This chapter will delve into three core pillars of Vietnam's pedagogical transformation. First, it will explore the paradigm shift in educational design philosophy, moving from a singular focus on "teaching" to the creation of "learning experiences." Second, it will analyze the application of technology-enhanced pedagogical models, particularly Gamification and blended learning, within the specific context of Vietnam. Finally, it will argue for the strategic importance of curricular co-creation, an approach that places students and other stakeholders at the heart of the innovation process.

From Instruction to Experience: A Paradigm Shift in Learning Design

The most fundamental change in modern education lies not in the technology employed, but in the philosophy behind the creation of learning environments. It is a shift from designing instruction to crafting experiences. This change necessitates a new understanding of the roles of the educator, the learner, and the nature of the learning process itself.

Differentiating Instructional Design and Learning Design

For decades, Instructional Design (ID) has been the dominant framework. ID is defined as a systematic, content-driven, and often linear process focused on the efficient and effective delivery of instructional materials (Blue Carrot, 2025). It is prescriptive, concentrating on matching specific learning objectives with corresponding strategies and assessment methods (Purdue University College of Education, 2024). This model views the learner as a vessel to be "filled" with knowledge and skills through a carefully engineered sequence of activities.

Conversely, Learning Design (LD), also known as Learning Experience Design (LXD), is a higher-level, holistic, and learner-centric approach (Schmidt, 2025). Instead of focusing solely on content, LD considers the user's entire experience, including emotional and motivational aspects. LD is grounded in learning theory, goal-oriented, and emphasizes the creation of an engaging environment tailored to the learner's needs, preferences, and context (Schmidt, 2025). The relationship between these two concepts is often viewed as sequential: LD sets the strategic and philosophical foundation, upon which ID executes the creation of detailed materials and activities (Blue Carrot, 2025).

Core Principles of Human-Centered Design in Education

The philosophical engine behind modern LD is Human-Centered Design (HCD). HCD is an approach that prioritizes human needs, behaviors, and experiences throughout the design process (BeBusinessed, 2025). When applied to education, HCD places the student at the center to foster positive learning outcomes (Instructure, 2025). Three core principles of HCD shape modern academic planning:

- Empathy: This is the foundation of HCD. It requires a deep understanding of students' thoughts, motivations, challenges, and needs. By acknowledging learners' strengths and weaknesses, empathetic design allows for the creation of flexible and personalized learning experiences (Instructure, 2025).

- Iteration: HCD is not a linear process. It is a continuous cycle of prototyping, testing, and refining educational tools, materials, and strategies based on real user feedback. This approach ensures that academic resources remain current and can evolve to meet students' changing needs (Schmidt, 2025).

- User Feedback: HCD demands active solicitation and integration of student feedback into decision-making. Learning experiences are planned based on students' preferences, experiences, and concerns, ensuring that the resources created are relevant and effective (Instructure, 2025).

The adoption of HCD in the Vietnamese educational context, with its tradition of revering the teacher as the primary source of knowledge, is not just a methodological choice; it is a cultural one. It challenges long-established power structures and demands a mindset shift from both educators, who must become facilitators, and students, who must become active agents in their own learning journeys.

Foundational Models: From ADDIE to Design-Based Research (DBR)

Two prominent models illustrate the evolution of design thinking in education. The ADDIE model (Analyze, Design, Develop, Implement, Evaluate) is a foundational and systematic framework (EdTech Books, 2025). Though originally conceived as a linear model, ADDIE is increasingly applied more iteratively and flexibly today (Stefaniak, 2020). It is effective for structuring the instructional process but is sometimes criticized for being overly prescriptive and potentially leading to superficial design if not applied with depth (Stefaniak, 2020).

Meanwhile, Design-Based Research (DBR) is a methodology that is also iterative and conducted in naturalistic settings like classrooms, but with a distinct primary goal: to generate new theories and frameworks, not merely to "refine what works" (AIU, 2025). DBR is seen as a bridge between learning sciences (theory building) and instructional design (interventionist practice), offering a powerful method for evidence-based innovation in complex learning environments (Greenhow, 2018).

Technology-Enhanced Pedagogical Models in the Vietnamese Context

The application of a learner-centric design philosophy is realized through specific pedagogical models, where technology acts as both a catalyst and an enabler. In Vietnam, two models that demonstrate significant potential and considerable challenges are Gamification and blended learning.

Gamification: Motivating the Modern Learner

Gamification is defined as the integration of game design elements into non-game contexts to enhance motivation and engagement (Nguyen & Do, 2023). A key study by Nguyen and Do (2023) surveyed 306 undergraduate and graduate students in Vietnam participating in gamified lectures, providing crucial insights into this method's efficacy. The research focused on three primary factors: Challenge, Enjoyment, and Competitiveness.

The key findings reveal a multifaceted picture of Gamification's impact (see Table 7.1 in the Online Appendix link https://tinyurl.com/he50Appendices). Both Challenge and Enjoyment were found to have a direct, positive influence on student engagement and satisfaction. Notably, the Challenge element also directly impacted learning effectiveness. This suggests that designing tasks of moderate difficulty—ones that stimulate critical thinking without causing frustration—is key to improving tangible learning outcomes. Furthermore, engagement and learning effectiveness act as mediators, meaning that when students feel challenged and enjoy the process, they engage more deeply and learn more effectively, which in turn leads to higher overall satisfaction (Nguyen & Do, 2023). These findings align with global meta-analyses, which indicate that the use of elements like points, badges, and leaderboards significantly enhances motivation, participation, and academic success (Putz et al., 2020).

Blended Learning: Navigating Flexibility and Challenges

Blended learning, which integrates face-to-face classroom instruction with online learning components, has been widely adopted in Vietnam, particularly in the wake of the COVID-19 pandemic. The benefits of this model are clear and highly valued by students. However, its implementation has also exposed significant challenges, creating a dichotomy in the learner experience (see Table 7.2 in the Online Appendix link https://tinyurl.com/he50Appendices).

The data reveals that while students deeply appreciate flexibility and rich resources, they are confronted with infrastructural barriers and, more critically, difficulties in self-regulating their learning. The time management challenge is particularly prevalent among students unaccustomed to the high degree of autonomy that blended learning demands (Le and Lai, 2024). On the instructor side, faculty face issues such as ambiguity regarding the concept of blended learning, increased workload pressure, and skepticism about students' capacity for self-directed study (Amiruddin et al., 2022).

A pivotal finding from this research is the strong positive correlation between self-regulated learning skills and overall satisfaction ($r=0.72, p<.01$) (Le and Lai, 2024). This is more than a statistic; it points to a core truth: the success of blended learning depends not on the technology, but on the learner's capacity for autonomy.

The Foundational Role of the Learning Management System (LMS)

The Learning Management System (LMS) is the core technological infrastructure that enables the deployment of both Gamification and blended learning. An LMS is a digital platform designed to manage, deliver, and track educational content and activities (Nguyen, 2024). Although LMS adoption was significantly accelerated by the pandemic (Nguyen, 2024), its practical effectiveness in Vietnam remains constrained. Key barriers include weak user IT competency, a lack of confidence and formal training, a preference for traditional methods, unstable internet connectivity, and a lack of timely technical support (Nguyen, 2024). A common situation is that even when an LMS is available, the level of participation from both faculty and students remains low, and the system's functionalities are not fully utilized (Riyath & Rijah, 2022). Successful LMS adoption is heavily dependent on user-psychological factors such as perceived usefulness, perceived ease of use, and the quality of support services (Al-Mamary, 2022).

The challenges encountered in implementing blended learning and the LMS are not isolated issues. They are symptoms of a deeper, systemic problem: a failure to integrate technology (the tool) with pedagogy (the method) and learner development (the mindset). Universities are deploying a technology (LMS) to support a pedagogical model (blended learning) that requires a specific student skill (autonomy), yet they have not invested adequately in training faculty to teach in this new way and students to learn in this new way. The technology is being implemented in a pedagogical and cultural vacuum, leading to the reported challenges. The problem is not the tool, but the lack of an integrated and holistic implementation strategy.

The Co-Creation Imperative: Rebuilding the Curriculum with Stakeholders

To truly transform the learning experience, innovation cannot be confined to classroom teaching methods. It requires a fundamental shift in how we build curricula—moving from a top-down model to a collaborative, co-creative process. Co-creation is a collaborative approach wherein all stakeholders, including students, faculty, alumni, and industry partners—jointly participate in the development process (Nasser, n.d.).

The theoretical foundation for this approach is Service-Dominant Logic (S-D Logic), which posits that value is not unilaterally created by a provider and delivered to a customer, but is always "co-created" through collaborative efforts (Vargo & Lusch, 2004). In an educational context, this means the value of a program lies not just in the content provided by the institution, but in how students interact with, engage in, and co-shape that learning experience.

A case study at Vietnam National University (VNU) applied this theoretical framework to analyze the co-creation process (Nguyen & Hong, 2023). The study examined two key inputs: Co-production (comprising knowledge sharing, equity, and interaction) and Value-in-Use (comprising experience, personalization, and relationships). The outputs were measured across three dimensions: Innovation, Knowledge, and Relational benefits.

The analysis revealed that co-creation positively impacts all three outcomes. However, a critical finding was the significant difference in perception and impact between faculty and students (see Table 7.3 in the Online Appendix link https://tinyurl.com/he50Appendices). For instance, the "Co-production" element had a stronger effect on faculty, which may imply a power imbalance in the collaborative process, where student input might be treated as "input" into a faculty-owned process rather than as a truly equal partnership (Nguyen & Hong, 2023).

This finding carries a crucial implication: in a hierarchical context like Vietnamese education, "participation" does not automatically equate to "partnership." If not designed carefully, co-creation initiatives risk reinforcing existing power structures rather than dismantling them. For co-creation to be truly transformative, institutions must proactively design processes that empower students and mitigate these power imbalances.

Case Studies in Vietnamese Higher Education Innovation

To illustrate the concepts and analyses presented, the following three case studies highlight how innovative pedagogical models and co-creation are being applied in practice in Vietnam.

Case A: Gamification to Enhance Student Satisfaction

At a university of economics in Ho Chi Minh City, a Principles of Marketing course, traditionally perceived as dry with low student participation, was completely redesigned using Gamification, drawing on principles from the research of Nguyen and Do (2023). Instead of traditional lectures, the instructor created a marketing "journey" on the LMS platform, where each chapter was a new "land" to be explored. The Challenge element was integrated through complex case studies of increasing difficulty, requiring students to apply theory to solve real-world business problems. Successfully completing difficult challenges not only earned students' higher points but also unlocked "expert badges," directly improving learning effectiveness. The Enjoyment factor was fostered through a visually appealing interface, engaging narrative videos, and group competitions to build a marketing plan for a fictional product. The end-of-term results showed a dramatic shift: forum discussion engagement increased by 300%, and overall student satisfaction with the course rose from 2.8/5 to 4.5/5. This clearly illustrates the mediating role of engagement: the game elements created a positive feedback loop, motivating students to participate more deeply, learn more effectively, and ultimately, become more satisfied.

Case B: The Blended Learning Experience at Hanoi Open University

An, a second-year English Language major at Hanoi Open University, enrolled in a foundational English program delivered via a blended learning model (Le & Lai, 2024). Initially, An was excited about the flexibility (valued by 83.2% of students) the model offered; she could study while holding a part-time job. The rich online resources (valued by 78.6%) available on the LMS made it easy for her to review lectures and materials anytime (Le & Lai, 2024). However, challenges quickly emerged. During a critical online test, an unstable internet connection (an issue for 31.9% of students) caused her to panic and perform poorly. The greater challenge was time management (a difficulty for 28.1%); without a fixed daily schedule, An often procrastinated and felt overwhelmed by the workload at the end of the week (Le and Lai, 2024). Recognizing the problem, An began using planning tools and setting small, daily learning goals. Gradually, she developed the skill of self-discipline and proactivity. By the end of the semester, An not only achieved a high grade but also felt more confident in her ability to learn independently. An's experience is a vivid testament to the strong correlation ($r=0.72$) between self-regulated learning skills and satisfaction in a blended learning environment (Le & Lai, 2024).

Case C: A Radical Partnership—The "Co-Design Year" at Fulbright University Vietnam

Fulbright University Vietnam undertook a landmark educational experiment with its "Co-Design Year" in 2018–2019 (Derby-Talbot and Ellis, 2024). This represents a pinnacle example of institutional-level co-creation. Before the university officially opened, a group of 54 pioneering students (called "Co-Designers") and 17 founding faculty members worked together to build the entire undergraduate curriculum from the ground up (Derby-Talbot & Ellis, 2024). Using the principles of design thinking, they engaged in joint activities to innovate education (Derby-Talbot & Ellis, 2024). Students were not consultants; they were true partners in shaping the educational philosophy, course structures, and assessment methods. The result of this radical collaboration was the establishment of clear learning goals, specific academic pathways, and a curricular map for 11 majors, all forged from the equal contributions of both students and faculty (Fulbright University Vietnam, 2024). Fulbright's "Co-Design Year" went beyond co-creating a single course to co-designing an entire university, standing as a powerful symbol of the potential of placing learners at the absolute center of educational innovation.

Synthesis and Strategic Recommendations for the Future

The journey of pedagogical transformation in Vietnamese higher education to align with the 5.0 model is a complex process, demanding more than the mere adoption of new technologies or the replication of Western models. The analysis in this chapter reveals that success lies not in wholesale importation, but in intelligent and sensitive contextual adaptation. Cultural nuances such as deference to teacher authority and the culture of "saving face," infrastructural limitations like internet quality and classroom equipment, and a pedagogical history centered on the teacher are contextual factors that cannot be ignored.

The success of Higher Education 5.0 in Vietnam hinges on achieving a delicate equilibrium between three forces: Global Best Practices (e.g., HCD, co-creation), Local Contextual Realities (culture, infrastructure), and Human Capabilities (student autonomy, faculty adaptability). Neglecting any one of these elements will lead to failed initiatives. Based on this synthesis, the following strategic recommendations are proposed:

For University Leaders:

- Foster a Culture of Pedagogical Experimentation: Create a safe environment that encourages faculty to experiment with new teaching methods without fear of failure.

• Invest in a Three-Pillar Strategy: Develop an integrated strategy comprising: robust technological infrastructure (stable LMS, high-speed internet), comprehensive faculty development (training in HCD, blended learning pedagogy, and facilitation skills), and structured student support programs (workshops on self-regulated learning, time management, and digital literacy).

For Faculty Members:

• Shift to a Facilitator Mindset: Gradually transition from the role of knowledge transmitter to that of an experience designer and learning process facilitator.

• Start Small: Introduce co-creative practices incrementally, such as inviting students to co-design a single assessment or a course module (Knaggs et al., 2021).

• Design Intentionally for the Vietnamese Context: Create "safe spaces" for students to provide feedback and ask questions without fear of judgment or "losing face," for instance, by using anonymous survey tools or private feedback channels.

For Policymakers:

• Continue to Support University Autonomy: Maintain and expand policies that grant autonomy to universities.

• Link Autonomy to Quality Assurance Frameworks: Develop quality assurance criteria that incentivize deep pedagogical innovation rather than the superficial application of technology.

• Fund Research on Cross-Cultural Adaptation: Invest in in-depth studies on adapting international educational design models and principles to the Vietnamese context to build a robust, localized knowledge base.

Ultimately, redefining the learning experience in Vietnam is a marathon, not a sprint. It requires persistence, commitment, and close collaboration from all stakeholders to build a higher education system that is truly human-centered and future-ready.

8

Exploring the teachers' and students' perceptions of the implementation of learning design on their blended learning experiences in Vietnamese higher education[17]

Nguyen Thanh Cong[18]

ABSTRACT

Blended learning, which integrates traditional face-to-face instruction with online learning experiences, offers a great flexible and dynamic learning environment that can cater to diverse learning needs. In Vietnam, though the implementation of blended learning has gained popularity in Vietnamese higher education institutions, the perceptions and readiness of both educators and students towards this approach remain varied and sometimes challenging. A critical aspect of this approach is learning design, which enhances student engagement by integrating interactive elements that promote collaboration and communication among peers and instructors. By focusing on these interactive components, blended learning can significantly enrich the overall educational experience for students in Vietnamese higher education settings. Acknowledging the potential benefits of learning design, this study investigates the perceptions of teachers and students regarding the implementation of

---

17 All references, tables, figures, author affiliation and biography used in this chapter are available on the Online Appendix link at https://tinyurl.com/he50Appendices.

18 Corresponding author: cong19082001@gmail.com

learning design in blended learning contexts within Vietnamese higher education. The research, using qualitative methods, involved semi-structured interviews among four participants, including two university teachers and two students at two separate higher education institutions in the Hanoi capital area. The results demonstrated the implementation of learning design in blended learning based on three aspects: flexibility, content delivery, and assessment. Particularly, from the perspectives of both teachers and students, the factor of flexibility has not reached the necessary level, while aspects such as content delivery and assessment have been implemented almost well.

Introduction - Context

Blended Learning (BL), which integrates face-to-face and online education, has gained significant traction in higher education globally (Anthony et al., 2022). This approach is seen as an "evolutionary transformation" supported by web-based systems in universities, enhancing student interaction in large classes and offering flexible, manageable, and cost-effective learning options (Gedik et al., 2023). In Vietnam, the Ministry of Education and Training (MOET) has acknowledged the potential benefits of blended learning amid rapid technological advancements, leading to policies that mandate the use of Information and Communication Technologies (ICTs). Consequently, Vietnamese universities are increasingly adopting BL to overcome the limitations of traditional face-to-face teaching methods (Nguyen, 2017).

However, for BL to be effective in higher education, it requires more than just the integration of online and face-to-face practices; careful consideration of its implementation is essential (Gedik et al., 2023). Smith and Hill (2019) argue that BL enriches classroom experiences and transforms the learning environment by providing students with greater autonomy to study independently, select content, and set their own pace, thereby enhancing their overall effectiveness. This raises critical questions about how to further promote learner autonomy and improve the effectiveness of BL in Vietnamese universities.

The COVID-19 pandemic has significantly accelerated the demand for blended learning options in higher education, as institutions worldwide shifted to remote instruction (Finlay, Tinnion & Simpson, 2022). During the pandemic, Vietnamese universities had to adapt to lockdown measures, leading to the rapid adoption of BL and online learning modalities. Post-pandemic, a flexible mix of face-to-face and online learning methods has been embraced to achieve educational goals. Learning Management Systems (LMS) have played a crucial role in managing students and tracking their academic progress, with educational resources such as PowerPoint presentations, videos, and online quizzes being shared through platforms like Google Classroom and SHub Classroom. In traditional classrooms, teachers follow structured lesson plans and assign assessments, while final exams and mock university entrance tests are conducted in physical settings.

Despite the growing body of literature on blended learning in Vietnamese universities, research often overlooks the specific nature of the "blends" between delivery methods. Previous studies have primarily focused on student characteristics and outcomes (Kintu et al., 2017), while the critical aspect of learning design—essential for the effectiveness of blended learning—has received less attention. Effective learning design can successfully integrate online activities with practical fieldwork, preparing pre-service teachers for their future careers (Nortvig, Petersen & Balle, 2018). Fegely et al. (2020) emphasize that intentional course design and appropriate digital tools can foster collaborative and inquiry-based learning relevant to field practice. By integrating online and face-to-face elements, educators can create engaging learning environments that cater to diverse student needs, ultimately enhancing educational outcomes. Thus, this research aims to examine the implementation of learning design in BL within Vietnamese higher education from the perspectives of university teachers and students, contributing to the enhancement of BL experiences in this context.

1. What are the teachers' attitudes towards the implementation of learning design in BL in Vietnamese higher education?

2. What are the students' attitudes towards the implementation of learning design in BL in Vietnamese higher education?

Literature review

Blended learning

Blended Learning (BL) is a topic of ongoing debate in higher education, primarily due to its intricate definition (Walker & Keeffe, 2010). Graham (2006) characterises it as a system that merges face-to-face (F2F) instruction with computer-mediated learning, placing a strong emphasis on inclusiveness. In contrast, Garrison and Kanuka (2004) view it as the combination of F2F and online experiences, prioritising quality and thoughtful integration. This latter perspective aligns more closely with the goals of the current study, which underscores the importance of meaningful integration between online and offline learning. Nevertheless, pinpointing the fundamental principles of BL remains a challenge because of its wide-ranging applications (Smith & Hill, 2019). According to Arbaugh (2014), effective integration strikes a balance in delivering educational content through both online and F2F methods. This strategy enhances learning by leveraging rich online resources while also providing immediate feedback in person (Roddy et al., 2017). Hence, the study suggests that BL should thoughtfully integrate different instructional methods, employ active learning strategies and a variety of pedagogical approaches, provide access to rich learning materials and course content, and facilitate rapid feedback on course progress of students through online resources and in-class meetings.

Learning Design

There have been two viewpoints on learning from Britain (2004) and Dohn (2010). Britain identifies three concepts in learning design: first, that active engagement enhances learning; second, that structured teaching activities improve effectiveness; and third, the potential for teachers to exchange or reuse learning designs. Dohn (2010) emphasises that focusing on learning designs is crucial for guiding learning activities. Together, they suggest that learning design fosters creative and analytical thinking in organising instructional practices. Wekerle et al. (2022) add that teachers should create courses encouraging active, technology-supported participation rather than relying solely on passive learning methods.

The concept of learning design is examined through various scholarly viewpoints to define it more clearly. Conole (2013) characterises learning design as a methodology that aids educators in making informed decisions about developing learning activities and interventions, stressing the importance of pedagogical knowledge and effective resource utilisation. This definition encompasses everything from individual activities to curriculum design. Tang et al. (2020) describe learning design as an educational process involving diverse activities in areas like computer-aided design and engineering. Laurillard et al. (2013) emphasise critical educational elements such as effective pedagogy, tools, time management, and learner reflection. Together, these perspectives reveal commonalities in learning activities, resources, and technologies crucial for improving learner effectiveness. Overall, it can be concluded that learning design is a methodology that requires knowledge of the subject matter, pedagogical theory, technological skills and practical experience to make effective use of learning activities, interventions, appropriate resources and technologies to facilitate the educational process.

Learning Design on BL

In this section, the important elements of learning design in BL will be discussed. First, in Boelens et al. (2017)'s study, flexibility appears to be an important factor in accommodating various learning styles and preferences, which is also a goal of BL. By allowing students to choose when and how they engage with blended courses, they can progress at their own pace and further encourage their self-regulation and autonomy (Julien et al., 2022). Second, Boelens et al. (2017) emphasise assessment as a key component to monitor students' and measure the learning outcomes effectively. When assessments are varied and aligned with learning activities, students not only participate actively in both online and F2F components but also achieve the learning objectives. Third, regarding 'content delivery', Muller et al. (2023) believed that this aspect is one of the important factors as it ensures that educational materials are accessible to all students. Muller et al. (2023) also suggested well-structured content delivery encourages active learning by inviting students to engage with the material through discussions, problem-solving activities, and hands-on projects.

Therefore, the study focusing on the learning design illustrates some proposed factors affecting the BL experience such as flexibility, content delivery, and assessment. In the following section, the definitions of each element will be discussed.

Flexibility

Flexibility in BL involves a balanced approach to the number, format, and duration of F2F and online activities (Vanslambrouck et al., 2018). In the future, it is forecasted that learners will take charge of deciding the type and format of their BL experiences to meet their individual needs (Bruggeman et al., 2022). However, research by Boelens et al. (2017) reveals a different scenario, where instructors predominantly dictate the blend's implementation in 85% of the courses studied, focusing on learning objectives. For effective BL, courses must be interactive and balanced in-person with virtual activities, aligning with student preferences (Faraniza, 2021). In Vietnamese higher education, literature indicates a lack of emphasis on flexibility in BL courses. Therefore, it is crucial to reassess how both students and teachers perceive this flexibility to better align expectations and enhance student-centred learning.

Content delivery

Content delivery in BL design refers to the methods and strategies used to provide students with access to educational resources and information (Medina, 2018). This approach merges traditional classroom experiences with various digital resources, including tutorial videos, online discussion forums, and instructional texts (Chen et al., 2022). Muller et al. (2023) emphasise that effective content delivery involves well-aligned learning resources that connect seamlessly with tasks in the learning environment. Similarly, Baytiyeh (2017) highlights that structured, collaborative activities yield better outcomes compared to passive tasks like watching videos or reading articles. Bliuc et al. (2007) further assert that successful BL integrates face-to-face interactions with technology-mediated exchanges among students and educators. Despite existing research on BL environments, there is a notable gap regarding the perceptions of content delivery among Vietnamese educators and students. This study aims to explore these perceptions to enhance teaching practices in BL contexts.

Assessment

Assessments in education are primarily categorized into formative and summative types (Ismail et al., 2022). Formative assessments aim at developmental goals, while summative assessments provide evaluative judgments (Chan & Tan, 2017). Nguyen (2017) highlights that all assessments should effectively measure student understanding and the connections between topics. Formative assessments are crucial for evaluating learning outcomes and improving course quality through feedback (McCallum & Milner, 2021). In Vietnam, technology enhances formative assessments by fostering active learning and enabling diverse evaluation methods and peer interactions (Hooda et al., 2022). However, effective implementation of formative assessments in Vietnamese universities requires further investigation. Conversely, summative assessments serve as final evaluations of student performance based on established standards (Nguyen, 2017). In blended learning environments, various summative formats, such as quizzes and group projects, are used, yet many assessments still prioritize memory recall over skill application (Vu & Peters, 2021). Addressing the gap between student expectations and teacher perspectives on assessments is vital for improving educational outcomes.

Methodology

Participants

This study employs a qualitative approach to investigate the perspectives of teachers and students on the impact of learning design in a BL context, focusing on four participants in Hanoi. Utilising phenomenology as the primary research strategy allows for in-depth descriptions of experiences through participants' narratives. The research examines the experiences of both learners and teachers regarding learning design in BL lessons, providing rich insights into the topic. Convenience sampling is adopted, involving two university lecturers - one teaching English and the other specialising in Economics - and two students from the University of Education, VNU. These participants engage with multimedia resources and various assignments formats, contributing to a comprehensive understanding of BL experiences.

Data collection procedures

Interviewing is a primary data collection method for this study. Participants were invited via email, informed of the research objectives, and scheduled for interviews using Microsoft Teams to accommodate geographical barriers. Semi-structured interviews were conducted individually in either Vietnamese. This one-on-one format also simplifies data management, transcription, and translation when necessary. Additionally, online interviews help mitigate the interviewer effect, which can negatively influence responses (Denscombe, 2021). This flexibility is essential for eliciting open-ended responses and fostering participants' engagement in the topic.

Data Analysis

After the interview sessions, the researcher employs thematic analysis to analyse the participants' raw data, identifying and elaborating on emerging themes from their responses. After conducting interviews with all participants, the researcher will transcribe the raw data and provide English translations of any Vietnamese content. Subsequently, the transcriptions will be imported for in-depth analysis. Initially, key ideas will be identified and extracted from the data, then categorised and compared to form themes. The initial dataset will then be reviewed to ensure all relevant data is included, followed by a final review and confirmation of the identified themes. Finally, the researcher will refine and define the themes and report the analysis results in the subsequent section.

Analysis and Discussion - Teachers' attitudes towards the impact of learning design in BL in Vietnamese higher education

Flexibility

In exploring Vietnamese teachers' perspectives on the impact of learning design in blended learning (BL), two key aspects emerge: the "combination of two learning modes" and "teachers' control." Firstly, regarding the combination of learning modes, both teachers reported a three-hour lecture divided between face-to-face (F2F) and online activities. Teacher 1 shared, "70% of my course activities were conducted online via Zoom Cloud

Meetings, with an initial in-person meeting, student presentations, and a final exam making up 30%." In contrast, Teacher 2 noted, "Each of my courses includes twelve obligatory seminars (70%) combined with online study packs (30%) distributed through Moodle." This reflects Teacher 1's preference for online instruction, which is suitable for self-regulated learners, particularly in language education. Conversely, Teacher 2's approach offers a more balanced format that caters to students who thrive in interactive classroom settings.

Secondly, regarding teachers' control over learning formats, both teachers indicated they primarily decide the mode of instruction. Teacher 1 stated, "I usually decide on the learning format and inform students at the start of the course," while Teacher 2 added, "My colleagues and I determine the learning format in advance and communicate this through the LMS and in the first class." This indicates a lack of student involvement in the decision-making process, aligning with findings by Boelens et al. (2017) that suggest instructors often dictate the implementation of BL based on course objectives. For effective BL, as highlighted by Faranize (2021), student choice is essential to meet individual needs, indicating that the current approach in Vietnamese higher education lacks the necessary flexibility for successful BL.

Content delivery

In examining Vietnamese teachers' perspectives on the impacts of learning design in blended learning (BL), two sub-themes emerged: learning resources and their suitability for teaching activities. Firstly, regarding learning resources, the data revealed how teachers delivered content. Teacher 1 utilized videos and online flashcards like Quizlet, while Teacher 2 encouraged the use of mind maps, videos, and professional articles. This demonstrates their effective use of multimedia to achieve learning objectives, aligning with methods discussed by Chen et al. (2022) and Walker et al. (2021). Secondly, concerning the suitability of learning resources for educational activities, both teachers provided valuable insights. Teacher 1 noted that students watched real-life situation videos to visualize new vocabulary and then created dialogues using these words, practicing with interactive flashcards. This multimedia approach supports English as a Lingua Franca (ELF) learners, as highlighted by Khan

(2022). Meanwhile, Teacher 2 allowed students to explore new terms through various resources on the LMS before guiding them to present their findings, encouraging active knowledge-seeking. Overall, both teachers effectively addressed content delivery in Vietnamese universities through their diverse learning resources.

Assessment - Formative assessment

Regarding formative assessment, formative assessment, teachers adopt various methods tailored to their practices. Teacher 1 shared, "I often use Google Drive for students to submit their homework, such as writing paragraphs, reading assignments, and listening exercises. I then provide feedback during class." This method leans towards traditional practices, emphasizing individual assignments. Conversely, Teacher 2 noted, "I use platforms like Quizizz and Miro for formative assessments, including multiple-choice questions, poster designs, mind maps, and group discussions". This diverse approach accommodates different learning styles and promotes teamwork and active engagement.

When discussing formative assessment in higher education, Teacher 1 emphasized that, "In blended learning, my principles of formative assessment should facilitate learning through reflection." Teacher 2 added, "In my class, formative assessment consolidates learning after class and assesses understanding." While Teacher 1 focuses on the learning process, Teacher 2 highlights measuring student progress. Both perspectives align with Baleni (2015), who noted that formative assessment enhances course quality by evaluating student progress. Teacher 1 also stressed the importance of timely feedback, which is crucial for student improvement (Clark, 2012). Overall, the implementation of formative assessment in Vietnamese higher education reflects positive practices among university teachers.

Final assessment

The experiences of two teachers reveal distinct assessment approaches. Teacher 1 stated: "I assess the students' outcomes through a real language test with four skills once the course finishes," indicating a formal and objective method aligned with language proficiency standards. In contrast, Teacher 2 mentioned, "I often use essays and personal portfolios on the LMS to assess students at the end of each course," showcasing a more flexible and subjective approach that encourages creativity. While both methods aim to ensure students meet learning objectives, they primarily test memory rather than practical abilities, as noted by Hift (2014).

Students' attitudes towards the implementation of learning design in BL in Vietnamese higher education

Flexibility

First, data regarding learner control revealed a lack of flexibility in the distribution of learning modes. Both students noted that offline classes made up 70 percent of the course duration, with no input on the balance between online and offline learning. This distribution was solely determined by teachers, missing an opportunity to involve students in decision-making. As Faranize (2021) highlighted, successful blended learning (BL) requires incorporating student choices to meet individual needs, aligning with Boelens et al. (2017), who emphasized the importance of collaboration between instructors and learners. Second, in terms of preferences, the students expressed differing viewpoints. Student 1 preferred online learning, stating, "I don't enjoy lectures at 7 am; nighttime is better for recorded lectures." In contrast, Student 2 favored traditional offline classes for interaction with peers and instructors. Despite these differences, both students maintained positive attitudes toward their BL courses, noting that offline attendance accounted for only 10 percent of their grade, allowing for a balance between academic and extracurricular activities.

Content delivery

In examining Vietnamese students' perspectives on the implementation of learning design in blended learning (BL), two key criteria emerged: the quality of learning materials and their relevance to learning activities. Student A shared their experience in the "Management of Facilities in Schools" module, where the teacher required engagement in various activities, such as reading articles and watching videos on the LMS about relevant regulations, alongside in-person lectures. However, this content delivery was often perceived as boring and passive. As Baytiyeh (2017) noted, such approaches can be less effective than interactive activities that promote active participation. The absence of teamwork and collaborative tasks diminished the overall effectiveness of the learning experience, indicating that this method is not considered best practice in Vietnamese higher education.

In contrast, Student B's experience in the "Design Thinking" course involved engaging with theoretical content through animated videos, interactive questions, and infographics. Student B remarked, "I also need to plan a demo startup in groups using only pen and paper in class." This multimodal approach catered to diverse learning styles, making the content more engaging and accessible. The integration of theoretical knowledge with practical application highlights the importance of applying concepts in real-life situations, aligning with successful BL principles outlined by Mildenberger and Steingruber (2023).

Assessment - Formative assessment

Regarding formative assessment in the blended learning (BL) environment, interviewed students shared their experiences. Student A noted, "In a traditional classroom, instructors often assign group presentations, while in online learning, teachers assess us through group assignments and final essays." Student B added, "In online courses, I answer short questions in interactive video lectures, and in class, the teacher conducts quizzes using Google Forms or Quizizz."

Both students emphasized the diverse assessment methods employed. These interactive tools enable Vietnamese university teachers to track participation and provide effective assessments, aligning with Boelens et al. (2017). Student A remarked, "I find answering short questions on Quizizz fun," while Student B felt these methods helped them concentrate better and gauge their understanding. Their positive attitudes reflect how technology-enhanced formative assessment promotes active learning, consistent with Nguyen (2017). Overall, the BL environment at the Vietnamese university effectively addresses formative assessment from learners' perspectives.

Final assessment

Students appreciate the variety of summative assessment formats in their courses. Student A noted, "Most courses require assignments to be submitted online via the LMS. For theoretical courses, I write essays, while for practical ones, I create videos, images, or personal webpages." Student B added, "In practical subjects, I complete projects for grading. For instance, in 'Entrepreneurship,' I work on a group startup project, present it to the teacher, and submit it on the LMS, where the teacher role-plays as investors to provide feedback".

Both students highlight the digital approach to education, showcasing diverse assessment methods that include constructive feedback. This reflects a broader trend in education, fostering creativity and collaboration while enhancing the overall learning experience. Their positive attitudes indicate that technology-enhanced formative assessment promotes active learning, effectively addressing formative assessment in the blended learning environment at Vietnamese universities.

Conclusion

First, regarding flexibility, it can be observed that most experiences have not yet achieved successful BL because of the integration of online and F2F learning in blended courses. This is due to decisions being made by teachers or instructors in the department without student involvement. Second, in terms of content delivery, it has been noted that most feedback from interviewees positively highlights the use of diverse learning resources in blended courses. However, a good example of content delivery must be well-linked to corresponding teaching activities, and only one case of feedback indicated that they have not done this well.

Third, regarding assessment, the findings are divided into two types: formative assessment and summative assessment. On the one hand, concerning formative assessment, it is noted that all interviewees have experienced interactive quizzes on technology applications. The use of technology not only automates the assessment process for teachers but also helps students maintain their interest. However, the author suggests that instructors should provide appropriate feedback to students to help them encourage self-reflection and facilitate instructional adjustments. On the other hand, regarding summative assessment, there are many forms of assessment used depending on the fields. However, these forms seem to only evaluate outcomes based on testing memory ability and do not focus on applying knowledge in practice.

Generally, this research has answered two research questions. Specifically, among the three factors including flexibility, content delivery, and assessment, only the aspect of flexibility has not yet met the typical example of good practice in BL. The other factors have been implemented quite well and are close to achieving successful BL.

9

Digital Transformation of Blended Learning in Vietnam's Higher Education 5.0[19]

Duc Hong Thi Phan[20] and Bruno Mascitelli

Abstract

This chapter examines the ambitious digital transformation of Vietnam's higher education system, framed within the global context of the 4.0 Industrial Revolution and the vision of Society 5.0. It analyzes the nationwide institutionalization of blended learning as the primary pedagogical vehicle for this change, a process significantly accelerated by the COVID-19 pandemic. The central argument posits that while Vietnam has established a robust policy foundation for this transformation, its ultimate success and equity are contingent upon strategically addressing the profound and persistent challenges of infrastructure inequality, human capacity development, and institutional adaptation. By analyzing the critical gap between the high-tech vision of Education 5.0 and the on-the-ground realities of the digital divide, this chapter outlines the strategic imperatives required to build a more inclusive, resilient, and effective higher education system capable of preparing all students for a complex future.

---

19 All references, tables, figures, author affiliation and biography used in this chapter are available on the Online Appendix link at https://tinyurl.com/he50Appendices.
20 Corresponding author: hongducktkt@gmail.com

Introduction: The Imperative for Transformation in a New Era

The global landscape is being reshaped by the Fourth Industrial Revolution, a convergence of digital, physical, and biological technologies that is fundamentally altering how societies function. A core component of this new era is the vision of Society 5.0, a "Super Smart Society" where technologies such as Artificial Intelligence (AI), the Internet of Things (IoT), and big data are seamlessly integrated to address societal challenges and enhance human life (Tran & Nguyen, 2024). In this context, education is not merely a sector to be updated with new tools but a critical engine for cultivating the human capital required to navigate and lead this transformation. Globally, AI in education is poised to automate administrative tasks, deliver personalized learning at scale, and empower educators to focus on higher-value activities like student mentoring (HolonIQ, 2023).

Responding to these powerful global currents, Vietnam has embarked on an ambitious national reform agenda. This endeavor is not simply about technological adoption but constitutes a comprehensive "digital transformation" - a holistic integration of digital tools, pedagogies, and administrative processes designed to create fundamentally new and more effective learning experiences (Nguyen et al., 2024). The primary modality through which this transformation is being realized in higher education is blended learning, a pedagogical approach that combines traditional face-to-face instruction with online learning components. Its widespread adoption, catalyzed by the global COVID-19 pandemic, has shifted it from a niche option to the "new normal" across the nation's universities (Nguyen & Tran, 2025).

This chapter argues that while Vietnam has laid an ambitious policy foundation for digital transformation in higher education, its success hinges on strategically addressing the profound and persistent challenges of infrastructure inequality, human capacity, and institutional adaptation. A significant gap exists between the high-tech, AI-driven vision of Education 5.0 promoted in official discourse and the on-the-ground reality of fundamental infrastructure deficits and varying levels of digital literacy. This tension between vision and reality risks creating policies that, if not implemented with a focus on equity, could exacerbate existing disparities rather than mitigate them. This chapter will, therefore, analyze the policy landscape driving this change, examine the post-pandemic paradigm shift toward blended learning, critically assess the core implementation challenges, and propose strategic pathways toward building a more inclusive and resilient higher education system for the future.

The Policy Landscape: Vietnam's National Digital Transformation Agenda

The digital transformation of Vietnam's higher education is not an organic, bottom-up evolution but a deliberate, top-down national strategy. It is a cornerstone of the government's broader vision to modernize the country and sustain its remarkable economic growth trajectory in the era of the Fourth Industrial Revolution (Le, 2020). The central pillar of this strategy is the "National Digital Transformation Programme to 2025, with an orientation to 2030" (Decision No. 749/QD-TTg), a comprehensive roadmap that aims to leverage technology to foster innovative teaching and learning environments across all educational levels (Nguyen et al., 2024). This program signals a strong political will to integrate digital technologies into the very fabric of the nation's educational and socio-economic development.

Vietnam's efforts are situated within a broader regional movement across Southeast Asia, where nations are increasingly looking to educational technology (EdTech) to address learning crises and meet development aspirations. Regional reports by UNESCO and the Southeast Asian Ministers of Education Organization (SEAMEO) highlight a shared landscape of rapid technological growth, alongside common challenges related to access, equity, and governance (UNESCO & SEAMEO, 2023). This regional context underscores that Vietnam's journey, while unique in its specifics, is part of a collective endeavor to harness technology for educational advancement.

However, the centralized, government-led nature of this policy push presents a double-edged sword. On one hand, it provides a clear mandate, mobilizes resources, and creates a powerful impetus for change that might otherwise be slow to materialize. It ensures a degree of national coherence and direction. On the other hand, this top-down approach risks promoting a one-size-fits-all model that fails to account for the vast diversity among Vietnam's higher education institutions (HEIs). The realities and capacities of a well-resourced, research-intensive university in Hanoi or Ho Chi Minh

City are vastly different from those of a provincial college in a remote, mountainous region (Nguyen et al., 2024). A centralized directive, unless designed with inherent flexibility and context-sensitivity, may be executed poorly at the local level, potentially leading to ineffective implementation or even resistance. Therefore, the success of Vietnam's national agenda will depend critically on its ability to balance central direction with institutional autonomy and local adaptation, a principle that is also central to the effective implementation of flexible learning models (Commission on Higher Education, CHED, 2020).

The Rise of Blended Learning: A Post-Pandemic Paradigm Shift

The COVID-19 pandemic served as an unprecedented catalyst, forcing a rapid and universal pivot away from traditional classroom instruction. This period of "emergency remote teaching" (Nobis et al., 2024) has since evolved into a more permanent and deliberate adoption of "flexible learning" as the new norm in Vietnamese higher education (Romero, 2021). As defined by policymakers, flexible learning is a learner-centered approach that encompasses a combination of delivery strategies - including online platforms, digital modules, and printed materials - to meet the diverse needs of students in terms of place, pace, and process (CHED, 2020). Within this broad framework, blended learning has emerged as the most prevalent and sustainable model.

This paradigm shift has brought tangible benefits. Students have reported appreciating the increased autonomy and flexibility that blended models afford, allowing them to better manage their time and learning pace. For institutions, it has opened up new possibilities for reaching a wider range of students and innovating in course delivery (Nguyen & Tran, 2025). However, the rapid, forced nature of this transition has also exposed significant pedagogical challenges. While many institutions have successfully adopted the *technology* of blended learning, the *pedagogy* often lags behind. A common pitfall is the replication of traditional, teacher-centered lecture methods in an online format, rather than a fundamental redesign of courses to leverage the unique affordances of a blended environment.

To analyze the effectiveness of these new learning environments, the Community of Inquiry (CoI) framework offers a valuable theoretical lens. The CoI model posits that a meaningful educational experience in an online or blended setting is built upon three interdependent elements: **teaching presence** (the design, facilitation, and direction of the learning process), **cognitive presence** (the extent to which learners are able to construct and confirm meaning through sustained reflection and discourse), and **social presence** (the ability of participants to project their personal characteristics into the community, thereby presenting themselves as 'real people') (Nguyen & Tran, 2025).

The challenge of the pedagogical lag is starkly illustrated by findings from a study on blended learning in Vietnam, which revealed that while teaching and cognitive presence positively impacted students' perceptions, social presence did not have a significant influence (Nguyen & Tran, 2025). This suggests that in the rush to move content online, the crucial human and community-building aspects of learning - the interactions and relationships that foster a sense of belonging and collaborative inquiry - are often being neglected. This indicates that the key challenge is no longer merely technological access, but pedagogical innovation. True transformation requires a fundamental shift in mindset for educators, moving from a role of content delivery to one of learning facilitation, where technology is used to intentionally design engaging and interactive experiences that foster all three presences.

Bridging the Gap: Confronting the Core Challenges of Implementation

Despite the clear policy direction and the widespread adoption of blended learning, the path to a fully realized digital transformation is fraught with significant and systemic obstacles. The success of Vietnam's Education 5.0 vision depends on confronting these barriers head-on. They can be categorized into three interconnected areas: the digital divide, the human capacity gap, and institutional inertia.

The Infrastructure and Equity Divide

The most fundamental barrier is the digital divide, a stark manifestation of deeper socio-economic inequalities. There is a significant disparity in internet access and quality of digital infrastructure between urban and rural areas. A 2023 report on technology in Southeast Asian education noted that while 85% of urban schools in the region have high-speed internet, only 56% of rural schools do; this gap is reflective of the situation in Vietnam, where urban educators and students benefit from far better access to digital tools and resources (Nguyen et al., 2024). While nine out of ten schools nationally may be connected to the internet, the quality and reliability of that connection vary dramatically, particularly in remote and mountainous regions (United Nations DCO, 2023).

This divide disproportionately impacts the most marginalized student populations. Students from ethnic minority communities and those with disabilities face compounded barriers to participation. For instance, a staggering 67% of school children in remote areas of Vietnam lack access to online education opportunities (UNICEF Viet Nam, n.d.). Furthermore, data shows that only 33% of people with disabilities in the country have internet access, compared to 83% of those without disabilities, effectively shutting them out of a learning environment that increasingly requires digital engagement (UNICEF Viet Nam, 2022). The lack of accessible digital content and assistive technologies further exacerbates this exclusion (UNICEF Viet Nam, 2022). Compounding these infrastructure issues are the financial constraints faced by many students, who struggle to afford the necessary devices and reliable internet plans required for blended learning (Nobis et al., 2024). This reality means that technology, intended as a great equalizer, risks becoming an amplifier of existing disparities, widening the learning gap into a participation chasm.

The Human Factor: Educator and Student Readiness

Beyond infrastructure, a critical challenge lies in human capacity. The effectiveness of any EdTech initiative is ultimately determined by the people who use it. In Vietnam, as in much of Southeast Asia, there is a significant shortage of digitally literate educators equipped with the pedagogical skills to teach effectively in a blended environment. Nearly 40% of teachers in the region report receiving insufficient training in the use of digital technologies for instruction (SEAMEO, 2023). Professional development, when available, often focuses on basic technical skills (e.g., how to use a learning management system) rather than on the more complex art of designing and facilitating engaging online learning experiences (Nguyen et al., 2024). This skills gap is compounded by a global shortage of talent with advanced AI and EdTech expertise, making it difficult for institutions to recruit the personnel needed to drive innovation (HolonIQ, 2023).

Students also face significant challenges. The shift to more independent, technology-mediated learning has been accompanied by reports of increased stress, anxiety, and difficulties with self-directed learning and time management (Nobis et al., 2024). Many students express a strong desire for more face-to-face interaction, highlighting the risk of social isolation in poorly designed blended courses (Nobis et al., 2024). Successfully navigating this new learning landscape requires not only digital literacy but also strong self-regulation and metacognitive skills, which many students have not yet developed. Without adequate support systems, the promise of flexible learning can become a source of frustration and disengagement.

Institutional Barriers: Overcoming Resistance to Innovation

At the institutional level, Higher Education Institutions (HEIs) face numerous barriers that hinder the transition from emergency technology adoption to strategic transformation.

A primary obstacle is financial. The initial and ongoing costs of technology - including hardware, software licensing, robust technical support, and cybersecurity are substantial (Keshavarz & Ghoneim, 2021). Many institutions report being under-resourced for major technology initiatives, a problem that has become more acute in recent years (HolonIQ, 2023).

Beyond funding, another significant challenge is the *deep-seated resistance to change* within the system. This is evident in how slowly curricula and administrative processes adapt. A truly effective blended learning ecosystem requires a holistic approach that aligns infrastructure, curriculum design, faculty support, assessment methods, and student services (Nguyen et al., 2024).

Implementing such a systemic change is complex, requiring strong leadership and a culture of innovation. However, in a period of financial uncertainty, many institutions are focused on stabilization and consolidation rather than accepting the risks associated with major innovations in technology or pedagogy (HolonIQ, 2023). This cautious attitude can stifle the very experimentation and adaptation needed to realize the full potential of digital transformation. To provide a clearer overview, Table 9.1 (see Chapter 9 in the Online Appendix link https://tinyurl.com/he50Appendices) synthesizes these multi-level challenges.

Charting the Course for Education 5.0: Strategic Pathways Forward

Addressing the complex challenges hindering Vietnam's digital transformation requires a coordinated, multi-stakeholder framework for action. Progress cannot be achieved through top-down mandates alone; it necessitates concerted efforts from policymakers, university leaders, and educators, all guided by the core principles of equity, sustainability, and pedagogical innovation. The ultimate goal must shift from a technocentric focus on platforms to a human-centric focus on people.

For Policymakers: Building an Equitable Digital Foundation

The government's role is to create the enabling conditions for an equitable digital ecosystem. This involves moving beyond broad policy statements to targeted interventions:

- *Prioritize Infrastructure Investment:* National resources must be strategically directed toward closing the urban-rural digital divide. This includes investing in high-speed internet connectivity for schools and communities in remote and underserved regions (Nguyen et al., 2024).

- *Establish Equity-Focused Support Schemes:* To counter the financial barriers faced by students, the government should develop and implement financial support programs, such as subsidies or grants, for the purchase of devices and data plans for students from low-income households (Chuc & Anh, 2022).

- *Develop National Competency Standards:* Clear, national standards for digital competency should be established for both educators and students. These standards would provide a benchmark for curriculum development and teacher training programs, ensuring a baseline of essential skills for participation in the digital age (UNICEF Viet Nam, n.d.).

-

For University Administrators: Cultivating a Culture of Innovation

University leaders are the primary agents of change at the institutional level. Their task is to translate national policy into effective practice by fostering a culture that embraces innovation and supports its people:

- *Invest in Sustained Professional Development:* Institutions must move beyond one-off technical workshops and implement long-term, continuous professional development programs for faculty. These programs should focus on digital pedagogy - course design, online facilitation, and new assessment methods - not just technical skills (Nguyen et al., 2024).

- *Foster Industry-Education Synergy:* To ensure graduates are prepared for Society 5.0, universities should actively build partnerships with industry. These collaborations can inform curriculum design, create opportunities for work-integrated learning, and ensure that educational programs are aligned with the evolving demands of the labor market (Tran & Nguyen, 2024).

- *Embrace Data-Driven Decision-Making:* HEIs should leverage data analytics to monitor student performance, identify learning gaps, and assess the effectiveness of different teaching strategies. This data-driven approach fosters a culture of continuous improvement and allows for more tailored and effective student support (Nguyen et al., 2024).

For Educators: Reimagining Teaching and Learning

Ultimately, the quality of learning rests in the hands of educators. They are on the front lines of digital transformation and must be empowered to become architects of meaningful learning experiences:

- *Adopt Student-Centered Pedagogies:* Educators should embrace pedagogical models that use technology to promote active learning, collaboration, and critical thinking. This means shifting from being a "sage on the stage" to a "guide on the side," facilitating learning rather than simply delivering content (Nguyen et al., 2024).

- *Design for Inquiry and Presence:* By consciously applying the principles of the Community of Inquiry framework, educators can design blended courses that intentionally foster cognitive, social, and teaching presence. This involves creating opportunities for meaningful student-student and student-instructor interaction, promoting collaborative inquiry, and building a supportive online learning community (Nguyen & Tran, 2025).

The common thread across these recommendations is the primacy of the human element. Technology is a powerful tool, but it is only a tool. The success of Vietnam's digital transformation will be determined not by the sophistication of its platforms, but by its investment in people - empowering teachers to become skilled facilitators of 21st-century learning and supporting students to become resilient, self-directed, and lifelong learners.

Conclusion

Vietnam stands at a critical juncture in the modernization of its higher education system. The ambitious vision of Society 5.0 provides a compelling direction, the national digital transformation program offers a strategic framework, and the post-pandemic normalization of blended learning has created an unprecedented momentum for change. The potential to create a more flexible, personalized, and effective learning ecosystem is immense. However, as this chapter has argued, this potential is shadowed by the profound challenges of a persistent digital divide, gaps in human capacity, and the slow pace of institutional adaptation.

The journey from the aspirational rhetoric of Education 5.0 to its equitable implementation on the ground requires a clear-eyed acknowledgment of these realities. The evidence strongly suggests that without a deliberate and unwavering commitment to equity, digital transformation risks amplifying existing disparities, leaving the most vulnerable students even further behind. An "equity-first" approach is, therefore, not merely a moral imperative but a pragmatic necessity for achieving the nation's human capital and socio-economic development goals.

Ultimately, the goal is not simply to build a "digital" university, but a better university - one that is more resilient in the face of future disruptions, more accessible to all learners regardless of their background or location, and more effective in preparing students with the critical skills needed to thrive in an increasingly complex and uncertain world. Digital transformation should not be viewed as a final destination but as an ongoing process of thoughtful adaptation and continuous improvement. By placing the human elements of teaching and learning at the center of this process, and by ensuring that technology is deployed "on our terms" (UNESCO & SEAMEO, 2023), Vietnam can harness its power to build a truly inclusive and dynamic future for its higher education.

10

Gamification in Higher Education: Boosting Student Learning at the Vietnam National University[21]

Trịnh Thị Phan Lan[22] and Lê Thanh Huyền

Abstract

The main purpose of this chapter is to evaluate the use of gamification to facilitate a student-centered learning environment at the university level. The chapter is using the findings of surveys (380 from students and 20 from lecturers) as well as the observation in the class to evaluate the engagement of students by applying gamification in class. The high level of active participation of students in class were observed, such as: pay attention, raising hand, making decision, sharing oppinion. Lecturers also recognized that there was a high level of homework completion and the reduction in school absences.

Introduction

The demands of students in the 21st century (those known as "generation Z") and the overall evolution of the world present new challenges in the learning and teaching process. Engaging students to learn is becoming a priority for many lecturers (Gibbs 2014), which has led to the creation of

---

21 All references, tables, figures, author affiliation and biography used in this chapter are available on the Online Appendix link at https://tinyurl.com/he50Appendices.

22 Corresponding author: trinhphanlan@gmail.com

numerous strategies, including student-centered approach (Baeten et al. 2010), flipped classes (McLaughlin et al. 2014), and technology-mediated learning (Hepplestone et al. 2011). In an effort to improve the effectiveness of teaching and learning in higher education, a question arises: how to provide an autonomous and flexible learning environment that can encourage students to pursue specific goals (Landers & Callan 2011) and engage in deeper levels of activities more persistently (Anderson et al. 2014).

In this context, gamification has increasingly attracted attention among researchers. A number of studies have investigated its effectiveness in different disciplines such as Engineering (Chaves et al. 2015), Physics (Adams 2016), Medicine (Dankbaar 2016), Nursing (Sarabia-Cobo 2016), Management (Geithner & Menzel 2016), Political Science (Jones & Bursens 2015), Education (Ke 2015), Language (Franciosi 2016), and Social Science (Cózar-Gutiérrez & Sáez-López 2016).

In the context of Vietnam, the general situation of most universities is that class days start early and end late. Students are required to study a huge amount of knowledge in class. Furthermore, students in generation Z lack concentration and learn best by doing and creating, with greater emphasis on creativity (Schwieger et al. 2018). In Vietnam, VNU Hanoi is one of the leading universities in teaching innovation. From 2018–2019, VNU coordinated with the Creative Academy, University College Dublin (UCD) the implementation of the VIBE project phase 1 on "Capacity building for teaching staff and managers at VNU using innovation and entrepreneurship thinking (performance-oriented thinking) to promote and strengthen 21st century skills and nurture the spirit of entrepreneurship and innovation in students." From 2020 to June 2022, VNU continued to coordinate with Dublin University to implement phase 2 on "Leading and bringing a culture of innovation into Higher Education: Preparing for the second industrial revolution." Phase 3 was also completed in August 2023. Last but not least, there are 9 universities under VNU Hanoi. Therefore, it was chosen as a case study in the research.

This study aims to examine the application of gamification in teaching and the engagement of students in class. The chapter is structured into five parts. After the introduction in part 1, the theoretical foundations of gamification are presented in part 2, followed by the research methodology in part 3. Part 4 describes the context of gamification application in VNU and the observation of one case conceived to apply gamification concepts at the university level. We then present the results of using gamification in teaching and learning through surveys of lecturers and interviews with students in part 4 and provide conclusions in Results and Discussion.

The concept of gamification

The term gamification is still very new to us. In the year 2008, it was first introduced by Brett Terill on his personal blog when he was writing about video games on the Cameron network. Brett (2008) uses the term gamification to define the actions of users using game mechanics and applying them to other web properties to increase player engagement. In current usage, the concept of gamification is not limited to web properties, but more generally refers to the use of game design elements in the context of non-games or the use of the game's aesthetics of thinking to engage people, or the use of educative games to spur action and solve problems. Healey (2019) argues that lecturers have long used games in teaching, so the definition of games in teaching can be considered in comparison with conventional video entertainment. Essentially, playing while learning can be fun and very engaging, but without voluntary participation, it is work. Compulsory participation in a game to learn is only counted as "play", not "game". Therefore, gamification is predicted to become a prominent trend in educational innovation in the near future.

Gamification is like a way of getting closer to education based on applying one or many elements that have "game characteristics", "game inspiration", or "game principles". Gamification is not a type of game but the concept of applying gaming aspects and mechanics into non-game contexts.

Studies on gamified learning often focus on researching the impact or merit of gamification, and currently, it may not yet provide the most comprehensive view of the bigger picture. The studies about gamified learning are intriguing and diverse in scope: from general studies to specific research; from simple testing to academic experimentation; multidimensional perspectives, varying from positive to neutral and negative viewpoints. Among them, many academic studies show the significant potential of gamification: Carpenter & Delosh (2006) argue that gamification enhances connections and forms pathways, thinking lines that make knowledge last longer. Cabeza (2013) examined brain activity using experimental effects and found that gamification enhances internal memory and combines the activity of different brain parts to increase creativity in learning. An FMRI (functional magnetic resonance imaging) analysis showed that gamification activates brain areas such as the anterior hippocampus and temporal cortex, activating certain nerve pathways.

The impact of gamification on student's learning

Bedwell (2015) reports that although categorizing game attributes shows a connection between specific game attributes and training outcomes, these training outcomes are based on pedagogical philosophy. In line with this, Lander's theory of gamification provides a framework for understanding the mechanisms of how gamification affects learning. According to the author, gaming does not directly affect learning but instead affects learners' behavior and attitudes, which in turn influence learning.

Similarly, De Smale (2015) systematically reviews 64 articles related to gamification and concludes that there is a positive or neutral relationship between the use of gamification and academic achievement. Building on this, Ritzhaupt (2014) provides a meta-analysis based on 73 articles, demonstrating the effectiveness of gamification in changing behavior, attitude, and emotion.

Sitzmann (2011) considers educationally oriented games that should be partially or fully integrated into the learning process as a complementary or essential part of the course. Implementing gamification requires high-quality mechanisms, student and faculty engagement, and consensus. Nevertheless, the integration of games depends on the instructor's contribution and how they design and incorporate games into their teaching activities. Therefore, instructors need to be equipped with knowledge and experience to guide learners through the process of how to play properly.

Clark et al. (2015) show that gamification promotes knowledge acquisition as well as the understanding of content and concepts. Moreover, students achieve better academic goals through joyful learning (Tsekleves et al., 2014). Ritzhaupt (2014) also notes that gamification influences students' motivation, participation, and satisfaction based on learning games. In terms of behavioral outcomes, gamification provides numerous opportunities for collaborative learning, enhanced interaction, feedback among players, and skills development including both soft and social skills. However, Young et al. (2012) document that games and simulations may have some or no positive effect on knowledge and skill acquisition when compared with traditional teaching methods.

Additionally, gamification has the ability to influence student motivation by creating enjoyable experiences, building links (community, sharing, understanding, increasing positive emotions), and creating competition (rewards, points, badges). In fact, gamification has the ability to motivate learners even if it does not help them improve their grades. As stated by Dicheva (2015), empirical research shows that gamification positively impacts learners' learning, including higher student engagement in activities, increased attendance, more contributions without reducing quality, higher pass rates, and closing the gap between low and high achievers. Generally speaking, students respond better in courses that include simulation tests that make learning more motivating, enjoyable, and easier.

Gamification can also encourage learners to maintain initiative rather than merely comply with "attendance" requirements. It thus provides a solution to a key educational challenge: students often start semesters engaged but participation declines significantly towards the end if not reinforced by grading or constraints. However, poorly designed gamification can negatively affect learning. For example, multiple rewards may encourage engagement beyond intended goals (JISC, 2017); blind application of gamification in schools can backfire (Lee & Hammer, 2011); and binge-playing may undermine long-term learning (Lee & Hammer, 2011).

Qualitative Research Methods

The study team conducted the in-depth interviews with 20 lecturers. Because of the available resources and time, we focus on 3 universities under VNU Hanoi (University of Technology, University of Economics and Business, University of Education, and Institute of Vietnamese Studies). They were chosen randomly based on their voluntariness and willingness to participate in the research. A meeting with the voluntary participants was arranged to seek their informed consent as participants in the study. See Table 10.1: Summary of Data from interview in the Online Appendix link https://tinyurl.com/he50Appendices.

Quantitative Research Methods:

Surveys were conducted with students who was in the game application classes. There were 380 respondents from the University of Economics and Business (150), University of Technology (129), and University of Education (101), which are all students of VNU Hanoi. These students' majors are as follows: Accounting includes Banking and Finance, Accounting, and Business Administration, Robot Engineering, Global Economy, and Educational Technology.The questionnaire focused on interest level, the level of engagement of students gained when using gamification in class time. See Table 10.2: Summary of Data from survey available in the Online Appendix link https://tinyurl.com/he50Appendices.

Observations:

To observe the application of gamification in class, the subject of Personal Finance (3 credits) was chosen. This is an elective subject in the courses offered to undergraduate students at University of Business and Economics, VNU Hanoi. Observations were made directly through the student's expressions, behaviours, and attitudes when participating in the classroom. These observations are made in both the traditional classroom and the online classroom. Four game elements considered prominent in higher education being used by lecturers at VNU to engage and motivate students are: narrative, challenge, progression and feedback. See Table 10.3: Game elements used in Personal finance Practice in the Online Appendix link https://tinyurl.com/he50Appendices.

The application of gamification on learning process at VNU Hanoi

VNU Hanoi has seen significant transformation since 2019 as it moves closer to realizing its vision of becoming a leading centre for teaching and learning. Numerous training sessions are held frequently to help lecturers improve themselves and enhance their creative capabilities. The course "Building capacity of academic staff members and senior leaders at Vietnam National University, Hanoi by entrepreneurship to foster 21st century skills and attributes in students" (VIBE) is organized by Innovation Academy, University College Dublin (UCD)-Ireland in collaboration with VNU, strongly promoting the innovation and entrepreneurial spirit of the faculty. The establishment of the Center for Teaching Excellence (CTE) also marked an important development in VNU Hanoi's innovation direction. Subjects like startups, innovation, and design thinking have quickly been included in the formal training programs of many member universities in VNU Hanoi. From 2021 innovation has become a strategic direction of VNU Hanoi.

The influence of COVID-19 is another element that demands rapid orientation and adjustment of VNU Hanoi lecturers' teaching strategies. In addition, continuous online learning for a long time requires lecturers to find solutions to create interest and improve learners' cognitive and receptive abilities. Gamification application in teaching is therefore an inevitable and promising movement as a result of innovation in university teaching strategies, student-centered self-study and the advancement of science and technology.

To address the question, "Innovation or death?", innovation in teaching is a new approach at a number of universities under the VNU Hanoi. The chosen solution is to create a gamified intervention in the form of a student-centered learning environment (Hannafin and Land, 1997). Gamification, as noted above, is the practice of incorporating elements of games into non-gaming contexts (Deterding et al., 2011). It means that gamification is not only for traditional or online classes. To apply gamification elements in teaching, VNU Hanoi lecturers have a number of educational platforms to inspire students. We use a long list of online learning platforms such as Duolingo, Khan Academy, Treehouse, Coursera, Newsmart, classroom management platform ClassDojo, Schoology, Google classroom, or role-playing games. This change can be observed in all university members of VNU Hanoi and for different subjects in different fields.

The applications of gamification in teaching

Below is the case study of the Personal Finance Subject at VNU -University of Business and Economics. The subject is prepared using the traditional method with 15 lectures. From the year 2020, a number of online lectures have been conducted, depending on the actual situation and within the outline of the subject. Although the prepared documents are available with this course, it is acknowledged that there is a low level of student engagement in the class.

From 2019, the application of gamification in teaching personal finance is evaluated based on four factors, namely: **narrative, challenge, progress, and feedback** with or without digital support. See Figure 10.1 in the Online Appendix link https://tinyurl.com/he50Appendices.

Narrative

Narrative is the use of stories that engage students in class, such as case studies or real-life situations. The "narrative" elements in this module are stories shared by the lecturers or students in the class. The lecturers' stories related to finance lessons and will enable students to understand the lessons quickly, and they can apply these lessons to their real life. The stories will be engaging because the subject's material is related to how each person and family manages their finances. The stories are more appealing because of the lecturer's confidence in the storytelling. These stories help them visualize the future problems they might face in managing their money and be well prepared for the future.

Another notable aspect of the "narrative" is a student's story about how to handle their finances. These narratives will cover both positive and negative situations that the students have had, particularly those that have to do with borrowing, spending, or saving. The instructors have seen that students are more engaged in the class when they have had difficult experiences as they have found their own identity somewhere.

In Figure 10.1 (available in the Online Appendix link https://tinyurl.com/he50Appendices), the "narrative" element is performed alternately in order to guide and link lessons together or connect with reality. The report is fully exploited in the lecture by giving possible financial scenarios as these situations are always associated with a specific context. Students discussed the situations that arise in a case study (for example: the case study in Table 10.4 (available in the Online Appendix link https://tinyurl.com/he50Appendices). It is so interesting that students were willing to share their family's financial situation, such as what difficulties their family faced and how to overcome those difficulties. (See Table 10.4 in the Online Appendix link https://tinyurl.com/he50Appendices).

Challenges

There are numerous tasks created specifically for students. The students are quite eager to take on these challenges because they are linked to their pocket money. In the area of personal finance, challenges are often designed around activities that are closely connected to students' daily lives, such as reading books, recording expenses, financial planning, and game-based learning. For example, reading books on money management helps students develop the habit of taking notes and acquiring fundamental financial knowledge. In addition, the challenge of recording expenses whether in a notebook or through applications such as Money Lover or Misa, encourages students to track their spending and categorize bills. Setting short- and long-term financial goals further supports students in practicing personal financial planning. Finally, simulation games such as "Prosperous Family," "Financial Race," or "Savings" provide opportunities for learners to experience real-life scenarios, prepare balance sheets, and achieve well-balanced financial reports. (See Table 10.5 in the Online Appendix link https://tinyurl.com/he50Appendices).

Progression

Taking on the challenge makes students feel a sense of conquest. Their management of their finances is reported to have increased. Students are more conscientious and thoughtful in their spending decisions. The percentage of students who know how to control their finances has increased, especially if they have a very clear sense of having to manage money. Before making a decision, students can distinguish between the amounts for various funds, create a budget, and understand their needs and desires. (See Table 10.6 in the Online Appendix link https://tinyurl.com/he50Appendices).

The results and discussion - The knowledge of lecturers about gamification

We obtained 20 responses of lecturers from the University of Technology, University of Economics and Business, University of Education, and Institute of Vietnamese Studies within VNU Hanoi, with 89.5% of the participants being female. The majority of lecturers have to undertake 6-7 subjects (accounting for 48.7%). However, they will normally teach 2-3 subjects in one semester. According to the survey results, most lecturers are aware of gamification. Only 10% of lecturers have never heard of or applied gamification in teaching. (See Figure 10.2 in the Online Appendix link https://tinyurl.com/he50Appendices).

The practice of applying game elements in class

One or more game components were employed in teaching by up to 94.7% of the lecturers who took part in the survey. The most popular game elements were bonus points, awards, try challenges, and competition. The proportions of real stories and responses were the same. Only 10% of lecturers did not use gamification in teaching.

The results show that 70% of teachers interviewed are willing to apply gamification to their lessons at a rate of 10-30%. About 15% of teachers apply gamification at a rate of 30-40%. Only 5% of lecturers apply 40-70% to their lectures. 5% of lecturers do not apply gamification in their classes. Subjects that use a lot of gamifications are said to be skill subjects such as creative thinking, designing your life, and teamwork. (See Figure 10.3 in the Online Appendix link https://tinyurl.com/he50Appendices link).

The implementation of game elements varies between classes, so the results obtained in terms of student experiences with these elements are different. The game elements that students experience the most are the point system (56.8%), Challenging and Competitiveness (37.8%) and the least are Feedback (8.1%) and Badges (10.8%). (See Figure 10.4 in the Online Appendix link https://tinyurl.com/he50Appendices).

Impact of gamification on students' learning experiences

The results of the application of gamification in teaching were significant. From the lecturers' point of view, we can see the students' positive changes in terms of the increase in percentage of students' participation, the faster completion of assignments, the higher test scores, and lower student absences (See Figure 5 in the Online Appendix link https://tinyurl.com/he50Appendices).

From students' point of view, the survey results also showed quite positive results regarding the application of gamification in the classroom. Table 10.6 (available in the Online Appendix link https://tinyurl.com/he50Appendices) shows that students are very attentive, ask questions and often raise their hand to respond to lecturers' questions. (See Table 10.6 in the Online Appendix link https://tinyurl.com/he50Appendices). In Vietnamese context, asking questions and responding by raising hands is a very popular teaching practice. When lecturers apply gamification in the class, students have more chance to make their own decisions and interact with other students.

According to the student survey, the frequency of student's engagement in the class is valuable. The rate of students focusing on the lesson and raising hands was very high (91.3% and 79% respectively). Students are also confident to share their opinions (30.3% in personal concern and 33.7% in academic concern). Furthermore, students who wanted to learn through games were "Review Knowledge" (71.1%) and "Ice Breaking" (36.8%). It was found that "tests" are an activity that students rarely want to do while playing the game (13.2%). (See Figure 10.7 in the Online Appendix link https://tinyurl.com/he50Appendices).

Conclusion

This study has explored gamification in higher education. Findings from the literature review on gamification in education suggest that the use of game elements is more suitable for lecturers than the whole game. Importantly, gamification does not require software applications and supportive technological infrastructure. Rather, this study identifies four game elements that can be used to enhance student engagement and motivation; these are narrative, challenges, progression, and feedback.

These elements can be used as means to encourage students to stay active during learning and promote deep approaches to learning in which students gain both declarative and functional knowledge. Thus, the purposeful use of gamification may enhance the learning process by creating interactive and fun teaching lessons; to motivate and engage students by placing the students at the centre of learning activities; and encourage students to engage with other students more actively in the classroom.

Gamification may not, however, help lecturers to reduce their workload. About 30% of lecturers anticipate facing challenges in terms of classroom management. 24.9% of lecturers fear not having enough time to meet the curriculum's academic standards when applying gamification. During the in-depth interviews, lecturers also shared some concerns in terms of time investment, recognition, class infrastructure and class size. Therefore, it may not be an approach to make teaching more efficient (e.g., fewer teaching hours) but rather to make teaching more effective, as it may contribute to students' learning outcomes as well as their overall experience at university.

11

A report on one year of applying Education 5.0 at a natural school in Hanoi, Vietnam[23]

Phan Thi Phuong Hoa[24]

Abstract

Education 5.0 has been applied at Spring Hill Primary and Secondary School in the 2023-2024 school year. Besides teaching the Vietnamese curriculum, we trained pupils in English following the Vietnamese Ministry of Education curriculum combined with online schools from grade K to grade 9 from the US. The power of technology and personalized learning, together with social-emotional learning, create an educational environment that helps pupils develop critical thinking, problem-solving, and social-emotional learning skills. In this study, 331 pupils and 25 teachers attended. Final tests in semesters 1 and 2 were recorded and analyzed, which factors lead to the successful implementation of Education 5.0 at Spring Hill school. Overall, results showed that in the first school year, using Education 5.0 had many benefits for pupils, and centered pupils achieved successful learning scores. However, some pupils did not improve much due to other variables, one including lack of responsibility from some teachers. While a good plan was put in place, implementing the educational plan depended on each individual teacher, with dedicated teachers being helpful to pupils in contrast to teachers who may neglect

---
23 All references, tables, figures, author affiliation and biography used in this chapter are available on the Online Appendix link at https://tinyurl.com/he50Appendices.
24 Corresponding author: phuonghoa@gmail.com

their duty. However, these variables did not significantly hinder the benefit of Education 5.0. One year of practice is not enough to achieve success, yet given more time and effort, the practice is projected to achieve even more success than it currently has. The results suggest that constantly training teachers ethically, emotionally, and academically is conducive to successfully implementing Education 5.0, and teachers are the key to success for schools applying Education 5.0.

Introduction

Nature schools, also known as Forest Schools, have gained prominence as a significant educational model addressing the global issue of children's growing detachment from nature (Cummings & Nash, 2015). This disconnection is linked to negative impacts on children's sense of place and self, with potential consequences for their spatial, emotional, and social development (Lanza et al., 2023). In response, Forest Schools offer outdoor learning experiences that emphasize play and holistic development, nurturing children's physical health, emotional intelligence, social skills, and environmental connectedness (Maynard, 2007).

Education 4.0 has shortcomings, including limited support for personal learning and distance learning through the Internet (Amad et al., 2023). Spring Hill School adopted Education 5.0 in the school year 2023-2024 to improve pupils' health and well-being. We designed to teach 50% of lessons in the classroom and 50% in nature classes, where pupils enjoy learning under the canopy of green trees (Askerlund, et al, 2016) in the forest of Spring Hill as much as possible. Spring Hill School is more than 45km (about 24.85 mi) from the center of Hanoi. It is a happy and nature school where students and teachers can live, study, and work amidst beautiful nature. The most important philosophy is to educate children to understand and love living with gratitude. Children use their senses to learn to love themselves, others, the land, and nature's beauty. When students understand and are passionate, they live with more gratitude and appreciation for what they have.

Spring Hill School

Spring Hill School's nature classes from the bottom of the hill to the top of the hill are listed below.

Peach is a flower of Spring in Northern Vietnam. The Peach Garden Classroom is situated beneath lush, cool, fruit-laden peach trees. This is a class where teachers prioritize using visual, artistic, and scientific activities to help students observe and actively learn knowledge. Under the canopy of peach trees, students can read books, do self-study, and work in a quiet green space. Occasionally, the cool breeze from the valley of green rice fields blowing up the hill is wonderful. The peach garden classroom is next to a sports space that trains endurance and concentration through basketball. (See Figure 11.1 in the Online Appendix link https://tinyurl.com/he50Appendices).

We organized a project practice garden. This is where children practice clean, sustainable agricultural projects. Students grow vegetables and fruits and measure them. Students learn through these activities to improve teamwork and develop thinking and social skills (Volpe, et al, 2019).

Hillside plum garden

Near the soccer field, where the lake's humid wind brings a bit of cold morning dew, the terrain is gentle and receives the morning sun, providing favorable conditions for plums to grow. This year, the hill plums have bloomed and fruited, and the plum garden promises many enjoyable learning experiences for Spring Hill School students.

The open football field has an area of more than 5000 m2. This is where students can freely play basketball and badminton and learn self-defense martial arts under the shade of the bright red fireworks of spring. Moving on, there are two rows of pink and white bougainvillea trees, as well as a swimming pool using spring water from the protective forest. Here, students can learn to swim and cool off in the clean spring water.

The pebble pit

The pebble pit is an ample, open space with many tall, green trees, providing shade to the playground, which is situated with its back against the mountain and offers a view down to the rice fields and village roads. The scene is as beautiful as a picture painted with natural colors. Every week, the entire school organizes emotional intelligence education classes in this pebble pit. Fig trees, jackfruit trees, whip trees, and wild orchids, blooming with beautiful, gentle yellow and purple flowers, shade the space of the pebble pit. Stepping into the pebble pit feels like stepping into a tropical forest, where wild orchids bloom, their fragrant scent mingling with that of jade orchids, wild chestnut flowers, and Japanese jasmine. For students of all levels, the pebble pit is also a place to play and create shapes during breaks. As we lie on the pebble pit and look up, we see a blue sky and white clouds, like cotton, floating by. Sometimes, many people altogether can feel Mother Earth's rotation and movement around the sun.

Dracontomelon, myrtle, and wild guava trees shade the walkway. Once you reach halfway up the hill, turn right. You can see a tree garden. The garden has many pineapples, mulberries, and some fruit trees. Students will be able to take care of the garden plants themselves and then work with teachers and uncles to farm and harvest the fruits. Learning about and making clean agricultural products, as well as bringing them home to give to your parents, will be one of the most memorable and meaningful lessons of your life. When you savour a delicious fruit, remember its origin and remember your parents, who made it possible for students to enjoy attending school every day.

Continuing both sides of the road to the top of the hill, we can see colorful fairy-hair flowers. Spring Hill School grows many types of fruit and flower trees, thereby creating attractive diversity. The diversity and richness of flowers and fruit trees will help train students' observation skills, artistic sensibility, and respect for differences. Each tree species will have its own beauty and value, so we all respect these differences.

In the forest of Spring Hill School, there are many wild guava trees. The smell of guava is so fragrant. We set up a "Guava Garden classroom", situated halfway up the hill, under a cool canopy of guava trees. The classroom offers breathtaking views. The wind from the front of the valley blows up the special fragrant scent of ripe hill guava. From here, we can look out into space and enjoy expansive views. Purple myrtle flowers bloom in harmonious clusters of purple, pink, and white, and bees diligently follow the students climbing the hill to suck nectar.

The classrooms at the top of the hill

In the open class of Combretum indicum Class, teachers and students will both learn about and observe the fragrant rose garden in front and the shaded flower trellis behind. The path to the right will lead you forward to the Pink Guava Class.

The classroom exudes a sweet and fragrant guava scent. Guava flowers bloom white and are extremely beautiful in all four seasons. During the ripe guava season, many wild birds come and eat fruit. The delicious taste of ripe guava is the most addictive flavor in the hills. There's nothing better than learning and being creative in that sweet-smelling classroom.

Walk through the bougainvillea trellis and shade the rows of Bombax ceiba trees that are nearly 100 years old. That is the Poinsettia class. It is in the heart of a luminous paradise that this classroom serves as a natural learning space, one that students adore. Lessons are vividly and uniquely staged between heaven and earth, amidst immense mountains and forests.

On the other side, there is the green bamboo classroom. Green bamboo is a symbol of the persistent will, solidarity, resilience, and indomitability of the Vietnamese people. Under the green bamboo classroom, memorable poems nourish the students' souls. The green bamboo's lesson of solidarity and overcoming difficulties in all circumstances will be a valuable one for each person, keeping in mind that the Vietnamese national cultural traditions are preserved.

The classroom, Bombax ceiba, conveys the clearest rhythm of nature's hills during the changing seasons. "When fireflies fly out and Bombax ceiba flowers fall, add sesame seeds". When the Bombax ceiba flowers bloom, crested birds and sunbirds feed and drink nectar. Students can use telescopes to observe the beauty of the birds flying to perch on the blooming Bombax ceiba flowers. The whole hill area is beautiful in March and April.

A gap in the sunflower class is a Fig tree classroom. The space is high, open on all four sides, and under the canopy of a large, cool fig tree. You can see the hillside, the valley, and the open classrooms below. Far away are hills and romantic floating clouds.

Next to it, the Paper flower class is a poetic 4-season class, where pupils studying under the shade of bougainvillea flowers bring endless inspiration for writing poetry and fine arts to teachers and students.

Sunflower Classroom

In the 2023-2024 school year, Spring Hill School did a project planting 1000 Sunflower trees on top of the hill, which we called Sunflower Classroom. This is a result of a solidarity lesson; the teachers and students at Spring Hill School transported 1,000 sunflower seedlings from the foot of the hill to the top of the hill for the 2024 Tree Planting Festival. Pupils were happy to be studying in a place where collective strength would make impossible things come true: 1,000 sunflowers planted on a high hill bloomed and headed towards the sunlight and good things.

Go through rows of blooming myrtles; that's the path leading to a soccer field with a view of Dong Bo Lake. The spacious outdoor natural soccer field is an ideal place to practice sports. The soccer field has natural ginger grass, overlooking a clean water reservoir flowing from a protective forest spring. Looking to the right is a mountain range of protective forests that are green all year round, protected forests, clean water, and a gentle climate for all the people here.

Pupils can also learn by taking care of friendly animals, and the Rabbit Barn Class is one of the favorite classes for Spring Hill pupils. The Spring Hill School students' daily climbing motivations are thanks to petting and playing with baby rabbits. The interesting experience, including observing mother rabbits, giving birth and caring for their babies provides students with vivid visual lessons that enhance their understanding of life.

Yoga class

Practicing yoga helps prolong youthful beauty and longevity, prevents joint degeneration, protects the spine, strengthens bones, helps blood circulate better, strengthens the immune system, and helps keep the heart healthy. Every day, students eagerly welcome lessons such as participating in sports and practicing yoga in nature classes under the shade of trees in the production forest.

Here, Spring Hill School offers two yoga classes. Yoga class 1, located right next to the pebble pit, features many vivid drawings of various yoga positions, sparking students' curiosity and creativity. With a large space shaded by green trees, the chirping of jay's blends with the students' practice rhythm in the yoga class next to the pebble pit. The second yoga class is a Peach Garden Yoga class, situated in a vast space surrounded by hills and valleys that are wide and airy. There's nothing better than practicing and admiring this majestic scenery.

Art classroom

In addition to providing physical development activities, Spring Hill School consistently instills in its students the importance of developing artistic vision every day. The art classroom is an open, spacious, and airy space that displays a variety of creative products from students and teachers, inspiring and artistically arranged in harmony with nature. The students have created many beautiful and aesthetically pleasing products. Students either sold these products to raise funds for charity or brought them home as gifts for their parents and family members.

Many people enjoy natural sounds, such as the chirping of birds, the buzzing of insects, the rustling of leaves, the gentle breeze, and the soothing sound of running water. All of these make people forget their fatigue. Energy is full of vitality. After lunch, the sound of piano and orchestral music resounded, shaking the mountains and forests. Even though the student's study on hills and mountains, the music they play every day contributes to the vitality of Spring Hill School, which, although far from the city center, still maintains a modern, international character thanks to the music. The piano, the guitar, and the echo of the brain come alive in a corner of the forest.

Rice fields stretch far apart but close to Spring Hill school; each season, the fields have different colors. The green sea of rice, stretching to the foot of the hill, marks the planting season. Following the harvest, the fields transform into a vibrant "golden sea, golden harvest," signaling the arrival of the bumper season. For all of these experiential activities, the vast valley field serves as the classroom. In the nature classroom, situated in the midst of the rice fields, students learned the lesson of gratitude to the farmers and had real-life experiences planting rice, weeding, and harvesting the "golden grains". The students understood and loved them, and from there they lived and practiced gratitude for all the good things present here, both given by people and Mother Nature.

"Homeland is a blue kite." "Spring Hill School was where I spent my childhood."

By learning and experiencing the natural environment, students will have a beautiful childhood they will never forget.

Study purpose and Data collection

The aim of this study is to test the hypothesis: "Does nature school nourish pupils to improve their standard scores at school?" We conducted the study and used the results of semesters 1 and 2 to analyse what factors are involved in the quality of pupils' education by measuring their test scores.

Research methods used to evaluate the study, in combination with teaching lessons in 50% of indoor classes and 50% of lessons in outdoor classes, included participant observation, student and parent questionnaires, child interviews, and teacher diaries (Volpe et al., 2019). We recorded the scores at the end of semesters 1 and 2 in the school year 2023-2024 to determine the improvement of pupils after implementing the study.

A total of 329 pupils and 18 teachers participated in this study and were divided into 16 classes, with the number ranging from 15 to 25 pupils per class. For primary classes (from grade 1 to grade 5), one Vietnamese teacher taught both math and language arts, and one English teacher taught English. In secondary classes (from grade 6 to grade 9), one teacher taught language arts, another one taught math, and one English teacher taught English. We designed to teach 50% of lessons in the classroom and 50% in nature classes, where pupils enjoy learning under the canopy of green trees in the forest of Spring Hill as much as possible. Details of each class are shown in Table 11.1 in the Online Appendix link https://tinyurl.com/he5oAppendices.

Data analysis

Teachers taught and designed the standard tests in semesters 1 and 2 in three subjects: English, Math, and Language Arts. We followed the curriculum of the Vietnamese Ministry of Training and Education. Besides those, teachers used accounts of online schools from grade K to grade 9 in the US, such as Acellus (https://www.powerhomeschool.org/), Study Island, and Education City, produced by Edmentum (https://www.edmentum.com/), to update pupils' English knowledge. We analysed the learning results to find out whether the hypothesis was correct or not.

Statistical analysis

A Fisher's exact test (Suresh, 2011) (Chi-Square Calculator) was used to test for differences in two semesters in 16 classes based on their tested scores in English, Math, and Language Arts (The curriculum of the Vietnamese Education Ministry). A p-value of b <0.05 was considered statistically significant.

Discussion

Results between two semesters of the 2023-2024 school year were summarized in Figure 11.2 (available in the Online Appendix link https://tinyurl.com/he50Appendices). Overall, teaching Vietnamese for math and language arts was effective in 14 out of 16 classes. Only the teacher in grade 2.1 did not help her pupils improve much because of lack of dedication. This may be a result of overwork from taking the responsibility of teaching more than three classes. Based on this, we concluded that a teacher should at most teach no more than two classes for the results to be optimal. (See Figure 11.2 in the Online Appendix link https://tinyurl.com/he50Appendices). Therefore, teachers in both Vietnamese and English who taught more than two classes do not have the ability to help students to enhance their standard knowledge. Furthermore, we observed two English teachers who taught six classes. They prepared the lesson plan well, but overworking in many classes did not benefit the pupils' improvement. One English teacher got 2/6 classes with a significant increase in the scores. However, the scores of 4 out of 6 classes decreased sharply in the second semester. The other English teacher had 3 out of 6 classes with improved pupils and 3 out of 6 classes with reduced scores. Several students dropped to scores under 5/10 (see Figures in the Online Appendix link https://tinyurl.com/he50Appendices).

In detail, English improved significantly in grade 1. The scores for Math and Language Arts were statistically not significant.

In Grade 1.1, English students improved their scores, although the improvement was not statistically significant. In contrast, Math and Language Arts scores increased significantly.

In grade 2, English scores increased, but the increase was not statistically significant. Math, containing zero pupils, had under five scores, and statistics cannot identify the score results. When we analysed scores above 5, the increase in score was not statistically significant.

In grade 2.1, English scores decreased significantly and were not statistically significant. That means pupils did not improve their English. Math and Language Arts scores decreased clearly and statistically but were not significantly. That means pupils did not improve their math and Language Arts either.

In grade 3, English scores seemed slightly elevated but were not significantly increased statistically. But Math and Language Arts scores were increased significantly in this class.

In grade 3.1, English scores did not improve significantly. Although no students achieved excellent scores, the class overall showed statistically significant increases in Math and Language Arts scores.

In grade 4, English scores decreased significantly. However, Math and Language Arts scores increased significantly.

In grade 4.1, Pupils did not significantly improve their English scores. In semester 2, no pupil got an excellent score, even though seven pupils had outstanding scores in semester 1. This suggests that the English teacher did not help pupils enhance their English despite their superb English background. On the other hand, one teacher helped students improve their math scores, but did not significantly improve them in Language Arts.

In grade 5, English, Math, and Language Arts teachers taught well, resulting in significant increases in pupil scores across all three subjects.

In grade 5.1, the number of pupils who got excellent scores in semester 2 increased to 11/15, but overall, their English improvement was not statistically significant. A similar trend was found in Math and Language Arts; the excellent scores increased in semester 2 but were not statistically significant in all classes.

In grade 6, the pupils' scores in English, Math, and Language Arts increased significantly.

In grade 6.1, the scores in three subjects, English, Math, and Language Arts, did not increase significantly. It stayed at its original level. In grade 7, it was found that the English scores increased slightly. However, this change was not statistically significant. In Math and Language Arts, the scores improved significantly in Vietnamese.

In grade 7.1, the English scores decreased in semester 2, but this change was not statistically significant. This suggests that English teachers did not help pupils improve their English after one year of implementing Education 5.0 in indoor and outdoor classes. On the other hand, Math and Language Arts scores tended to increase slightly, but it was not statistically significant.

In grade 8, the scores of all three subjects did not increase statistically significantly.

In grade 9, English scores were not statistically significantly different, while Math and Language Arts scores were improved considerably.

Analyzing the English scores, it was noted that 4/16 classes had pupils improve statistically significantly, 8/16 classes showed higher scores in semester 2 but not statistically significantly, and 4/16 classes saw pupils decrease their scores in semester 2. The 10/16 classes with Vietnamese math and language arts scores improved statistically significantly; 4/16 classes with scores increased but not statistically significantly; and 2/16 classes with pupils dropped their scores significantly (Table 11.2 - see the Online Appendix link https://tinyurl.com/he50Appendices).

Conclusion

The results of this study revealed that the nature school at Spring Hill helps pupils improve their standard scores in certain classes, possibly attributed to an improved study environment. Especially teaching Vietnamese in outdoor classes brought many benefits. For English, the circumstances depended on the usage of electronics within indoor classes, but moving the teaching to outdoor classes might be helpful to pupils, where they can practise the obtained knowledge indoors, and express it seamlessly without depending on electronic devices. The results agreed with some previous research, which showed that the implementation of Education 5.0 poses some challenges, and one of these challenges is teacher competencies. Observing the teaching methods in educators, we found that the effort put into teaching should also be as heavily emphasized. One year after the implementation of Education 5.0 in a nature school in Spring Hill, the apparent results we cannot deny were that pupils' health and well-being have improved. Children were happy to go to school, and most parents were content with the outdoor classes, even though the distances to the commune ranged from 5 to nearly 100 km by bus. The scores of pupils, therefore, were partly contributed to by their well-being, but also, at the same time, they still relied on the teachers' contribution and dedication. Combining both efforts previously mentioned is the main goal of Education 5.0.

12

The relationship between QC and internal QA: A case study at Vietnam National University, Hanoi[25]

Nguyen Thanh Tu and Nguyen Thi Nham[26]

Abstract

This study explores the relationship between Quality Culture (QC) and Internal Quality Assurance (IQA) at Vietnam National University, Hanoi. In the context of higher education, ensuring academic and administrative quality requires effective coordination between QC and Internal QA mechanisms. Through a case study approach, data were collected document analysis, and observation of quality management practices. The findings reveal that while QC focuses on operational compliance and performance monitoring, Internal QA emphasizes systematic evaluation, continuous improvement, and strategic planning. The study highlights areas of synergy and gaps in coordination between the two functions, suggesting that enhanced communication and integrated procedures can strengthen overall institutional quality. The results provide practical implications for policy development and quality management practices in Vietnamese higher education institutions.

---

25 All references, tables, figures, author affiliation and biography used in this chapter are available on the Online Appendix link at https://tinyurl.com/he50Appendices.

26 Corresponding author: nguyenthinham1310@gmail.com

Introduction

Over the past few decades, the global higher education landscape has undergone rapid transformation. This transformation is characterized by the diversity of educational institutions and the increasing number of students, especially with the development of cross-border educational institutions. The issue of educational QA is not only significant for universities but also a mandatory requirement and accountability for all educational institutions. For each country, the higher education QA system plays a very important role in orienting the strategy for developing educational quality to adapt to the requirements of the times, and at the same time must be consistent with the development characteristics of each country. Educational QA includes internal QA (IQA) and external QA (EQA), playing an important role in managing, monitoring, evaluating and improving the quality of education. In which, IQA helps to evaluate, measure, and control overall quality, thereby ensuring and improving the quality of the school (Hou et al., 2015).

However, focusing only on QA is not enough. As higher education develops strongly, fierce competition between universities requires continuous quality improvement. From there, the philosophy of continuous quality improvement was born with the total quality management model (TQM) to continuously improve quality and increase efficiency. An effective solution to implement TQM is to build a QC so that all members of the organization can join hands to continuously improve quality and efficiency, to ensure the organization's existence and sustainable development. QC is a tool to effectively implement TQM, playing a very important role in improving and enhancing the continuous quality of education of educational institutions in general and higher education institutions in particular. Developing a QC always goes hand in hand with building, perfecting and developing the IQA system of a higher education institution. IQA is the first factor to promote the development of QC. There is always an interaction between these two factors to promote the continuous development of the quality of university education.

In Vietnam, the quality of education in general and the quality of higher education in particular is always a matter of great concern. Society expects an advanced higher education system, which provides high-quality human resources for the country, plays a leading role, promotes the progress and development of society. However, it seems that higher education has not yet fully met expectations, especially in the context of educational institutions being increasingly given autonomy and self-responsibility. One of the main reasons for the low quality of higher education is due to weaknesses in management due to the lack of quality management and improvement measures (Do et al., 2017). In addition, although the IQA system has been formed and implemented in Vietnamese higher education for nearly 20 years. However, many studies and practices have shown that the effectiveness of QA activities has not been truly guaranteed and met national, regional and international standards. International experience shows that the formation and development of a QC along with the formation and development of a university's internal QA system will help the university achieve its goals and missions (Hien & Huong, 2021). Based on the premise that QA and the surrounding QC are two closely related processes and that IQA is a component of QC (Loukkola & Zhang, 2010), this study will track the development of an IQA system and QC at the leading university among Vietnamese universities in implementing QA activities and QC, Vietnam National University, Hanoi (VNU Ha Noi). The questions raised are: What is the relationship between QA and QC? What measures promote the development of QC and QA in higher education in Vietnam? This study will clarify the relationship and interaction between IQA and QC at VNU Hanoi to analyze and evaluate the connection between internal QA and aspects of QC of universities. The results of this analysis and evaluation provide additional perspectives on IQA of the international higher education system and its implementation in Vietnam, thereby helping universities build and develop a QC, aiming at overall quality management, creating social trust in the quality of education.

Overview of QA and QC in Vietnamese higher education

Quality is an important issue in higher education in Vietnam. According to TCVN 5814, QA is defined as "all planned and systematic activities, implemented within a management system, demonstrated to be adequate to provide adequate confidence that an entity will fully satisfy the quality requirements". That is, QA in education is all policies and procedures to maintain and improve the quality of higher education, while providing evidence and QA to stakeholders in higher education. This shows two issues: First, the main purpose of QA in higher education lies in two aspects: one is to promote the maintenance and improvement of quality, and the other is to provide quality evidence to stakeholders in higher education such as: government, employers, students, parents, society... to demonstrate that the quality of products and services provided by higher education institutions is reliable and to enhance their confidence in the quality of higher education. Second, to achieve the above goals, a series of specific policies and procedures must be adopted, such as establishing a QA agency, developing quality standards, developing assessment tools and processes.

The issue of QA in higher education began to be concerned from the late 20th century to the early 21st century and was implemented more drastically when the Ministry of Education and Training of Vietnam issued a set of standards for assessing university quality, including 10 standards and 53 criteria. The model of educational QA in Vietnam is influenced by many countries in the world that have experience in implementing these activities. First of all, it is influenced by the QA model of the United States and North American countries; influenced by the QA models of European countries, which are many years ahead of Vietnam in implementing the model of educational QA; especially influenced by countries in the Asia-Pacific region due to many similarities in culture, making it easy to share and exchange practical experiences. The influence of other countries on Vietnam's QA model is mainly through bilateral cooperation support and support from international organizations, especially the World Bank, Asia-Pacific Quality Network (APQN), SEAMEO and some countries such as the United States, Australia, and the Netherlands.

In the process of approaching many models of QA and quality assessment of education in the world, the model of education QA in Vietnam is gradually being formed, in line with the QA models of many countries in the world, especially the models of Europe, Asia - Pacific, AUN, models that continue to develop on the common model of Europe. The model of education QA in Vietnam consists of 3 basic components:

(1) The internal QA system of the school;

(2) The external QA system of the school (external assessment system including policies, processes and assessment tools);

(3) The system of QA organizations (external assessment organizations and independent accreditation organizations).

This model originates from the European QA system, developed by the Asia-Pacific Quality Network (APQN) and encouraged to be applied to countries in the region. In Vietnam, the work of QA in higher education is carried out under the regulation of the Government, the Ministry of Education and Training through the Department of Quality Management (formerly the Department of Testing and QA of Education) which performs the state management function of testing, assessment and QA of education. Since its inception, the Department of Testing and QA of Education has registered to become a member of the Asia-Pacific Quality Network (APQN), the International Network of Higher Education Institutions (INQAAHE), and is a founding member of the ASEAN QA Network (AQAN).

The IQA system of universities in Vietnam includes: (1) The school's policies, plans for improving educational quality, a specialized unit for QA (for universities and colleges), activities and coordination between units within the school; (2) Mechanisms for approving, monitoring and periodically reviewing and evaluating educational programs (for universities, colleges and vocational training institutions); (3) Strategy for continuous improvement and enhancement of educational quality; ensuring the quality of the teaching staff; (4) Public disclosure of information on teaching, programs and educational and training results.

In 2012, Vietnam had 156 universities (accounting for 75.3%), 145 colleges (accounting for 67.7%), 48 vocational secondary schools (accounting for 16.3%) establishing specialized units on QA, including 5 centers supported by the Dutch Government established at Thai Nguyen University, Hue University, Da Nang University, Vinh University, Can Tho University and operating from 2005 to present; and 2 centers of the Viet Nam National University have been operating since the late 1990s; 63 departments of education and training have Examination and Education Quality Management Departments. From 2009-2013, VNU Hanoi and VNU Ho Chi Minh City were official members of AUN and had 18 programs evaluated by AUN (Thanh, 2012). To ensure the construction of a system of accreditation organizations that meets practical requirements and forms a "network", the Department of Quality Management has coordinated to develop regulations related to public accreditation organizations and recognize the operations of three foreign accreditation organizations in Vietnam, including: ASEAN University Network-QA (AUN-QA); High

Council for Evaluation of Research and Higher Education (Hcéres) and The QA Agency for Higher Education (QAA) in 2022. In 2022, Vietnam will have 5 Vietnamese higher education institutions in the 2022 Best Global Universities Rankings; in 2023, 2 more institutions (a total of 5 institutions) will be listed in the QS World University Rankings 2023; 10 institutions in the Webometrics rankings and 5 educational institutions in the rankings of universities in emerging economies 2021 (The Emerging Economies University Rankings 2021). According to the latest announcement of Times Higher Education (THE), Vietnam has 6 higher education institutions in the world university rankings in 2024 (THE WUR 2024).

Efforts to build a QA system within educational institutions are aimed at gradually forming a QC within those educational institutions with the aim of making all members of the school understand, care about and desire to improve the quality of education.

The issue of building and developing QC has initially been focused on throughout the system, from state management agencies to universities. With the goal throughout the 2017-2020 period, the Ministry of Education and Training determined to "focus on assessing the quality of educational institutions and training programs to improve quality, gradually forming and building a school QC" (Vietnam MOET, 2019). Accordingly, universities have also paid attention to investing in building a QC within the school. The view of QC as a system of organizational values to create a favorable environment for establishing and continuously improving quality; building a QC is essentially establishing an environmental system for quality activities and continuously improving the quality of the organization, while requiring all members of the school to build quality working habits (Hien & Huong, 2021). A university can only build and develop a QC when it simultaneously meets both the factors of awareness and action as mentioned above (Huong, 2017).

QA and QC at Viet Nam National University, Hanoi

Vietnam has two national universities: Viet Nam National University - Hanoi and Viet Nam National University Ho Chi Minh City. Viet Nam National University, Hanoi ranked 1 st in the Top 10 higher education institutions in Vietnam in the ranking edition published in January 2023.

According to the January 2023 ranking edition, VNU continued to improve its rank, up 97 places compared to its rank in August 2022, placed in the Top 700 globally and 137th in Asia, and 11th in Southeast Asia. In 2022, according to the QS World University Rankings, VNU Ha Noi won the Recognition of Improvement Award - an award given to institutions for their significant improvements in rating results based on the improvement in their average ranks. VNU was the first Vietnamese higher education institution presented with this award. VNU Ha Noi has the mission of "Training high-quality, highly qualified human resources, nurturing talents; scientific research, technology development and multidisciplinary and multidisciplinary knowledge transfer; contributing to the construction, development and protection of the country; as the backbone and locomotive in the Vietnamese higher education system" (VNU website, ND).

VNU Ha Noi has a lot of experience in the field of QA and educational quality assessment. VNU has 9 Universities, 6 Research Institutes, 4 Affiliated Schools, 2 Training and Research Centers, 16 Service units and other units. VNU Ha Noi has 2 main units responsible for QA: the Institute for Education Quality Assurance and the Center for Education Accreditation. In which, the Institute of QA is the management agency for educational QA, educational quality assessment, university governance, and educational organization quality assessment of VNU Ha Noi. The Center for Quality Assessment provides public services on educational QA, consulting, and monitoring the assurance and improvement of educational quality according to national, regional and international standards with a vision to become a prestigious quality assessment center in the region by 2035, meeting the standards of international educational quality assessment organizations. By the end of 2023, VNU Ha Noi had had 172 undergraduate programs, 183 master's programs and 113 doctoral programs. Currently, VNU Ha Noi has a student body of 5,075 including 113 foreign students. VNU Ha Noi is a trusted destination for nearly 1,200 international students studying short-term and long-term courses. VNU Ha Noi international staff, undergraduate and graduate students have contributed and brought diverse cultural pieces to the VNU Ha Noi community. Starting its training journey with majors only in basic sciences, to date, with over 400 training programs at undergraduate, master, and doctoral levels, VNU Ha Noi has already developed the following training structure: Natural sciences and medicine - pharmacy: 25%; Social sciences and humanities, economics, foreign languages, law and education: 45%;

Technology – engineering: 15%; Interdisciplinary and pilot programs: 15%. VNU Ha Noi has been actively transforming its training structure from basic sciences to those linked with engineering, technology and practice. Thanks to that, VNU's training programs have quickly matched with those around the world, closely linked with industries and businesses, which helps increase graduate employability.

The QA system of VNU Ha Noi is tightly structured, ensuring unified operation from the leadership level to the smallest structural units, which are the departments. The internal QA system structure of VNU Hanoi is implemented according to the following hierarchical model:

At the VNU Ha Noi level: As a member unit of VNU, all activities of the University are carried out in accordance with the regulations of VNU. Regarding QA work, VNU Ha Noi assigns the Institute for QA as the focal unit to deploy QA work to all member units of VNU Ha Noi. Member units are responsible for implementing and reporting QA activities to the Institute for QA, VNU Ha Noi in accordance with regulations.

At the member university level: Member universities establish a QA Council consisting of leaders, experts in the field of QA, heads of functional departments, and heads of vice-deans of faculties. The QA Council is responsible for advising the President on educational QA work in accordance with current regulations of the Ministry of Education and Training, VNU Ha Noi. In addition to the QA Council, the University of Education also assigns the Vice President to monitor, supervise, direct and implement the QA activities and also be the promotor of the quality for the whole school.

Professional unit level: the permanent unit for QA work is the QA Department of member universities. The QA Department has the following tasks:

a) Take the lead in processing the results of evaluating the quality of graduates through investigating the employment status and continuing education after graduation, the level of satisfaction of employers with the capacity of graduates.

b) Take the lead in collecting feedback, evaluating and monitoring teaching work through evaluating learners' feedback, the level of students' acceptance of the quality of teaching for the entire course or each module, student learning outcomes, and the rate of meeting the requirements of each module.

c) Coordinate with other units in the school to evaluate scientific research work, evaluate the quality of staff, administrative work and school services, research solutions to improve quality such as innovation in teaching methods, learning methods, innovation in testing and evaluation methods.

d) Preside over the periodic self-assessment of all activities and training programs of the school (according to the standards of the Ministry of Education and Training, VNU Ha Noi and AUN) and register for educational quality assessment as well as external assessment.

e) Preside over and coordinate with faculties to organize and implement self-assessment activities of lecturers.

f) Preside over the construction and maintenance of the database of self-assessment activities according to quality assessment requirements.

g) Develop QA processes (standards and criteria for evaluating the activities of units) of the university and monitor the implementation of quality policies (QC, quality goals, etc.).

At the level of faculties, units and units under the University: in addition to the staff of the Department of QA specializing in QA work, each functional department and training faculty must have a leader directly in charge of QA work and assign at least 01 specialist to concurrently perform QA work at their unit. All members of the internal QA system of the University must be trained in QA work, many lecturers and managers are trained in QA and have QA cards to participate in many external assessment teams of educational institutions and external assessment of training programs at higher education institutions across the country.

The approach to QC of VNU Hanoi from a systemic perspective, standard values and quality working habits from the daily practical work of each unit and individual is also similar to the approach of Harvey (2004). QC must be imbued in the rules of action and habits of performing well the assigned tasks of all staff, lecturers and learners in order to create high-quality training and scientific research products that meet social requirements.

VNU has identified the levels of QC and the contents of implementing QC building for member universities (VNU, 2011) at two levels:

At the unit level (member universities), QC is expressed through the effective construction and operation of the QA system, including the construction of a good strategy for QA of the unit, the construction of a permanent department for QA that works effectively.

At the individual level, it is expressed through completing high-quality work, on time, ensuring sufficient quantity of products, meeting requirements, reasonable costs, meeting teamwork skills, solidarity, democracy... This viewpoint is consistent with the study of Lanarès (2009). In order to achieve the goals, VNU has agreed on 6 contents to implement the steps to build and develop a QC at member schools.

Since 2021, VNU Ha Noi has launched the Higher Education and Vocational Quality Channel. This is a forum for education managers, higher education experts, researchers, lecturers, and staff working in the field of QA, quality assessment and university ranking to clarify theoretical and practical issues in QA; update and disseminate new trends in QA - assessment and university ranking activities; identify the current situation and evaluate the effectiveness of policy implementation on university autonomy, university governance in general, quality accreditation - assessment and university ranking in particular in Vietnam; and share experiences and good practices in QA, assessment and university ranking activities. The ultimate goal of the Channel is to create a foundation for developing a QC in Vietnamese universities and colleges.

Existing issues and causes

Although VNU Ha Noi and Vietnamese universities have fully recognized the work of QA and have carried out a number of activities, there are still many difficulties in implementation, especially in building and developing a QC. The main shortcomings and causes are:

1) The QA model within the units is not clear; the QA system of the organizations is not complete; awareness of the QA system, mechanism, and activities is not complete; the functions and tasks

of the QA department are not clearly defined. The conditions for QA have not been fully met, especially the team of lecturers and staff have not really understood and imbued with their roles and tasks in QA work (Hien & Huong, 2021). IQA work is mainly carried out according to the regulations of the Ministry of Education and Training, according to the standards of the Southeast Asian University Network (AUN - QA) without referring to and applying the quality assessment standards of countries with advanced education (Tran Thuy Anh, 2021).

2) The attention of leaders of units to QA work is not adequate; this is not considered a central task of the unit; awareness of the work is still vague (often responding to instructions from above without truly caring about learners); funding for activities is still too limited and unstable and the awareness of the majority of officials and civil servants about the role and importance of QA work as well as the responsibilities and tasks of individuals for this work is not high, leading to the implementation being formalistic, even perfunctory (Cuong et al., 2017).

3) Some regulations and plans for QA have not received due attention from universities during the implementation process. Especially the development of regulations and criteria for emulation and rewards in QA work, building QC, and regulations on quality improvement work. 4) Some universities have pioneered in building and forming a QC associated with the development of a sustainable internal QA system, but many universities are facing difficulties in mechanisms, operating conditions and human resources for implementing QA work. If autonomy is enhanced and accountability is improved, universities with appropriate strategies and solutions will be able to create and develop a QC, thereby successfully building and ensuring the effective operation of the QA system within the university.

Orientation for developing quality higher education in Vietnam: Resolving the relationship between QC and QA

The internal QA system and QC are closely linked. QC creates an organizational culture that aims at sustainable quality improvement. A QA system alone cannot create sustainable quality. But when combined with QC and an internal QA system (processes, systems of documents, necessary sanctions), it will create a habit of voluntarily participating in QA work. The QA structure can create habits, expectations and common values that everyone shares. QC is one of the key elements of the internal QA system and QC determines the sustainability of QA activities.

To build a QC in a university, both psychological factors are needed: voluntary implementation and management (imposed from above). If quality is imposed from above, and members of the organization do not voluntarily implement it, quality will not be sustainable (it will only be implemented when supervised). If only a few individuals make efforts, it will not be widespread enough, and without the support of the entire system, there will be no conditions for the formation of an organizational culture. The commitment of the top leadership is a prerequisite for the success of quality. The role of leadership in building a QC in a school is very important. The university leader is the one who decides on the policy of building a QC to lead the organization towards a new direction and is the one who inspires and influences all members to attract and lead them to follow in order to achieve that vision. To implement the building of a QC, leaders need to attach importance to the implementation of leadership, consulting, guidance, motivational activities... for members of the school to carry out the set goals and tasks with a spirit of volunteerism, self-awareness, creativity and high responsibility. Specific QA activities such as developing an overall QA strategy; organizing training courses to raise awareness of educational quality assessment and accreditation for managers, lecturers, support staff and students; collecting feedback from stakeholders on training quality; assessing the capacity and classifying lecturers... gradually contribute to the formation and establishment of a QC.

The relationship between QA and QC is expressed in two aspects: action (QA) and cognition (QC).

In terms of cognition: QC is an element of QA (cognition in action).

In terms of action: QA is an element of QC (action in cognition).

QA activities aim at continuous quality improvement. Therefore, there cannot be a QC in a university without implementing QA and educational quality assessment activities. On the contrary, once a QC has been formed, it will contribute to maintaining, consolidating and developing QA and educational quality assessment activities, contributing to orienting appropriate development strategies, aiming at implementing the mission, vision and development strategy of the university. In order for QC to become a permanent value in all thoughts and actions of individuals and units, the first important thing is to form correct perceptions of quality. Therefore, when implementing the construction of a QC, the first activity that needs to be implemented is to widely disseminate to relevant parties the regulations on educational QA and QC in the unit such as discussing, organizing conferences, workshops, seminars to disseminate quality assessment and quality surveys to civil servants, public employees and learners of the school. In a university, when all members from leaders to management staff, lecturers, staff and learners and organizations and units follow the values, standards, processes and commitments towards quality, it will be the premise for developing a QC. This is the factor that ensures the success of the university in implementing activities to ensure the achievement of its strategic goals.

The next step is to build and complete the internal QA system of the unit, including a system of management and operation documents, strategies, policies, and plans for QA; the QA system such as organizational structure, personnel, functions, tasks, and plans for training staff; a database system for quality assessment and comparison; and at the same time, deploy, review, evaluate, and improve QA activities in the unit. In addition, it is necessary to implement overall quality management, often following the PDCA process clearly and systematically. This is the tool and mechanism to measure, evaluate, ensure, and improve the quality of a university. For a university's internal QA system to develop sustainably, QC must become a permanent value in all activities of the organization.

The close connection between QA activities and the formation of QC in schools will be systematic, interacting with the internal environment (organizational culture; mechanisms, forms and capacity to implement QA activities) and the external environment (socio-economic environment, socio-culture, university education system) will change the capacity and awareness of quality of individuals and groups in the university.

Conclusion

Up to now, it can be concluded that the work of QA and QC in Vietnamese universities has been gradually formed. Although it can be affirmed that the internal QA system of Vietnamese universities has been relatively stable, the issue of QC has just been formed and is not yet solid. The article considers QA and QC consisting of two main components: QA represents action, QC represents awareness and has a close relationship with each other. There is much evidence that QA is a component of QC (from action to awareness) and QA is a component of QC (from awareness to action), in which the quality capacity of individuals and groups determines the success of the process of converting action into awareness or QA can be seen as a manifestation of human resource quality capacity (quality capacity of all individuals and groups in the university). That is, when the human resource quality capacity in the university is large enough, QC will be formed. However, for QA activities in each university, depending on each university, it is up to each school to choose to implement QA activities and build a plan to form QA in accordance with the general level of quality awareness of the whole school in order to achieve the desired quality values. (Ehlers & Schneckenberg, 2010). In particular, activities are being implemented simultaneously at Vietnamese universities such as self-assessment of schools, self-assessment of training programs, collecting feedback from learners on lecturers' teaching activities, developing and publishing output standards for training majors.

13

University Education 5.0: Creativity and Innovation for the Future[27]

Nguyễn Minh Tuấn[28]

Abstract

University Education 5.0 marks a significant step forward in reshaping the educational system to meet the demands of the technological era and intelligent society. In the context of the Fourth Industrial Revolution and the rapid development of new technologies such as artificial intelligence, big data, and virtual reality, universities must innovate and adapt to equip students with 21st-century skills. This includes critical thinking, creativity, collaboration skills and problem-solving abilities. This study employs a literature review method to explore the challenges faced by the educational system in the 5.0 Era and identifies potential opportunities for innovation and transformation. Furthermore, the research emphasizes the need to foster critical thinking, creativity, collaboration, and other 21st-century skills in students to prepare them for future challenges and opportunities. Finally, this research will highlight the transformative potential of education in the 5.0 era.

Introduction

The rapid technological advancements of the Fourth Industrial Revolution

---

27 All references, tables, figures, author affiliation and biography used in this chapter are available on the Online Appendix link at https://tinyurl.com/he50Appendices.

28 Corresponding author: tuannm@uef.edu.vn

(4IR), including artificial intelligence (AI), big data, and virtual reality (VR), are reshaping various sectors, and education is no exception. These developments underscore the emergence of University Education 5.0, which envisions an education system that meets the needs of a "super smart" society, or Society 5.0. This concept originated in Japan, emphasizing a harmonious integration of digital and physical worlds to create human-centered, socially responsible innovation. Education 5.0 thus calls for a paradigm shift in university education, equipping students with the skills to navigate a technology-rich and interconnected future.

Equally Industrial Era 5.0 represents a progression from Era 4.0, emphasizing the collaboration between technology and humans. Modern manufacturing aims are achieved through cutting-edge technologies like artificial intelligence, advanced robotics, augmented reality, and cyber-physical systems. Industry 5.0 seeks to strike a balance between merging human capabilities with robotic advancements (Intyas et al., 2022). The technologies of Society 5.0, such as robots and AI based on big data, are employed to replace or assist human labour, generating new value that transcends social, age, gender, and language disparities. Unlike the primarily business-focused Industrial Revolution 4.0, Society 5.0 aims to reconcile corporate and economic progress with the social environment (Megayanti et al., 2022).

The evolution of society shown in Figure 1 depicts how society moved from an industrial society in the 18th century to an information society in the latter half of the 20th century, and with rapid technological advancement, we will move towards a super-smart society (S5.0), a new era of the seamless integration of human society with advanced technology. (See Figure 13.1 in the Online Appendix link https://tinyurl.com/he50Appendices).

A critical aspect of Education 5.0 is the curriculum, a plan and arrangement regarding the objectives, content, learning materials and methods used as guidelines for organizing learning activities to achieve specific educational goals (Rapanta et al., 2020). The higher education curriculum, as one of the levels of education that plays a role in producing quality, relevant and competitive human resources, must be able to adapt and innovate according to the challenges and needs that exist in the Education 5.0 era (Darmaji et al., 2019).

In this context, it is important to consider the global and regional implications of technological transformation on society. This transformation encompasses changes in lifestyle, economy, interpersonal relationships, and culture on a global and regional scale. Additionally, Era 5.0 presents both challenges and opportunities for education. The challenges include the need for curriculum changes, innovative teaching methods, the development of 21st-century skills, and the integration of technology in the learning process. On the other hand, the opportunities offered by Era 5.0 lie in the potential to enhance the relevance of education to the demands of the time and produce quality graduates prepared for the evolving job market.

This study aims to explore the concept of educational transformation in Era 5.0, examine the innovation challenges faced by education in this era, and identify possibilities and strategies for addressing these challenges. This research will delve into important themes concerning the difficulties and possibilities of educational transformation in the 5.0 Era.

Key Themes in Education 5.0

Technology and academic institutions have been running in parallel for the transformation of education. Development of modern tools and techniques are also being updated in parallel for better education standards. Education 5.0 is the next generation of the previous four versions (Mustafa Kamal et al., 2019). All parties involved who could play a role in teaching such as teaching staff, students and administration, define the core of Education 5.0 as learning. Learning is connected to the learner, focused on the learner, demonstrated by the learner and driven by the learner (University Teknologi Mara, 2019). As such, the learner is seen as a whole person whose values, beliefs, knowledge and skills are not seen as separate fundamentals to be nurtured and trained. Dynamic technology surrounds the learner and provides options for the learner's core decisions of what, where, when, how, why and with whom to study (Melluso et al., 2020). Details are available in Figure 13.2 in the Online Appendix link https://tinyurl.com/he50Appendices.

Education 5.0 has the following key areas for implementation to obtain maximum benefits:

- Focused learning to become a professional;

- Improved and blended concept of personalized learning;
- Applying creative thinking for solving the problems;
- Developing value-based learning culture.

The following are the key pillars of Education 5.0 and their outcome:

Curriculum Innovation and 21st-Century Skill Development

University Education 5.0 requires substantial innovation in curricula to prioritize skills relevant to the 21st century. The integration of technology-oriented subjects, such as AI, data analytics, and digital literacy, is essential for preparing students for modern workplaces. Studies show that curriculum transformation is essential to incorporate 4IR technologies while fostering critical skills, including creativity, collaboration, problem-solving, and adaptability. Project-based learning, flexible course structures, and learner-centered approaches enhance students' engagement and competency development in a technology-mediated learning environment.

Adapting the Curriculum

One of the primary difficulties in the 5.0 era is adapting the curriculum to align with technological advancements and the evolving demands of the workplace. The curriculum needs to incorporate 21st-century skills such as problem-solving, collaboration, data literacy, and digital skills (Jang & Paulson, 2016). It is crucial to equip students with the competencies necessary for effective participation in 21st-century life (Rahayu, 2021). To achieve this, teachers need to adopt a learner-centered approach, promote collaboration, connect learning materials to real-world problems, and foster responsible citizenship (Devi et al., 2018). The curriculum should include subjects like information technology, the Internet of Things, big data, computerization, entrepreneurship, and internships to develop graduates with essential skills (Putriani & Hudaidah, 2021).

Developing 4C Abilities

The 4C abilities, namely communication, collaboration, critical thinking, and creativity, are crucial in the 5.0 era. Problem-solving forms the foundation of critical thinking, while creativity involves exploring novel methods of problem-solving, innovation, and invention. Collaboration refers to the ability to cooperate, synergize, and adapt with others to achieve common goals, and effective communication involves expressing and sharing thoughts, questions, ideas, and solutions (Anas & Mujahidin, 2022). These abilities are essential for success in Era 5.0, which emphasizes adaptability, good communication, teamwork, critical thought, and innovation. Education needs to employ creative and contextualized teaching strategies, such as group projects, practical assignments, and simulations, to develop these skills in students (Anas & Mujahidin, 2022). Moreover, education should prioritize the development of Higher Order Thinking Skills (HOTS) to enable complex and systematic thinking (Uyun et al., 2021). Character development, including attitudes towards collaboration and problem-solving, should also be emphasized to provide students with both hard and soft skills (Hashim, 2018).

Technological Integration and Adaptive Learning Environments

Technological integration is revolutionizing education in the 5.0 Era by leveraging advanced tools to create adaptive learning environments that cater to diverse learner needs. Virtual Reality (VR) immerses students in interactive simulations, enabling them to experience real-world scenarios and practical applications in a controlled setting. Artificial Intelligence (AI) enhances personalization by analysing individual learning patterns and offering tailored educational content, thereby fostering deeper engagement and understanding. Similarly, the Internet of Things (IoT) facilitates seamless connectivity between devices, providing dynamic, data-driven insights into student performance and behaviour.

Big data analytics plays a crucial role in refining these innovations by enabling institutions to analyse vast amounts of information. This allows educators to design curriculum strategies that align with various learning styles, ensuring no student is left behind. For instance, predictive analytics can identify at-risk students and suggest timely interventions to improve academic outcomes.

By integrating these technologies, universities can shift from traditional teaching models to more dynamic, student-centric approaches, enhancing the effectiveness of the learning process. According to a report by the World Economic Forum (2020), these advancements in educational technology significantly improve student engagement and retention, ensuring learners are better prepared for the demands of the modern workforce.

Interaction with Robots

In the era of Society 5.0, there is a possibility that students may interact directly with robots in the learning process, either as replacements for educators or under remote supervision (Megayanti et al., 2022). This paradigm shift in education requires educators to focus on the learning materials' purpose and empower students through motivation (Megayanti et al., 2022). The use of robots in education suggests that teaching and learning can occur anytime and anywhere, with or without a physical teacher present. In the age of information and communication technology, teachers need to evolve into learning managers alongside their role as instructors (Aspi & Syahrani, 2022).

Addressing Challenges in Transition to Education 5.0

The shift towards Education 5.0 presents a range of challenges that institutions must address to ensure effective implementation and equitable access. A major obstacle lies in the substantial investments required to develop and maintain digital infrastructure, such as high-speed internet, learning management systems, and advanced technological tools like Virtual Reality (VR) and Artificial Intelligence (AI). Faculty re-skilling is another critical area, as educators must be equipped with the knowledge and skills to integrate emerging technologies into teaching and learning processes effectively.

In developing countries, these challenges are magnified by limited financial resources, insufficient infrastructure, and unequal access to technology, further widening the education gap. Rapid technological evolution compounds these difficulties, as universities must regularly update curricula and policies to remain relevant and responsive to industry demands.

Collaborative partnerships among universities, industries, and governments are essential to overcoming these barriers. Such alliances can pool resources, provide funding, and share expertise to support the transition. For example, industry collaborations can offer practical training programs, while governments can create policies and incentives to promote digital equity in education. As highlighted by UNESCO (2021), fostering multi-stakeholder cooperation is crucial for ensuring inclusive, quality education in the 5.0 Era.

The Role of Universities in Sustainable Development and Social Responsibility

Society 5.0 aims to balance economic advancement with social well-being, and University Education 5.0 reflects this goal by embedding sustainability and social responsibility into educational practices. Through initiatives such as community-engaged projects and sustainability-focused research, universities can cultivate a sense of social responsibility in students. Adopting frameworks like the Quintuple Helix Model, which emphasizes partnerships across academia, industry, government, society, and the environment, universities can drive innovation that supports sustainable development goals (SDGs). This model fosters interdisciplinary collaboration, aligning university research and activities with societal needs and sustainability priorities.

Key Role of the Teacher in Education 5.0

This is also helping the teachers to improve their teaching methodologies aligned with the international standards and market requirements. Teacher's role has become an essential part of modern education; following are some of the key roles of teachers in Education 5.0:

• Resource Specialist: Teacher must fulfil the requirements of a resource specialist because modern education more relies on the source of knowledge instead of just knowledge. Therefore, it is the teacher's role to provide sources of information for the students and to help them to use that information.

• Support Person: Teacher will be playing a role of support person, instead of traditional way of delivering lecture etc. Students need support while learning new skillset of informative knowledge both technical and otherwise. A teacher's job is to facilitate the student whenever some information is needed like a coach, leader or a counsellor to help the student in learning and acquiring the knowledge in a specific subject.

• Mentor: In modern education, a teacher's role is more towards presenting himself as a mentor, having all capabilities of admiring a student, shape the student's behaviours; expand the required work ethics, provide leadership skills for their continuous growth in developing their personality as a true professional, which will influence the student to be more motivated towards learning. Students will always look for a role model instead of a traditional instructor.

• Learner: One of the very important roles of the teacher is to be open always as a learner because learning is a continuous and life-long process, this will add value to the teacher's personality and will help the students to learn better from the teacher.

Opportunities for Innovation and Sustainable Development in Education 5.0

The opportunities for educational change in Era 5.0 are immense. In the era of Technology 5.0, education has the chance to align itself with the demands of the modern world (Fricticarani et al., 2023). Cutting-edge technologies such as artificial intelligence, virtual reality, augmented reality, and the Internet of Things are integrated into learning, providing students with quick and easy access to information and personalized data recommendations. These advancements are expected to produce graduates with marketable skills (Munandar, 2019).

Moreover, Era 5.0 strongly emphasizes the value of collaboration between industries and educational institutions. This cooperation can take the form of internships, company visits, joint curriculum development, and project-based learning, fostering real-world problem-solving abilities. Society 5.0 offers diverse career opportunities based on information technology and artificial intelligence, which depend on individuals' soft and hard skills, creativity, abilities, and work attitudes. Educational institutions encourage technology use among faculty and students (Yunus, 2022).

Enhancing Student Competencies through Innovative Learning Approaches

The literature underscores the potential of University Education 5.0 to enhance student competencies by embracing innovative learning methodologies. Key opportunities include the expansion of project-based learning and experiential learning modules that promote critical thinking, creativity, and adaptability. By engaging students in practical, real-world challenges, universities not only improve skill development but also make education more relevant to societal and industry needs.

Fostering a Global Education Ecosystem through Collaboration and Digital Platforms

Education 5.0 emphasizes the creation of a global education ecosystem where collaboration and digital platforms play a central role in breaking traditional boundaries. Digital learning platforms enable institutions to share resources, teaching methodologies, and innovations across borders, providing students with access to diverse and high-quality learning materials. These platforms facilitate the exchange of best practices, allowing universities to learn from one another and adopt strategies that enhance educational outcomes.

Collaborative networks among universities, industries, and governments further strengthen this ecosystem. Through partnerships, institutions can co-develop courses, conduct joint research, and share expertise, ensuring that students acquire skills aligned with global industry standards. Open Educational Resources (OERs) are particularly impactful in addressing disparities, as they provide free and accessible learning materials to underserved communities, fostering inclusivity in Education 5.0.

By leveraging these opportunities, universities can build a more interconnected and equitable education system. A report by the OECD (2021) highlights that digital platforms and international collaboration significantly improve access to education, reduce costs, and promote lifelong learning opportunities worldwide, contributing to a more inclusive knowledge society.

Building a Digital and Sustainable University Model

Building a digital and sustainable university model is critical for fostering innovation while addressing global environmental challenges. A digital-first strategy enables universities to integrate advanced technologies like AI, IoT, and big data analytics into their operations and curricula, enhancing efficiency and providing tailored learning experiences. For instance, smart campus initiatives utilize IoT to optimize energy consumption, improve resource allocation, and enhance campus security.

Sustainability is equally essential, as universities play a pivotal role in modelling environmentally responsible practices. By investing in renewable energy systems, green building designs, and waste reduction programs, institutions can significantly lower their carbon footprints. Integrating sustainability into research and teaching further prepares students to address future environmental challenges, aligning with the principles of Society 5.0, which aims to balance technological advancements with social and ecological well-being.

Combining digital infrastructure with sustainable practices not only improves operational efficiency but also demonstrates a commitment to creating a better future. According to the International Association of Universities (IAU, 2021), universities that embrace sustainable and digital transformations are better equipped to lead societal change, ensuring education contributes to both technological progress and environmental stewardship.

Recommendations for Implementation in University Education 5.0

To transition effectively to University Education 5.0, the following strategies are recommended:

1. Curriculum Reform: Incorporate interdisciplinary subjects and adapt curricula to include technology-centered competencies. Regularly update curricula to stay aligned with industry trends and societal needs.

2. Investment in Digital Infrastructure: Prioritize the development of smart classrooms and digital laboratories, especially in under-resourced regions. Partnerships with industry and government can support funding for technological upgrades.

3. Faculty Development: Equip faculty with training programs focused on using educational technologies and fostering critical skills in students. Faculty members must be prepared to adopt new roles as mentors and facilitators in a technology-rich learning environment.

4. Collaborative Networks and Platforms: Promote collaboration among universities, industry, and government to share resources, knowledge, and

innovative practices. Digital platforms can connect students and faculty across borders, enhancing educational access and diversity.

5. Commitment to Sustainable Development Goals: Embed sustainability in curricula and research agendas, aligning educational objectives with broader societal goals. Universities should prioritize research that addresses critical global challenges, fostering a socially responsible and sustainable mindset among students.

6. Factors Influencing Curriculum Development: Several factors shape the development of innovative and adaptive higher education curricula:

a. Vision, Mission and Goals. Universities' strategic direction influences curriculum design, and precise alignment with Education 5.0 principles drives curriculum innovation.

b. World of Work and Society Demands. Curricula respond to industry needs, preparing graduates for real-world challenges. Societal expectations drive curriculum relevance and impact.

c. Science and Technology Advancements. Curricula adapt to technological shifts, integrating digital literacy and emerging fields. Science and technology developments inform curriculum content and methodologies.

d. Government Policies and Regulations. National policies guide curriculum development. Compliance with quality standards ensures accountability and credibility.

Discussion

University Education 5.0 offers a transformative framework for reimagining higher education by integrating technological innovation with human-centered values. This model aims to create an adaptable, inclusive, and socially responsible educational system that equips students to navigate a complex, digitally interconnected world. Through the integration of advanced technologies such as Artificial Intelligence (AI), the Internet of Things (IoT), and Virtual Reality (VR), combined with a focus on sustainability and human-centric approaches, Education 5.0 seeks to redefine the teaching-learning paradigm to meet the demands of the modern era.

One of the primary opportunities brought by Education 5.0 is the potential to enhance the learning experience through advanced technologies. For instance, AI-powered personalized learning platforms enable institutions to tailor educational content to individual students' needs, fostering better engagement and improved outcomes. Similarly, immersive VR simulations allow students to gain practical experience in controlled environments, making theoretical knowledge more applicable to real-world contexts. These technologies not only improve accessibility but also provide diverse learning resources that empower students globally.

Education 5.0 also emphasizes the promotion of 21st-century skills, including critical thinking, creativity, problem-solving, and digital literacy. These competencies are vital for preparing students to succeed in an evolving job market characterized by automation, artificial intelligence, and rapid technological advancements. By integrating these skills into curricula, universities ensure that graduates are equipped to address complex challenges.

Another opportunity lies in fostering stronger collaboration between academia and industry. Partnerships with industries can provide valuable insights into current market demands, enabling universities to design courses that align with workforce requirements. Such cooperation also facilitates internships, mentorship programs, and real-world project experiences, bridging the gap between academic learning and professional application. Moreover, Education 5.0 highlights the importance of sustainability, urging universities to adopt green technologies and promote environmentally responsible practices within their operations and curricula.

Despite these opportunities, the transition to Education 5.0 presents several challenges. Adapting curricula to incorporate emerging technologies is a complex task that requires continuous updates and significant financial investment. Institutions must regularly revise their programs to remain relevant in a rapidly changing technological landscape. This demands collaboration among educators, policymakers, and technologists to ensure effective implementation.

Another significant challenge is the digital divide. While advanced digital tools offer immense potential, disparities in access to technology can hinder equitable adoption. In many developing countries, limited infrastructure, lack of funding, and unequal distribution of resources exacerbate this issue, leaving some students without access to the benefits of Education 5.0. Bridging this divide requires targeted investments in digital infrastructure, affordable internet access, and comprehensive policies to ensure inclusiveness.

Faculty readiness is another crucial factor. Transitioning to Education 5.0 requires educators to be proficient in digital literacy and innovative teaching methodologies. Reskilling and upskilling faculty members demand time, resources, and effective training programs. Institutions must invest in professional development initiatives to ensure that educators are prepared to integrate technology effectively into their teaching practices.

To successfully navigate the transition to Education 5.0, educational institutions must adopt proactive strategies. Prioritizing the development of 21st-century skills in students is paramount. Universities should embed these competencies into their curricula through project-based learning, interdisciplinary courses, and experiential learning opportunities. Hybrid learning models that combine online and in-person instruction can further enhance flexibility and accessibility, catering to diverse learner needs.

Equipping educators with the necessary digital skills is equally critical. Comprehensive training programs, workshops, and peer mentoring can empower faculty to embrace technological innovations confidently. Furthermore, institutions should establish collaborative networks with industry partners, governments, and other universities to share resources, expertise, and best practices.

Addressing the digital divide is essential for fostering inclusivity. Governments and institutions should prioritize investments in digital infrastructure, particularly in underserved regions, to ensure equitable access to technology. Open Educational Resources (OERs) can also play a vital role by providing free, high-quality educational materials to learners worldwide.

While Education 5.0 provides a promising framework, further research is needed to explore its full potential. Conceptual studies, such as the one discussed here, lay the groundwork for understanding the key challenges and opportunities. However, expanding this research into quantitative and qualitative studies can provide deeper insights into the practical implementation and outcomes of Education 5.0. For example, longitudinal studies could assess the long-term impact of AI-driven personalized learning on student performance, while case studies could explore successful models of industry-university collaboration.

Recommendations

The researchers propose the following recommendations to enhance the quality and adaptability of universities in the Education 5.0 era:

Innovating and developing curricula suitable for Education 5.0

Universities must continue to innovate and adapt their curricula to meet not only the quality standards set by governments, industries, and society but also the challenges and opportunities brought by Education 5.0. This involves incorporating advanced technologies into educational programs, fostering creativity, and encouraging critical thinking among students. Additionally, universities should provide students with tools to adapt to the rapidly changing societal and labour market demands.

Strengthening collaboration with stakeholders

Universities need to establish and maintain strong partnerships with industries, governments, and communities. Through such collaborations, educational programs can be tailored to align with the demands of the workforce and societal needs. Furthermore, universities should contribute to economic, cultural, and social development through research projects, technology transfer, and community service.

Enhancing the quality and capacity of lecturers

The role of lecturers is pivotal to the success of educational programs. Therefore, universities must focus on improving the quality and capacity of their teaching staff through professional development, soft skills training, and innovative teaching methodologies. Lecturers should act not only as knowledge providers but also as facilitators, motivators, and lifelong learners who inspire students to excel in academic, research, community service, and personal development.

Implementing continuous evaluation and accreditation

To ensure the quality, relevance, and impact of educational programs, universities must carry out continuous evaluation and accreditation processes, both internally and externally. Employing reliable, valid, and accurate assessment tools will enable institutions to identify areas requiring improvement and implement necessary adjustments to meet societal and labor market expectations effectively.

Conclusion

In conclusion, Education 5.0 represents a paradigm shift in higher education, blending technological innovation with human-centered values to create a more relevant, engaging, and effective learning environment. By addressing challenges such as curriculum adaptation, the digital divide, and faculty readiness, and by seizing opportunities through advanced technologies, industry collaboration, and sustainability, educational institutions can prepare students to thrive in a digitally interconnected world. As Education 5.0 continues to evolve, ongoing research and innovation will be crucial for realizing its transformative potential, shaping a competent and adaptable workforce, and advancing sustainable development in an intelligent society.

14

Virtual Personal Space: Leveraging Virtual Reality/Augmented Reality for Stress Relieving and Mindfulness Practice within Higher Education in Vietnam[29]

Bao Gia Truong, Khoi Hoang Truong[30], Trang Quynh Kong Nguyen and Duc Hong Thi Phan

Abstract

Virtual Personal Space (VPS) is a personal cyberspace where people can express themselves freely. Observing students at present, their VPS has been occupied by pressures from the excessive academic achievement rivalry. Educational stressors are rising but remaining unsolvable in the digital era, leading to several negative student impacts. Due to the thriving of Virtual Reality/Augmented Reality technologies, the researchers wonder how these technical alternatives can be applied to address the problem. An interview has been conducted with 19 student-aged participants, and two practitioners to gain a qualitative dataset. Besides, an online survey reaching up to 402 valuable samples nationwide provided a quantitative dataset for comparison and supplement. We found that students avoid sharing feelings from the barrier of intrapersonal issues such as insecurity, shyness, or the fear of being judged. Even though these youngsters are often assumed as "digital natives", the result revealed that

---

[29] All references, tables, figures, author affiliation and biography used in this chapter are available on the Online Appendix link at https://tinyurl.com/he50Appendices.

[30] Corresponding author: truonghoangkhoi.work@gmail.com

they still struggle with communicating and prefer interacting with non-human assistants than sharing with human-being strangers. Moreover, personalization and the feeling of being attracted by the product's displays are two key factors engaging students to use app-based mindfulness and mental healthcare. The outlook and recommendations are given for improvements and developments shortly since the Vietnamese process of intelligent cities is promoted. The chapter discovers hurdles within applying AR/VR for practicing mindfulness and relieving stressors in the Vietnamese higher education environment which is plausible to accelerate the progress of tech-applied education access for students. It aligns with Vietnam's endeavours to fulfill the SDGs by raising awareness about mental healthcare for educational workers and students.

Introduction

Virtual Personal Space (VPS) has been increasingly developed and applied in multiple sectors, including education. Entering the 1990s, when cyberspace surged, the space promptly transferred from physical to virtual experience (Strate, 1999). Until the early 2000s, thriving virtual reality (VR) and augmented reality (AR) marked a new chapter for Virtual Personal Space (VPS), evolving up to the mainstreaming applied in a diversity of industries in the last two decades (Kruse et al., 2013). Many VR/AR applications are implemented broadly in classrooms for teaching and learning, explored in many studies such as the current study of Han and Bailenson (2024). Within higher education (HE) environments prone to stressors, these technologies support individuals in mental health management (Singh, 2024).

Stress and mindfulness are correlated and increasingly popular in the educational environment. As regards stress, the term "stress" is ubiquitous and indiscriminately labelled for any sort of mental issue regardless of the earliest attempt in the 1950s until now to understand and conceptualize it (Robotham & Julian, 2006). Under the societal pressure of "study hard to get a well-paid job", characterized in Asia-rooted cultures, the stress in learning has risen as a detrimental cause leading to mental degradation and emotional deficit of students (Robotham & Julian, 2006). Even though some researchers appreciate in-moderation pressures as a motivational stimulus for determination and persistence (Ji et al., 2024), solutions to help students cope with stressors remain. Several scholars have proposed the idea of using mindfulness in the educational environment (Mettler et al., 2024). In particular, mindfulness has become popular and professionally appreciated in business throughout the 2000s when many giants adopted this practice to ensure employees' well-being (Butterfield et al., 2000). This concept expanded into other aspects of human life from the 2010s to the present, especially harnessing its potential in education (Yosep et al., 2024). This practice fosters and protects the cognitive and emotional competencies of students from risks of social and educational actors (Diamond, 2024). Young generations increasingly enjoy immersive experiences, as demonstrated by the widespread popularity of role-playing games, particularly those based on VR/AR technology. This trend suggests that applying VR/AR to mindfulness and stress-relief practices for students holds significant potential and promise. At a glance VR (Virtual Reality): Replaces your world. It puts you in a completely different, digital environment. AR (Augmented Reality): Adds to your world. It overlays digital information onto your real-world view.

However, VR/AR applications for educational purposes face a considerable number of hurdles. In Vietnam, the barriers to facilitation and societal acceptance towards applying VR/AR-based products in education-wise situations are quite genuine but not decisive factors in implementation (Le et al., 2024). The result contributes to the literature repository relating to not only stressors in learning in general but also relieving stressors ensued from HE environments through virtual personal space. As regards the combination of mindfulness practices and VR/AR to create a VPS for relieving educational stressors, this chapter seeks to answer the two questions:

(1) How can educational practices adopt VR/AR to manage the mental status and stress extent of students through virtual mindfulness?

(2) What are the challenges in its implementation as well as recommendations for improving mental healthcare within the HE environment in the near future?

This chapter will explore hurdles when applying AR/VR for practicing mindfulness and relieving stressors in the Vietnamese HE environment which is plausible to accelerate the progress of tech-applied education access for students. Based on the UN sustainable development goals

(SDG) of Good Health and Well-being, the findings also raise awareness among educators and students about mental healthcare.

VR/AR application to create VPS in the educational environment

Due to the accelerating spread of applied technologies, VR/AR has become popular and potentially utilized for educational purposes. In Vietnam, the barrier to VR/AR implementation in the Vietnamese school system is the cost besides human interaction, infrastructure, and technical issues (Le et al., 2024). Nevertheless, Le et al. (2024) also pinpointed that it is paramount for VR/AR appliers in the educational environment to overcome those obstacles. The inconvenient lockdown-rooted restriction during Covid-19 pandemic has proven Vietnamese adaptability from both teachers and students towards technologies when dealing with the pressures of keeping everything on track regardless of stressors (Pham & Ho, 2020). However, youngsters seem to scuffle with the consequences of being over-active in the digital world. Young people reportedly have better skills on social media or VPS than in real life; yet these "digital natives" - a term mentioned in the 2010 study of Bennett and Maton, are vulnerable to mental issues which are reactions during the process of emotion regulation. They perceptually underestimate their own competencies and self-values by focusing on social media comparisons for unreal values which leads to a penury in proper self-awareness (London et al., 2023). It genuinely reflects the fact that young generations are struggling with bad self-awareness besides emotion regulation. Resolutions must be explored to support these new generations to cope with mental issues through a more digital and personal method.

VPS, through app-based products, is a proper solution that is interestingly adaptable and friendly towards students. Adolescents appreciate experiencing app-based mindfulness because they are empowered to personalize and retrench the external control as much as possible (Webb et al., 2022). VR/AR-induced relaxation simulates serene personal space which mitigates cortisol levels and maintains physiological calm, integrating biofeedback and real-time adjustments (Wieczorek et al., 2024). Seizing the trend of virtual interactions on VPS, several app-based mindfulness suppliers appeared where users can customize their courses and experiences during mental healing. For example, HeadSpace based in the USA, delivers online-accessible guided meditations and other relevant mental healthcare products that attract millions of global users. A study by Flett et al. (2019) on a group of 208 university students has proved the effectiveness of HeadSpace in mindfulness. Hence, the potential for app-based mindfulness within VPS to integrate and penetrate educational practices becomes accentuated.

Data collection

A mixed method approach was used in this study and divided into two phases yet simultaneously implemented - the interview (qualitative) and the online survey (quantitative). The survey process lasted longer than the interview phase to cover a large number of samples up to 440 samples yet remaining only 402 after eliminating improper responses (from May 5 to August 12, 2024) (see Table 14.1 in the Online Appendix link https://tinyurl.com/he50Appendices); the interview covered up to 19 samples from students from the age of 17 to 23 (from May 24 to June 24, 2024), and used Vietnamese for better linguistic expression and explanation within the communication. In particular, there are two segments of the interview: (1) student-aged interviewees are divided into two categories as low concept awareness (LCA), and high concept awareness (HCA) (see Table 14.2 in the Online Appendix link https://tinyurl.com/he50Appendices), (2) psychology-wise practitioner interviewees, including one expert working in the domestic environment, and one psychologists working in the foreign environment (Canada) who also works as a community worker (see Table 14.3 in the Online Appendix link https://tinyurl.com/he50Appendices).

Interview results

Observing the result from the 19 individuals interviewed, 2 common problems were found: (1) LCA and HCA are exposed to stressors ensuing from overload or pressure at school or the loss of life balance, and (2) they are both shy to share feelings, even with those close to them. However, there are many differences between LCA and HCA. Basically, perceptions promote thinking, leading to actual decisions and actions. Therefore, the reaction of LCA and HCA when coping with stressors is distinguishable.

Educational stressors from student's common problems

All interviewees provided similar answers when interviewers asked about facing stressors recently: they do struggle with stress. However, LCAs feel stressed and overloaded because their expectations in major or study results are not fulfilled and their life balance is eroding; meanwhile, some HCAs admitted that their mental health has deteriorated due to external pressure yet still manage to overcome and create a life balance. For instance, interviewees have responded:

"I study at school and have a part-time job at the same time… recently, I have struggled with work-life balance… I still cannot find something proper to do for relaxing… I tend to let it happen, keep and manage it by myself instead of sharing… I also heard from my teacher that lots of students are stressed when they are forced by their parents to study too much even until midnight…" [LA6]

"There are many things to learn at school which made me so stressed out… I don't usually share my personal issues, but I used to write a diary or just reduce my workload to give me time for relaxing…" [HA2]

As a matter of fact, HCAs also struggle with educational stressors as LCAs do; nevertheless, they choose to get used to those inconveniences. Unlike HCAs, LCAs persist in figuring out a way to escape mental issues yet unintentionally capture them in a cage of resolutions. Here is an answer from an LCA because he admitted to not knowing too much about mental health, yet the process of his thoughts potentially transferred him to the HCA segment since he recognized mental health is not about forcing yourself to be "on-display happy".

"At first, I was so stressed out when I was a freshman… I was tired and bored of studying because I couldn't understand too much and the workload was horrible at that time… yet I guess I'm getting used to it now… I am able to balance my life… even though I am not really into sharing personal issues, especially on social media, I sometimes tell my close friends to release the emotional burden… I guess we should ask for help from people around us such as mentors specializing in mental health (psychologists) in universities or even in the dormitory, making an appointment with therapists, or just getting motivated by KOLs on social media who are spreading meaningful messages about taking care of mental health…" [LA5]

The status of "follow-the-flow" from LA5 does not resemble LA6's. LA5 strived to address educational stressors at first and soon dealt with disappointment when he felt bored of continuing to confront. He then chose to halt and familiarize himself with the study life at the university which helped him adapt to the environment. Whereas LA6 simply surrendered to the situation which led her to the feeling of being bewildered.

Barriers for students to address stressors

What makes Vietnamese students shy of sharing or accepting that they are mentally stressed? After analysing the result, the researchers explore that youngsters are so sensitive and confidential with their personal issues. Remarkably, regardless of Vietnamese collective culture, some cases show that the more intimate people are, the more young generations choose to keep secrets from them. Although HA8 knew about mental healthcare and stressors, she confessed that sharing with family is still something awkward and strange to her. It also derives from the external environment. People often share their problems when they have overcome them as empirical learnings instead of sharing while they are enduring to ask for help or empathy:

"I don't usually share my personal issues with my family; I am used to bearing them alone... sometimes with friends... mostly just smiling at myself... people around me usually share their stories as an experience when they have already overcome them... not spreading the negative feelings..." [HA8]

The researchers realize that there are two main hurdles for students to share and ask for help to deal with educational stressors. Firstly, external actors considerably manipulate the perception of students. Confucianism prejudiced boys to be mentally strong, thus male students are too shy to speak out about their issues while studying. Especially, the respect of hierarchy contributes to the generation distance which emphasizes the neglection from students when mentioning sharing with parents. Some Asia-rooted cultures, including Vietnam, obsessively appreciate scholarly achievements, leading to the normalization of educational stressors which is gradually destroying the young generations (Lueck & Wilson, 2010). LA6 shared the same story mentioned above that Vietnamese parents force their children to study excessively hard just for achievements that could satisfy their parental ego. Secondly, the intrapersonal issues hampered young people's ability to cope with educational stressors. HA8 is the epitome of inner problems holding back actions. She does not share with family members because she feels uncomfortable and strange; she does not share with friends or acquaintances while problems are occurring yet only when they end because she wants to follow the concept of sharing with people she has met. Frankly, it consumes a huge amount of time and effort for her to deal with educational stressors alone.

Findings within the practitioner interview

In this section, we summarized and classified the inputs of two interviewed practitioners. The researchers divided information into four segments: (1) add-in features enhancing user's experience, (2) interference features to manage behavioural and attitudinal issues amid the community, (3) developing an ecosystem to foster communication interactions, (4) potentials for applying VR/AR (metaverse). These inputs are used to discuss the improvements and outlook of leveraging VR/AR for stress relieving and mindfulness practices in learning. See Table 14.4 in the Online Appendix link https://tinyurl.com/he50Appendices.

Survey results

Table 14.5 Student's assessment based on reactions towards app-based mindfulness product's features and using experience (relating to the 1-to-5 scale, data is re-grouped: blank answers, 1 and 2 are counted as "negative response; 3 is counted as "neutral response"; 4 and 5 are counted as "positive response")

Based on descriptive statistics analysed and tabulated (See Table 14.5 in the Online Appendix link https://tinyurl.com/he50Appendices), the researchers identified that Vietnamese students most prefer an app-based mindfulness product to have (1a) features for personalization, which bolsters the feeling of intimacy and comfort while experiencing ($M = 2.746606$; $SD = 0.521405$), (2a) an online/virtual mental coaching zone where they can access mental services conveniently and privately ($M = 2.737557$; $S = 0.559132$), (3a) a virtual assistant to communicate and mentor them implementing mental practices (M = 2.606335; SD = 0.656267). Moreover, these students also appreciated having (4a) an online/virtual zone for stress relief (M = 2.574661; SD = 0.680969) rather than having (5a) a zone for practicing mindfulness and yoga (M = 2.572687; SD = 0.696231). It reflects the tendency in online/virtual practices with personalization among Vietnamese students, which can be explained by the exposure to technologies gradually popularized nowadays. On the contrary, most respondents refused to (6a) talk with anonymous strangers within an online/virtual zone (M = 2.511312; SD = 0.736150). It means youngsters embrace several mental barriers in sharing feelings. It is essential for students to have good reactions while experiencing app-based mindfulness products. Most respondents want (1b) the FOA, which means they commonly appeal to attractive appearances (M = 2.755656; SD = 0.508140). Regardless of the lowest response on (4b) the FOP (M = 2.515837; SD = 0.684884), surveyed students answered a remarkable extent of preference or (2b) the FOB (M = 2.529412; SD = 0.671020).

Discussion

Seeking the answer to the first question "How can educational practices adopt VR/AR to manage the mental status and stress extent of students through virtual mindfulness?" and a part of the second question "What are the benefits and challenges of the implementation...?", this study has discovered insights of Vietnamese students in dealing with educational stressors as well as their reactions and preferences towards app-based mindfulness products. In general, we discuss (1) barriers for students to address educational stressors, and (2) actors promoting students to adopt VPS through app-based mindfulness products integrated with VR/AR to their mental healthcare sections.

Intrapersonal challenges for students to address educational stressors

Understanding the answer of interviewee HA8, the researchers explored that she does not share because she does not want to regardless of her parents' encouragement. It is a sort of personal characteristic-based reaction towards "situational catalysts". HA8 has mentioned:

"I think it roots from my personal perspective… I have a weird perspective… my parents always encourage me to hang out with friends, but I'd rather do it alone like go for a walk… I'd like to enjoy the feelings alone…" [HA8]

We found that these personal issues are called "intrapersonal barriers". The term "intrapersonal" was then defined as "communication within the self, and of the self to the self…" by Graeme and Dimbleby (2006) mentioned in the study of Deveci & Nunn (2018). When the inner voice warns about something based on empirical and perceptual actors, people tend to avoid reacting or practicing. This relates to the quantitative result in the lowest ratio of response (see Table 14.6 available in the Online Appendix link https://tinyurl.com/he50Appendices) upon (6a) having a zone to talk with anonymous strangers which aligns with a part of the qualitative result indicating that youngsters embrace several mental barriers in sharing feelings. However, they do appreciate whether app suppliers deliver a (3a) virtual assistant to communicate with them. It is unusual that students would rather talk to virtual subjects than interact with real-life people. In other words, Vietnamese students are demanding a VPS where they can escape from reality and interpersonal communication which displays the differences between the two app-based mindfulness features (See Table 3 in the Online Appendix link https://tinyurl.com/he50Appendices).

As regards societal and culture-rooted judgments, students assume themselves to be ashamed when sharing their feelings. Consequently, they prefer talking with an unreal subject in their tailored VPS who does not judge or taunt them for being "beyond the social norms". The self-restriction in the sharing of young people can lead to negative thoughts and decisions, not only bound to educational stressors but also transferred to lethal issues. Parents are sometimes the main reason for the mental closure and sensitivity of students, such as the sharing of LA6:

"I also heard from my teacher that lots of students are stressed when they are forced by their parents to study too much even until midnight… one student wants to communicate with parents but they are too busy to talk together and prefer taking a rest after work… pressures from study and the parental inattention has led the student to the suicidal decision…" [LA6]

It is paramount for us to take action to help young generations escape from inner insecurities and shyness when sharing feelings. This is the most common and historical method for releasing bad emotions. Educational stressors these days come from not only academic achievement rivalry but also interpersonal (communicating with friends, school bullying, or isolation) and intrapersonal (self-awareness, self-esteem, or extent of being open-minded in sharing personal issues) dilemmas. Educators and educational workers must pay attention to this rising but unsolvable aspect, applying technologies to facilitate the process.

Actors affecting students to apply VR/AR-based or app-based mindfulness

As regards technology, students demand several sorts of feelings when experiencing VPS with certain VR/AR-applied features. Noticeably, (4b) the FOP ranked the lowest tier of student preference; it reflects that Vietnamese youngsters pay less attention to privacy policies. In contrast, (2b) the FOB recorded a high ratio of response which conflicts with the result of privacy. This can be explained by the status quo of Vietnamese privacy ignorance upon non-rigidly regulatory and socially perceptual facets. Vietnamese concerned less about privacy and confidentiality while experiencing VPS despite numerous cases of bank card fraud and phone-based scams from 2010 to 2018 analysed in the study by Nguyen and Luong (2021). The comparison between (2b) and (4b) implies a phenomenon: Vietnamese, including students, exude complete trust in VPS suppliers about privacy policies, otherwise, it simply derives from the ignorance of this aspect of digital habituation. This could facilitate the application of VR/AR-based mindfulness in VPS among educational environments, yet endangering student's digital safety of personal information and interest.

Another actor is (1b) the FOA which is outstanding compared to others (see Table 3 available in the Online Appendix link https://tinyurl.com/he50Appendices). In addition, the (1b) result aligns with the (1a) personalization preference from students ranked at the first tier of each segment. It proves that young people care a lot about the app displays, even demanding customization to suffice visual requirements for their VPS. The findings accentuate the DE's input to (DE1) implement customizations (see Table 2 available in the Online Appendicies link https://tinyurl.com/he50Appendices). This aligns with findings from the study of Webb et al. (2022), indicating that adolescents while experiencing app-based mindfulness respond to a higher extent of rumination reductions only when they are allowed to personalize and under no external control. If criteria of (1a) and (DE1) are met, VR/AR-based mindfulness products potentially enhance customer experience by upgrading (3b) the FOH while experiencing VPS. However, empowering users to create what they prefer could face several managerial shortfalls, especially for students who are incompletely developed in emotional and mental status. In particular, both DE and FE are concerned about this aspect demonstrated by suggestions for (DE2) a community code of conduct and (FE2) moderate interferences to address student's behavioural and attitudinal incurrences on VPS. As such, the HE environment requires improvements in time for urgent student mental healthcare.

Recommendations for Future Improvements

Processing the rest of the second question "What are... the outlook and recommendations?", the answers are proposed based on the combination of qualitative analysis from student and expert interviews together with the quantitative analysis from the survey. Firstly, students reportedly prefer app-based mindfulness within VPS to have (1a) personalization and (2a) mental coaching virtual zone applied in VR/AR-based or app-based mindfulness products; educators, thus, should focus on mining and developing these two features. Besides, according to the practitioner's inputs of (FE1) providing templates or tutorial materials to facilitate the user's adoption, the method should integrate with (3a) virtual assistants to accompany students throughout the mental healthcare journey in their own VPS. These practices are expected to attract and engage students into understanding the concept and benefits of mental healthcare as well as leveraging VR/AR in implementations as they enjoy digital and virtual interactions. As regards technological support, VR/AR applications require sufficient competencies within operational individuals. Although students pay less attention to (4b) the FOP, app-based mindfulness suppliers must strive to bolster VPS privacy and security to prevent users from information leaks. Both DE and FE agreed to have experts or seasoned practitioners specializing in psychology and technology, joining the development process, as mentioned in (DE4) and (FE4) (see Table 2 in the Online Appendicies link https://tinyurl.com/he50Appendices). Vu and Hartley (2018) stated: "Vietnam has made strong policy efforts to embrace ICT and SCD in pursuing development...", in which ICT stands for Information Communication and Technology, and SCD stands for Smart City Development. Technologies soon penetrated broadly into Vietnamese citizens' lives, and favourably applied in schools, colleges, and universities. It fosters the implementation of VR/AR-based mindfulness and mental healthcare practices in VPS within educational environments targeting students.

Conclusion

In short, this study has sought to address two research questions posed at the beginning. Educational stressors derive from environmental and intrapersonal barriers indicated and discussed by the researchers. Adjacently, students prefer personalization and online mental coaching features of VR/AR-based mindfulness and mental healthcare applied in VPS which is attached with virtual assistants to enhance the interactivity. As regards engaging students in using this technological method of mental healthcare, the result suggests prioritizing delivering the FOA which means the focus on UX/UI experiences and displays, together with the FOH. Due to the positive trend of smart cities in Vietnam and the exposure of students towards digital habituations, VR/AR technologies are designed to achieve educational integration. However, it is important to gather well-trained and seasoned practitioners in psychology and technology to improve and develop VR/AR-based mindfulness and mental healthcare applications for VPS in not only the educational sector but also other fields. These practices are expected to promote tech-applied education to be accessible to Vietnamese students as well as raise the awareness of educators and students about mental healthcare as a part of SDG goal of Good Health and Well-Being.

15

Tech-Savvy from the Get-Go: Enhancing University Teachers' Digital Competence (TDC) in Higher Education 5.0[31]

Phan Thi Anh Nga[32], Bui Van Hong and Nguyen Quang Giao

Abstract

The chapter delves into the pivotal role of digital competence in the transformation of higher education within the context of the emerging era of Higher Education 5.0. As universities increasingly adopt advanced technologies to foster personalized, collaborative, and innovative learning environments, the need for educators to develop robust digital skills becomes paramount. The objectives of this study are threefold: Firstly, it provides an overview of the various ways in which digital competence has been and continues to be employed to enhance teaching and learning activities both globally and within the present context of Vietnam's tertiary education. Secondly, this study examines the core components of digital competence for university teachers, including technological proficiency, pedagogical innovation, data literacy, AI competency and ethical considerations. It provides practical strategies and frameworks to support educators in enhancing their digital capabilities, ensuring they are well-prepared to navigate the challenges of the digital age. The study concludes with a comprehensive set of recommendations, useful suggestions, and inspiring constructive ideas on enhancing the Digital Competence of Vietnamese University Teachers in the Age of Digital Transformation.

---

31 All references, tables, figures, author affiliation and biography used in this chapter are available on the Online Appendix link at https://tinyurl.com/he50Appendices.

32 Corresponding author: ngapta@huflit.edu.vn

Introduction

The United Nations Educational, Scientific and Cultural Organization (UNESCO) anticipates that information and communication technology (ICT) will fundamentally alter the educational system in the 21st century. The Fourth Industrial Revolution (Industry 4.0) with its characteristics like robotics, the Internet of Things, Big Data, 3D printing, and Artificial Intelligence is impacting and shaping the future of education, especially higher education. Education needs to transform to seize opportunities and mitigate challenges, creating Education 5.0 (E5.0). There is a prevalent notion that the field of education is perpetually on the cusp of a transformative "revolution" driven by emerging technologies. In 1922, Thomas Edison predicted that television would predominantly supplant textbooks. Benjamin Darrow believed that radio would significantly challenge the traditional role of educators in 1932. In 1984, Seymour Papert anticipated that the computer would emerge as the primary instructional device. In 2019, the COVID-19 pandemic, also designated as the Great Online Transition, was perceived as a catalyst for a substantial shift towards digital modalities in teaching and learning. Presently, there is an ongoing reevaluation of education within the context of Artificial Intelligence. Although these predictions of radical and widespread changes in education have not yet come to fruition, it is evident that teaching and learning have evolved considerably and have embraced new technologies. These modifications are influenced by various social, strategic, human resource, and technological factors. Education needs to move from a "for employment" model to a "for entrepreneurship" model. Universities should focus on training skills, nurturing talent, and developing a vision for learners, rather than simply providing rigid curriculum-based knowledge.

Digital competence has become increasingly important in education due to the growing use of technology and the importance of efficient and appropriate use of ICT for professional development. In Spain, the National Plan of Digital Competences (MINECO, 2021) aims to promote sustainable and inclusive economic growth by identifying the acquisition of Teachers Digital Competencies (TDC) at all educational levels, including universities. Teachers play a crucial role in integrating technologies and implementing ICT in the classroom, as the transformation and improvement of education depends on educational action. Thus, it is imperative for educators to possess proficient digital competencies that enable them to effectively integrate and utilize technologies in a pedagogical manner, thereby safeguarding the future of society.

In Vietnam, digital transformation is an inevitable development trend, bringing both opportunities and challenges. It has a strong impact on all levels, sectors, fields, economic and social life, national security and defense. Digital transformation in higher education is being vigorously implemented in accordance with the National Digital Transformation Program by 2025, with an emphasis on 2030, as stipulated in Decision No. 749/QD-TTg dated June 3, 2020 of the Prime Minister and Decision No. 131/QD-TTg dated January 25, 2022, approving the Project to Enhance the Application of Information Technology and Digital Transformation in Education and Training for the period 2022-2025, with an emphasis on 2030. The implementation process of the program has clearly identified the requirements for digital transformation in higher education, including the requirement for developing the digital competence of teachers at universities in Vietnam at present.

Universities have had to shift away from mostly in-person to full-time online instruction, and both facilitators and students have experienced both advantages and disadvantages with different types of online instruction and support. However, even after the end of the coronavirus epidemic, higher education will continue to require instructional innovation that leverages technology. Hence, what competencies are necessary for higher education lecturers to achieve the necessary innovation employing IT? Although there has been extensive research on digital competencies for instructors across a range of industries, there has not yet been a comprehensive list of the competencies needed to use IT to accomplish innovative teaching techniques in higher education. According to research conducted by Rodrguez-Abitia and Bribiesca-Correa in the year 2021, it has been observed that digital competence at universities is lagging behind other fields due to ineffective leadership, limitations in culture, innovation, and financial support. Researchers have employed several models to assess stakeholders' digital competence, focusing on the most basic skills for practical application in learning, working, and daily communication (Nguyen & Marquet, 2018).

Digital Competence

Digital competency is a new concept that has been used in recent years and is closely related to the concepts of information technology and communication competency in the context of digitalization. According to Griffin et al. (2012), digital competence pertains to an individual's capacity to live, learn, and work in a digital society. It encompasses competencies for online information retrieval, problem-solving, sharing, and collaboration. It is a systematic process for developing capabilities in the modern world while ensuring information security. Although there are certain differences in the way it is defined, "digital competency" can be understood as: "The ability to access, manage, understand, integrate, communicate, evaluate and create information safely and rationally through digital technologies in order to serve learning, research, entertainment, and other professional work purposes. The necessary digital proficiency is closely linked to computer skills, information technology skills, digital information skills and media skills" (UNESCO, 2018). Particularly, the EU defines "digital competence" as: "the safe, critical and responsible use of and interaction with digital technologies for learning, at work and for participation in society. It includes information and data literacy, communication and collaboration, media literacy, digital content creation (including programming), security (including digital well-being and cybersecurity-related skills), intellectual property issues, problem-solving and critical thinking" (Council of the European Union, 2018, p. 9).

Research on digital competence in specific scientific fields faces limitations due to a lack of consensus (Varga-Atkins, 2020). Some perspectives view it as technical (Hinrichsen & Coombs, 2013), while others view it as a combination of scientific, social, and cultural practices with higher knowledge, creativity, and innovation (McDougall et al., 2018). Many studies have established, utilized, evaluated, and adjusted digital competence frameworks suitable for research contexts (Basantes-Andrade, et al., 2022). One study found that digital competence development is dependent on age, with younger individuals possessing higher technological knowledge levels (Basantes-Andrade, et al., 2020). To effectively develop digital competence, IT training courses should be designed to match the content and level of participants.

Digital literacy or digital competence?

Gilster (1997) introduced the term "digital literacy," defining it as the ability to access, manage, and modify digital information. The concept has expanded with technological advancements, intertwining with terms like information literacy, computer literacy, and media literacy. In teacher education, digital literacy traditionally emphasized technical skills, but these approaches have faced criticism for being narrow and contextually inadequate. Digital literacy and digital competence are interconnected but distinct. Digital literacy is prevalent in English-speaking contexts, while digital competence is more commonly discussed in European studies (Spante et al., 2018). Digital competence focuses on societal skills (Ilomäki & Lakkala, 2018) and includes UNESCO's three-level framework: digital literacy as a foundation, deepened knowledge for interdisciplinary learning, and effective knowledge management for innovation. Teachers' and students' digital literacy supports effective technology use, requiring knowledge of ethical and societal ICT implications. Recent studies advocate for broadening teacher education to include socio-cultural aspects, legal and ethical knowledge, and attitudinal elements (Esteve-Mon et al., 2020). Reviews of digital competence and literacy reveal diverse approaches but highlight challenges in fully understanding their implications in higher education (Marta-Lazo et al., 2020). This underscores the need to integrate technical, dispositional, and critical perspectives on digital technologies.

Artificial Intelligence (AI) Competence

This article seeks to achieve this by exploring the competencies that are enhanced through the effective use of AI across various fields, particularly in education. It is clear that as AI develops, the associated competence frameworks must necessarily change so that teachers (and students) have the skills they need for the environment in which they will exist. This, from the wider dimension of education, Faruqe et al. (2022) by introducing a competency model that goes beyond understanding (nonprofessional knowledge) towards a multi-layered framework that extends to multi-stakeholder assessments (e.g., consumers, collaborators). A critical model, for instance, for creating course content that equips people for work in an AI future. Ng et al. (2023) strengthen this by emphasizing how important it is for teachers to have digital competencies when integrating AI into their teaching, creating an environment for AI learning. Additionally, the impact of AI in recruitment processes, as noted by Vivek (2023), provides insight that AI can improve inclusion and minimize bias, yet a balanced approach using both technological advancements and human oversight will be more effective. This is consistent with the prescription by Aghaziarati and Darbani (2023) for a workforce that is technologically literate and socially responsible. The rise of AI across diverse sectors, especially education, demands a strong competency-based framework that integrates technicality with ethicality. With the ongoing impact of AI on work and education, it is critical for educational institutions across the world to prioritize AI literacy and prepare students and educators for the challenges of living in an AI-enhanced world.

The Teachers' Digital Competence (TDC)

Digital technologies are transforming education, necessitating teachers' digital competence to integrate technology effectively into classrooms and enhance students' digital skills. The COVID-19 pandemic further highlighted this need, emphasizing hybrid and digital teaching scenarios. Research underscores the importance of early exposure to technology during university studies (Tomte et al., 2015) and its role in teachers' professional success (Instefjord & Munthe, 2017). Teachers lacking digital skills negatively impact educational outcomes (Yazar & Keskin, 2016), while those with high competency improve learning quality and motivation (Caena & Redecker, 2019).

Digital competence, identified as a key skill for lifelong learning (OECD, 2010), supports active learning methodologies like flipped classrooms, enhancing educators' roles as facilitators. The EU's DigCompEdu framework and other models (e.g., ISTE, UNESCO ICT standards) define educators' digital teaching competence (DTC) across areas like professional commitment, digital resources, teaching, assessment, and student empowerment. Effective digital competence enhances teacher-student interaction, feedback, and learning processes in higher education.

Frameworks like DigCompEdu (Carretero et al., 2017) and UNESCO's standards (2018) guide teachers in mastering skills such as data management, communication, content creation, safety, and problem-solving. Measuring and addressing gaps in teachers' digital profiles is critical for systemic educational improvements (Hanell, 2018). As technology evolves, ongoing professional development remains essential (Starkey, 2020).

Teachers' Digital Competence Frameworks

Different organizations and institutions have identified indicators or standards for describing teacher digital competence. To classify competencies, teachers must develop them with different dimensions and descriptors. This work presents the most frequently used international indicators and highlights the competencies that teachers must develop, along with their various dimensions and descriptors.

European Framework of Digital Competence for Teachers DigCompEdu

DigCompEdu, published in late 2017, aims to align European educational policies with a digital competence model. It is a synthesis of scientific studies at local, national, European, and international levels. DigCompEdu is a digital competence model with six differentiated competence areas, each focusing on competencies that teachers must have to promote effective, inclusive, and innovative learning strategies using digital tools (Figure 15.1 available on the Online Appendix link https://tinyurl.com/he50Appendices).

The competencies include professional commitment, digital resources, digital pedagogy, evaluation and feedback, empowering students, and facilitating competence. Each area has a series of competencies that "teachers must have in order to promote effective, inclusive and innovative learning strategies, using digital tools" (Redecker & Punie, 2017, p. 4). The DigCompEdu framework consists of six areas:

- Facilitating Learners' Digital Competence - Enabling learners to use digital technologies in a safe, creative and critical manner. Professional commitment involves using digital technologies to improve teaching processes and interact professionally with colleagues, students, parents, and other educational community agents.

- Digital Resources - Sourcing, creating and sharing digital resources.

- Digital pedagogy - Designing, planning, and implementing digital technologies in all teaching phases, promoting student-centered approaches.

- Assessment and feedback - Using digital technologies and strategies to enhance assessment.

- Empowering Learners - Using digital technologies to enhance inclusion, personalization and learners' active engagement.

- Facilitating Learners' Digital Competence - Enabling learners to use digital technologies in a safe, creative and critical manner.

DigCompEdu proposes six progressive competence levels, ranging from novice (A1) to pioneer (C2), to identify a teacher's digital competence level (Figure 15.2 available on the Online Appendix link https://tinyurl.com/he50Appendices).

ISTE standards for Teachers

The ISTE (International Society for Technology in Education) Standards for Teachers are a framework developed by ISTE to define the skills and knowledge needed by teachers to effectively integrate technology into their teaching practices. The ISTE Standards for Teachers consist of seven standards:

Learners - Continually improve their practice by learning from and with others and exploring proven and promising practices that leverage technology to improve student learning.

Leaders - Seek out opportunities for leadership to support student empowerment and success and to improve teaching and learning.

Citizens - Inspire students to positively contribute to and responsibly participate in the digital world.

Collaborators - Dedicate time to collaborate with both colleagues and students to improve practice, discover and share resources and ideas, and solve problems.

Designers - Design authentic, learner-driven activities and

environments that recognize and accommodate learner variability.

Facilitators - Facilitate learning with technology to support student achievement of the ISTE Standards for Students.

Analysts - Understand and use data to drive their instruction and support students in achieving their learning goals.

Similar to the DigCompEdu framework, the ISTE Standards define the essential conditions, knowledge, skills, and attitudes for teachers to effectively leverage technology in teaching and learning. They provide guidance for teachers to develop and demonstrate digital age learning competencies.

UNESCO ICT Competence Framework for Teachers (ICT-CFT)

The UNESCO ICT-CFT is a framework developed by UNESCO to provide guidance on the competencies teachers need to integrate information and communications technologies (ICT) into their professional practice. This framework presents "a wide range of competencies that teachers need in order to integrate ICT in their professional practice" (Butcher, 2022, p. 2). The ICT-CFT consists of three main approaches to ICT integration:

Technology Literacy - Enabling students to use ICT to learn more effectively.

Knowledge Deepening - Enabling students to acquire in-depth knowledge of their school subjects and apply it to complex, real-world problems.

Knowledge Creation - Enabling students, citizens and the workforce they become, to create the new knowledge required for more harmonious, fulfilling and prosperous societies.

Within each of these three approaches, the framework is organized across six dimensions:

- Comprehending ICT in educational policies: Applying ICT to assist the curriculum's particular goals and participating in the assessment procedure.

- Curriculum and evaluation: Developing ICT-related competencies to promote efficient teaching and learning strategies.

- Pedagogy: The application of ICT to enhance efficient teaching and learning strategies.

- Application of Digital abilities: Developing ICT skills to incorporate them into the teaching and learning processes.

- Organization and administration: Taking care of the education center's digital gadgets and safeguarding its users.

- Professional learning: Making use of digital literacy in work settings.

For each dimension and approach, the framework defines a set of teacher competencies at three different levels - Emerging, Applying, and Transforming. The ICT-CFT aims to provide a comprehensive set of guidelines to support the development of national and institutional policies, strategies and programs for the professional development of teachers in the pedagogical use of ICT.

Digital competency framework for Vietnamese University Teachers: Navigating the evolving landscape

The digital competence of Vietnamese university teachers is essential for adapting to the rapidly evolving digital landscape. Based on frameworks such as UNESCO's and the EU's digital competence models, this study examines Vietnamese teachers' strengths and areas for improvement (see Figure 15.3 available in the Online Appendix link https://tinyurl.com/he50Appendices):

1. Information and Data Literacy: Teachers exhibit strong abilities in identifying, organizing, and analyzing digital information, assessing reliability, and retrieving relevant data. However, areas such as personal data management and digital identity protection require further development.

2. Communication and Collaboration: Teachers demonstrate commendable digital communication and collaboration skills, fostering effective interaction with peers and students. They understand the importance of

appropriate tools and cultural context but need to deepen their awareness of digital identity and online reputation management.

3. Digital Content Creation: Teachers display creativity and adaptability in creating and re-elaborating digital content, enriching lectures with multimedia elements. However, a better understanding of copyright and licensing protocols is necessary for responsible digital resource use.

4. Safety: Teachers show awareness of protecting devices, personal data, and privacy while promoting healthy digital practices. Yet, greater emphasis on security protocols and fostering a safe digital environment is needed.

5. Problem-Solving: Teachers effectively identify and address digital competence gaps, leveraging tools for innovation and knowledge creation. Maintaining adaptability is crucial for future advancements.

6. Career-Related Competencies: Teachers effectively use digital technologies for teaching, research, and academic administration. However, continuous professional development is needed to stay at the forefront of educational innovation.

While Vietnamese university teachers exhibit a solid foundation in digital competencies, areas such as data literacy, digital content creation, safety, and career-specific digital skills require ongoing investment and development. By addressing these gaps, they can better equip students with the skills needed to succeed in the digital era.

Helpful suggestions for leveling up the Digital Competence of Vietnamese University Teachers in the Age of Digital Transformation

Equipping lecturers with digital skills is crucial to ensuring high educational standards. Training programs focusing on creating electronic lectures, conducting virtual classes, and accessing online learning resources are essential. Such initiatives enable lecturers to adopt more effective teaching methods, aligning with global integration and the demands of Industry 4.0. Conferences and professional events allow educators to enhance their ability to incorporate technology into scientific research and education. Additionally, fostering self-education and self-research among lecturers boosts their capacity to utilize digital tools effectively.

Artificial Intelligence (AI) offers transformative benefits for teaching and learning. Automating administrative tasks like grading and lesson planning enables educators to focus on personalized instruction and student engagement (Zhang & Zhang, 2024). AI tools streamline assessment and feedback, offering timely insights into student performance (Mahligawati, 2023). Adaptive learning technologies cater to diverse learning styles, enhancing engagement and addressing challenges such as neurodevelopmental disorders (Barua et al., 2022). Predictive analytics further empower educators to identify and support at-risk students (Göçen & Aydemir, 2020). AI also fosters professional growth. Training programs on AI literacy improve educators' confidence and creativity, promoting interactive learning environments (Zhao & Zhang, 2022). However, challenges like data privacy and ethical concerns must be addressed to ensure AI complements traditional methods (Tiwari, 2024).

To address these challenges and leverage the opportunities of digital transformation, a range of targeted solutions must be implemented to improve the digital capabilities of university lecturers. In addition, it is necessary to create favorable physical conditions for lecturers to access and apply technology. Providing sufficient technological equipment such as computers, screens, projectors, along with ensuring high-speed internet connectivity will help lecturers use digital applications flexibly and effectively. Universities ought to prioritize and guarantee a robust technical infrastructure, specifically the information and communication technology system. This is a crucial factor, serving as the foundation for digital transformation, ensuring connectivity and interoperability across the entire university, as well as the capability to utilize, update, and share databases and digital data repositories in accordance with pertinent regulations and policies in the field of education. Simultaneously, this is also a significant solution to enhance the digital capabilities of the teaching staff and education management staff in universities.

To encourage creativity and sharing of experiences, educational institutions can organize competitions, workshops, and forums for lecturers. These activities will provide opportunities for lecturers to exchange ideas, learn from each other, and apply innovative digital solutions to teaching and learning practice. Furthermore, the development of digital platforms such as learning management systems (LMS), Moodle, digital libraries, and web portals will also support teaching and learning activities in the digital age. These platforms help improve the interactivity, convenience, and effectiveness of the teaching process.

Lastly, enticing lecturers to engage in networks and communities that facilitate the exchange of knowledge regarding the implementation of digital technology in teaching is a significant activity. This will broaden their perspectives and create opportunities for learning, exchange, and collaboration between lecturers across the country. The simultaneous implementation of the above solutions will significantly improve the digital capabilities of the teaching staff, thereby improving the quality of teaching and learning in the digital age. It will also meet the needs and development trends of modern education. Teaching staff must continually explore self-development and enhance their digital capabilities as well as enhance communication and collaboration on digital platforms alongside gradually establishing a culture of communication in the digital realm and establish efficient and civilized academic collaborative relationships.

Conclusion

In the era of Higher Education 5.0, it is essential to enhance university teachers' digital competence from the beginning in order to create a dynamic and future-ready educational landscape. By empowering teachers with advanced digital competencies and innovative pedagogical approaches, we can significantly enhance teaching effectiveness and enhance student learning experiences. These initiatives are crucial for preparing both facilitators and students to excel in a technology-centric world. AI plays a transformative role in enhancing teaching and learning. AI can help university teachers become better at using technology and change how they teach. AI-powered tools help teachers create personalized lessons, do repetitive tasks like grading, and use data to understand student performance. This helps teachers focus on teaching new ways of teaching and engaging students in meaningful ways. Also, AI helps teachers by giving them real-time feedback on how well they teach. Virtual teaching assistants, powered by AI, are capable of providing assistance to educators in managing large class sizes, responding to routine inquiries, and ensuring consistent communication with students. These technologies not only save time, but they also enhance the quality of interaction between educators and learners. Moreover, AI fosters professional growth by providing opportunities for educators to engage in lifelong learning. Adaptive learning tools and AI-guided professional development programs can help teachers stay current with the latest developments. As Alvin Toffler aptly stated in his landmark 1970 book *Future Shock*, "The illiterate of the 21st century will not be those who cannot read and write, but those who cannot learn, unlearn, and relearn." As the educational landscape continues to evolve, leveraging digital competence will ensure that teachers remain at the forefront of innovation, equipped to inspire and guide students in a technology-driven world.

16

Open Access Publications of Vietnamese Technology and Engineering Universities in the Context of Higher Education 5.0[33]

Trung-Thanh Nguyen and Ngoc-Thi-Bich-Tran[34]

Abstract

This study investigates the role of Open Access (OA) publications in advancing the transformative vision of Higher Education 5.0, focusing on Vietnamese technology and engineering universities. Higher Education 5.0 emphasizes innovation, inclusiveness and interdisciplinary collaboration, necessitating equitable access to knowledge and robust academic ecosystems. By employing bibliometric analysis of over 8,500 OA articles indexed in Scopus from 2013 to 2023, this study identifies trends, challenges, and opportunities in OA publishing. It highlights the role of governmental policies, such as Circular No. 08/2017/TT-BGDĐT and Decision No. 37/2018/QĐ-TTg, in fostering significant growth in OA outputs. The findings underscore the transformative potential of OA in bridging knowledge gaps, reducing financial barriers, and enhancing global research collaboration. However, challenges persist, including limited international funding and the need for strengthened global partnerships. The chapter concludes with actionable recommendations to optimize OA integration, such as subsidizing publication costs, expanding institutional repositories, and incentivizing international research collaborations.

---

33 All references, tables, figures, author affiliation and biography used in this chapter are available on the Online Appendix link at https://tinyurl.com/he50Appendices.

34 Corresponding author: ngoctransta@gmail.com

By aligning OA strategies with the principles of Higher Education 5.0, Vietnamese universities can contribute to a sustainable, innovative, and inclusive global academic landscape.

Introduction

Higher Education 5.0 represents a paradigm shift in academia, combining technological innovation with a human-centric approach to address global and societal challenges. This model emphasizes interdisciplinary collaboration, sustainability, and adaptability, fostering an academic ecosystem that integrates advanced technologies such as artificial intelligence, robotics, and game-based learning into the core educational framework

Simultaneously, Open Access (OA) publishing emerges as a pivotal tool for enhancing global collaboration, fostering innovation, and ensuring equitable access to knowledge. Open Science has emerged and developed through initiatives such as the Budapest Open Access Initiative (BOAI, 2002), the Bethesda Statement on Open Access Publishing (2003), and the Berlin Declaration on Open Access to Knowledge in the Sciences and Humanities (2003). In 2021, the UNESCO Recommendation on Open Science was unanimously adopted by all 193 member states, marking Open Science and Open Education as irreversible trends in today's world. Open Science represents a paradigm shift in how research and scientific inquiry are conducted, transitioning from traditional models of publishing findings in scientific journals to openly sharing and utilizing all forms of knowledge for the benefit of society" (The European Commission, 2016).

Open Access publishing involves the release of publications whose content can be accessed freely via the internet, with readers granted the copyright to republish or reuse the content as they wish, as long as proper attribution is given to the authors and publishers. In Vietnam, the State has issued numerous documents affirming the importance of science and technology (S&T). development, and have consistently created favourable conditions for the advancement of S&T. On September 25, 2023, the Prime Minister approved Decision No. 1117, which issued the program to build a model for open educational resources (OER) in higher education, with specific objectives and solutions. Then, OA publications at universities of technology and engineering make substantial contributions to the development of Higher Education 5.0, particularly due to the rapid pace of technological innovation and the necessity for continuous access to the latest research. This study investigates the role of OA publications in advancing these goals, particularly within Vietnamese technology and engineering universities.

Research Objectives and Methodology

This study aims to evaluate the impact of OA publications on fostering innovation and adaptability in Higher Education 5.0. It also examines the current state of OA publishing in Vietnamese universities and provides actionable recommendations for optimizing OA integration within the Higher Education 5.0 framework.

The study employs bibliometric analysis to examine OA publications from Vietnamese universities indexed in Scopus. Data was collected on publication trends, research areas, and collaboration networks over a 10-year period (2013–2023).

Step 1: Selection of Engineering and Technology (E&T) Universities in Vietnam. We reviewed universities under the Ministry of Education and Training (MOET) of Vietnam (Prime Minister, 2018) that offer the five E&T majors defined by the Vietnamese MOET (MOET, 2022). (See Table 16.1 in the Online Appendix link https://tinyurl.com/he50Appendices)

Step 2: Selection of Subject Areas Indexed in Scopus. We matched the E&T training programs of Vietnamese higher education institutions with the subject areas indexed by Scopus. These E&T majors correspond to 9 subject areas.

Step 3: Since the downloaded data from Scopus does not include subject area information, we proceeded to download the publication data for the 27 E&T universities separately by subject area. The search criteria are listed (See Table 16.2 in the Online Appendix link https://tinyurl.com/he50Appendices), including time span, document type, subject areas, language, publication type, and affiliations. The final dataset consisted of 8,519 documents.

*The selected time frame from 2013 to 2023 corresponds to the period after Vietnam implemented Resolution No. 29-NQ/TW issued by the

Party Central Committee in 2013, which aimed for a fundamental and comprehensive renewal of education and training, including the task to "Enhance the quality and effectiveness of scientific and technological research and application" (Party Central Committee, 2013). Key metrics include publication volume, international co-authorship and fundings for Open Access Publications.

Results and Findings

From a total of 8,519 OA articles in English were published in journals indexed in the Scopus database, we found some main issues on this topic. Note: a document can be classified in more than one Open Access category.

Table 16.3 (located in the Online Appendix link https://tinyurl.com/he50Appendices) describes the trend of OA publication in 27 universities in the T&E (Technology and Engineering) field in Vietnam from 2013 to 2023. A total of 8,519 OA articles in English were published in journals indexed in the Scopus database. The number of articles increased from 93 in 2013 to 1,752 in 2023, an 18.84-fold increase over a decade. The average annual growth rate was 36.63%, with the highest growth rate in 2019 at 92.20%, followed by 68.67% in 2016 and 51.24% in 2020. After 2020, the publication growth rate showed a downward trend, with the lowest increase in 2022 at only 3.12%. Although the growth rate was not as high as in the previous period, the number of published articles remained over 1,500 per year during this period. The 2018-2023 period marked exceptional growth, from 462 in 2018 to 1,752 in 2023, with the number of articles in this period accounting for 88.85% of the total publications from 2013 to 2023. The significant growth of OA can be linked to changes in Vietnam's policies on education and scientific research. Specifically, Circular No. 08/2017/TT-BGDĐT, later replaced by Circular No. 18/2021/TT-BGDĐT, established standards for doctoral supervisors and dissertation defence conditions linked to international publications indexed in scientific databases such as Scopus or Web of Science (Ministry of Education and Training, 2017), (Ministry of Education and Training, 2021). Additionally, Decision No. 37/2018/QĐ-TTg (Prime Minister, 2018) and Decision No. 25/2020/QĐ-TTg (Prime Minister, 2020), which set the standards for the appointment of associate professors and professors, considering the candidate's international publication record, may have been contributing factors driving international publication activities in universities across Vietnam, particularly in T&E universities.

Within Higher Education 5.0 context, it highlights the collaboration among authors from different countries in the field of technology and engineering. During the 2013–2023 period, the top collaborating countries with the 27 universities were not only those with long-standing partnerships, such as France, China, and Belgium, but also included expanding collaborations with countries like Japan, South Korea, Taiwan, and the United States. In recent years, Vietnam's government has issued documents emphasizing the need to enhance international research collaborations, including international publications (National Assembly, 2018; National Assembly, 2019). This has attracted the participation of new research groups and scientists from Europe, such as Ireland, the Czech Republic, Romania, and Hungary; the Middle East, including Iran, Iraq, Saudi Arabia, and the United Arab Emirates; and Africa, such as Egypt and Algeria.

The 27 universities in the E&T field in Vietnam are represented by the Vietnam node. See Figure 16.1 (in the Online Appendix link https://tinyurl.com/he50Appendices) which visualizes the global research collaboration network of 27 Vietnamese technology and engineering universities, highlighting connections with international researchers from 2013 to 2023. Each node represents a country participating in these collaborations, with larger nodes indicating higher publication output, and thicker lines denoting stronger collaborative ties. The intensity of nodes and lines reflects the duration of collaboration, with lighter shades representing more recent partnerships and darker shades indicating long-standing relationships.

This network embodies the principles of Higher Education 5.0 by showcasing the role of Open Access (OA) in creating a globally interconnected academic ecosystem. Through OA publishing, Vietnamese universities break down geographical and financial barriers, enabling equitable knowledge sharing and fostering interdisciplinary innovation. Figure 16.1 (in the Online Appendix link https://tinyurl.com/he50Appendices) underscores the capacity of OA to align academic efforts with the human-centric and innovation-focused goals of Higher Education 5.0, fostering a sustainable and inclusive academic landscape.

OA Publications reduce financial barriers, particularly for underfunded institutions

In the context of international integration, technical and technological universities in Vietnam are advancing Open Access (OA) publishing to enhance the accessibility and dissemination of scientific knowledge. From 2013 to 2023, funding from domestic and international sources has significantly supported OA publications. Domestic funding, spearheaded by the National Science and Technology Development Fund (NAFOSTED), exemplifies the government's commitment to fostering innovation and global collaboration—cornerstones of Higher Education 5.0. NAFOSTED-funded projects accounted for 788 documents, representing 9.25% of the total OA publications from these universities (table 16.4). This highlights the prioritization of science and technology development through public funding mechanisms aimed at fostering research excellence. Similarly, the Ministry of Education and Training (MOET) supported 641 documents (7.52%), underscoring the state's pivotal role in promoting research activities and aligning education systems with the technological and human-centered objectives of Higher Education 5.0.

These funding initiatives not only increase the quantity and quality of research outputs but also advance the integration of Vietnamese universities into global academic networks. By prioritizing OA publishing, funding bodies enable universities to embrace the pillars of Higher Education 5.0: accessibility, adaptability, and inclusivity. These efforts align research outcomes with societal and technological demands, reinforcing Vietnam's position in the international academic community.

Organizations such as the Vietnam Academy of Science and Technology, Hue University, and Hanoi University of Science and Technology have actively supported technology and engineering universities in conducting research and publishing in OA journals. This reflects a collective effort to develop sustainable scientific resources, aligning with Higher Education 5.0's focus on fostering innovation and societal impact. Prioritizing engineering and technology—sectors with significant economic growth potential—these organizations contribute to a research ecosystem that bridges academia and industry.

A noteworthy development is the involvement of private enterprises, exemplified by the Vingroup Innovation Fund. Funding 111 articles

(1.03% of total funding sources), the fund signals a growing interest from private corporations in advancing research and innovation. This trend aligns with Higher Education 5.0's emphasis on collaborative ecosystems where public and private sectors converge to drive progress.

Domestic funding sources, including NAFOSTED and MOET, remain the backbone of OA publishing, underscoring Vietnam's autonomy and internal capacity in science and technology. However, achieving the global standards envisioned by Higher Education 5.0 requires expanding investment from international funding sources. By fostering partnerships with global research organizations, Vietnam can enhance its publishing capabilities, integrate into international academic networks, and contribute to a more inclusive and innovative global education system. This approach aligns with Higher Education 5.0's goals of accessibility, adaptability, and interdisciplinary collaboration.

Table 16.5 (in the Online Appendix link https://tinyurl.com/he50Appendices) provides statistics on the top 10 international organizations that have contributed the most funding to universities in Vietnam for publications in OA journals. According to the statistics in the table above (in the Online Appendix link https://tinyurl.com/he50Appendices), the National Research Foundation of Korea leads with 218 documents, accounting for 2.56% of the total number of funded documents. The Taiwan Ministry of Science and Technology and the Japan Society for the Promotion of Science are also strong international funding organizations, with 181 and 176 documents funded, respectively. Several organizations from the United States, such as the Oregon Department of Agriculture and the National Science Foundation, have also contributed to funding publications from universities in Vietnam's technology and engineering sectors.

Despite the availability of both domestic and international funding sources, the number of documents supported by international organizations remains relatively low compared to other countries in the region. This presents a challenge for Vietnam in expanding international collaboration and attracting more foreign funding.

Domestic funding sources, particularly from NAFOSTED and the Ministry of Education and Training, have played a crucial role in supporting scholars at Vietnam's technology and engineering universities in publishing in OA journals. However, to enhance international publishing capabilities, increased collaboration and the attraction of more funding from major international organizations are needed.

Although many international organizations participate in supporting OA publishing, the total amount of funding from international sources remains modest compared to developed countries in the region. Of the 3,442 research funding organizations, the National Research Foundation of Korea is the largest international funder, supporting 218 documents (2.56%) out of a total of 5,367 funded publications. However, this percentage is still much lower compared to domestic support. Other international organizations, such as the Taiwan Ministry of Science and Technology and the Japan Society for the Promotion of Science, contribute less than 2%. While international organizations have made notable contributions to OA publication funding in Vietnam, the scale of funding remains low. This may be due to the lack of strong collaboration networks between Vietnam's technical and engineering universities and international research funds, or the limited access to foreign funding programs. Developing an internationalization strategy and creating more opportunities for collaboration with international organizations will be necessary steps to expand research potential.

One of the major challenges for universities in Vietnam is attracting international funding sources. Compared to developed countries in the region such as South Korea, Japan, and China, international funding for Vietnam remains limited, accounting for only about 2-3% of the total published documents. This not only affects the quantity of research but also limits the quality and impact of these studies on the international stage. The growth of funding sources for OA publications in Vietnam is a positive sign for the domestic science and technology sector, particularly in the fields of engineering and technology. However, to fully realize its potential, Vietnam needs to strengthen cooperation with international organizations and improve its domestic scientific funding system. Technical and engineering universities need to develop long-term strategies focused on enhancing partnerships with international organizations, creating opportunities for young researchers to access global funding programs. Additionally, significant investment from the government is needed to support researchers in joining international networks.

Aligning with Higher Education 5.0, greater foreign funding can enable Vietnamese universities to adopt global best practices and produce impactful research. It needs to be building robust networks with international research funds, providing training for researchers to access foreign funding programs, and ensuring alignment with global academic standards. Such efforts will not only improve the quality and visibility of Vietnamese research but also reinforce the principles of Higher Education 5.0.

Discussion

The findings underscore the transformative potential of OA in Higher Education 5.0. By reducing barriers and promoting inclusivity, OA enables universities to bridge knowledge gaps between developed and developing regions and foster interdisciplinary research and international collaboration, it removes access barriers, enabling researchers worldwide to collaborate seamlessly on innovative projects. It aligns with the inclusive goals of Higher Education 5.0, which ensures that knowledge and research outcomes are accessible to all and driving innovation by enhancing knowledge-sharing speed, empowering researchers to build on existing work.

From 2013 to 2023, the number of OA articles from 27 Vietnamese technology and engineering universities increased nearly 19-fold. This reflects enhanced academic productivity and alignment with global publishing standards, largely driven by supportive government policies like Circular No. 08/2017/TT-BGDĐT and Decision No. 37/2018/QĐ-TTg.

Additionally, the internationalization of Vietnamese technology and engineering universities is evident in their partnerships with institutions across Asia, Europe, and North America. Such collaborations have enriched academic output and fostered knowledge exchange, essential for meeting Higher Education 5.0 goals of inclusivity and adaptability.

Particularly, OA publishing reduces financial burdens on readers and promotes equitable knowledge dissemination whereas, authors often face article processing charges (APCs). Even though domestic funding from organizations like NAFOSTED and MOET plays a central role in supporting OA initiatives, international funding remains modest, representing only 2-3% of total publications. This underscores the need for strategies to attract more international investment and develop robust collaboration networks. OA publishing fosters innovation and human-centric education by enabling global knowledge sharing. It bridges geographical and financial divides, aligning academic efforts with the transformative vision of Higher Education 5.0. Although some findings have been found, this study has not mentioned yet to perceptions and awareness of scientists and lecturers of technology and engineering universities in Vietnam about the importance of OAP in promoting innovation creation and interdisciplinary collaboration in the context of higher education 5.0. To fully harness the potential of OAP within Higher Education 5.0, the following strategies are recommended. Governments and institutions should subsidize APCs and invest in developing institutional repositories to lower financial barriers for researchers. Training programs on OAP benefits and technical tools can empower researchers to publish and collaborate effectively. Collaborating with international funding agencies and academic networks can enhance the quality and impact of research. National policies should incentivize OAP contributions, linking academic promotion criteria to open-access publishing.

Higher Education 5.0 and Open Access Publications represent complementary forces driving the transformation of global academia. By embracing the principles of innovation, inclusivity, and collaboration, Vietnamese universities can set a benchmark for integrating advanced educational models with equitable knowledge dissemination. The journey to a sustainable, interconnected academic future hinges on strategic investments in technology, human capital, and global partnerships.

Conclusion

In conclusion, the study emphasizes the transformative potential of Open Access Publications in advancing Vietnamese universities toward the ideals of Higher Education 5.0. By leveraging OA's strengths, global collaboration, inclusivity, and innovation—universities can overcome financial and infrastructural challenges to achieve sustainable academic excellence. Prioritizing strategic investments in OA platforms, enhancing researcher capacity, and strengthening international partnerships will be crucial for Vietnam to establish itself as a leading contributor to the global academic community. Together, Higher Education 5.0 and Open Access Publications create a future-focused academic environment that is inclusive, innovative, and globally interconnected.

17

Learning analytics with AI: Theory and Models for Smart Higher Education[35]

Nguyen Thi Thu Hang and Pham Kim Chung[36]

Abstract

With the strong transformation of higher education to 5.0, learning analytics is an important tool to help personalize and optimize the learning experience. Artificial intelligence (AI) can analyse large amounts of data about learners' learning behaviour, predict students' ability to succeed, detect risks of falling behind, and help teachers provide timely support measures. This chapter will analyse the basic theories and models of using AI to support learning data analysis; collecting, processing, predicting, and making personalized recommendations for learners; and improving the quality and effectiveness of the educational process. At the same time, it presents the challenges and opportunities that arise from applying AI to learning analytics, as well as directions for future research and development in this field.

Introduction

The application of technology in teaching and learning improves the quality of education and promotes educational equity and lifelong learning opportunities. Digital teaching technologies offer many opportunities and

---

35 All references, tables, figures, author affiliation and biography used in this chapter are available on the Online Appendix link at https://tinyurl.com/he50Appendices.

36 Corresponding author: chungpk@vnu.edu.vn

great possibilities for facilitating and meeting the growing demand for personalized learning to suit the individual needs and abilities of each student.

The development of technology in the digital transformation process also leads to the formation of "Smart School" models. "Smart Education" is an educational model that uses information technology to change education in the future, with the expansion of time, space, learning materials and learning methods, surpassing the limits of conventional classroom lectures. Along with these opportunities, there are several challenges in integrating new smart technologies into teaching and learning. 'Smart' devices, such as the Internet of Things (IoT), help education managers, lecturers, and education researchers collect, measure, and analyse learning; help understand the learning context; monitor learner progress and identify learning risks and difficulties; predict learner performance to provide feedback to students; and evaluate learning effectiveness and personalize learning (Uskov et al, 2018).

Digital technologies have generated huge amounts of data (big data) from student learning activities, requiring the use of multiple measures on a system and combining with data from other system sources, requiring data processing tools and applying responsible data and artificial intelligence principles to learning analytics to ensure appropriate and ethical use of data by education systems.

Smart universities use smart technologies such as artificial intelligence, machine learning and data to analyse data collected during student learning to better understand how students learn and interact with learning materials, or set up smart classrooms with AI technology to monitor and analyse student engagement and performance in the classroom to support students in courses with strong interaction between students and technology, allowing students to access learning materials through online learning systems such as chatbots and artificial intelligence to support students in finding information, academic advising and time management and personalization in the student learning process, helping students succeed in their studies.

Smart higher education

Smart education connects the real world with digital space to create an interactive, flexible, and personalized learning environment, combining education and digital technology to create a personalized learning experience. From the perspective of smart technology, smart education effectively connects digital resources, social media, and smart devices through communication, cloud computing, and other technologies to provide new knowledge to improve learning methods (Singh & Miah, 2020).

From a holistic perspective, smart education system can be transformed into three levels (Figure 17.1 (available in the Online Appendix link https://tinyurl.com/he50Appendices): the smart learning environment, instructional model, and smart education system. The education system continuously improves knowledge generation from three aspects: efficiency, effectiveness, and benefits by promoting educational equity and improving educational quality by adapting the educational system and educational goals (UNESCO IITE, BNU & ISTE. 2022).

The Smart Education Framework takes a multi-pronged approach with three key levers: 1) refocusing on transformative education through technology, 2) building a digital learning infrastructure that facilitates smart education, and 3) ensuring future-minded policies and governance. In this way, students and teachers define learning goals and choose ways to demonstrate their mastery with appropriate guidance. Teachers guide, support, and use flexible measures and learning analytics to provide timely and personalized feedback (Demir, 2021).

Using technology for smart education requires the collection and processing of personal data. Learner analytics provides insights into the effectiveness of teaching methods, helping teachers and administrators make data-driven decisions. This poses challenges in terms of learner profile analysis, security, privacy protection, and so on.

Psychological theories in learning analytics - Behaviourism and learning analysis

Learning analytics focuses on collecting and using data to understand and improve the learning process, requiring the collection, measurement, analysis, and reporting of data on learners and their learning environments to understand and optimize learning in a given context. Behavioural theory was developed by representatives of psychologists Watson (1913), Pavlov (1928), Guthrie (1930), B.Ph. Skinner (1938), Hull (1943), Estes (1950), and learning analytics are based on the behaviour of learners in specific situations, expressed through certain words and gestures, focusing on factors that can be observed, measured, highly objective, and controllable. Costa et al. (2021) argued that learner behaviour, learning styles, and learning performance can be easily described through analytics collected in online learning environments. It enables and encourages educational research, software application development, and online educational practices towards personalized and adaptive learning (Ajzen, I. 1991).

Some studies have used behavioural and cognitive parameters, cognitive states, and emotions to analyse learning; for example, Yousef and Khatiry (2021) conducted behavioural studies for each group of students participating in computer-supported collaborative learning based on the analysis results of neural network models to provide personalized intervention solutions (Kovanovic et al. 2018).

Macfadyen and Dawson (2010) used learning behaviour logs, such as the number of hours online, number of interactions in discussion forums, and duration and time required to complete online tests, as meaningful data for analysis. This study investigated learners' reading behaviour in an online context using behavioural sequence analysis, which is a learning analysis technique. Zhao (2021) analysed the current state of learner models, the ideas for building learner characteristics models, and studied four learner characteristics models: basic characteristics, cognitive level, learning style, and learning emotions.

The study of Ricardo A. Ramírez Mendozal et al. (2022) on the set of behavioural indicators allows for a comprehensive view of student interactions and experiences, with each indicator providing a unique perspective on their learning process. Learner characteristics can be classified as shown in Table 17.1 (available in the Online Appendix link https://tinyurl.com/he50Appendices), (Yousef & Khatiry, 2021).

Constructivist theory and learning analytics

Constructivism theory was developed by Jean Piaget (1896-1980), Vygotsky (1896-1934), A. N. Leontev (1904-1979), J. Brunner (1915-2016). Learning analysis based on this theory must focus on how learners construct knowledge from their personal experiences. Changhua and Chunqiao (2021) used blockchain technology to connect learners' learning records and provide HTCNH roadmaps. It is also used to evaluate learners' learning achievements, work suitability, and intelligence. Vytasek et al. (2020) focused on student engagement. Student engagement is considered to be highly relevant to teaching and learning quality.

Richards (2011) showed that as online learners interact in online environments, they leave behind a data trail of time and location, what materials they accessed, who they talked to, and how well they did on web-based quizzes. Analysing these data provides more specific information about a learner or interactions from which progress can be measured, engagement can be inferred, and learning outcomes can be predicted. Integrating AI and Learning Analytics for Data-Driven Pedagogical Decisions and Personalized Interventions in Education analysed student behaviour in learning and indicators including engagement, emotional states, and learning progress (Table 17.2 available in the Online Appendix link https://tinyurl.com/he50Appendices) (Ramteja et al. 2020).

Learning analytics, with the aim of understanding and optimizing learning and the environment in which it occurs, as reflected in this definition, will depend primarily on providing information about learner learning in relation to the availability, quantity, speed, and type of data in the learning environment. Martin (2016) studied the types of data that can be collected through assessment and learning analytics techniques, which are described in Table 17.3 (See the Online Appendix link https://tinyurl.com/he50Appendices).

Table 17.3 (available in the Online Appendix link https://tinyurl.com/he50Appendices) presents an assessment of the effectiveness of the learning process. However, these metrics and indicators are not diagnostic tools and should be interpreted with a full understanding of their limitations. For clarity and transparency, a range of metrics and indicators was used, including student engagement, emotional state, and learning progress. Engagement metrics assist in understanding the level of student engagement and interaction, thereby indicating how active they are (Chen, Weiqin. 2019).

AI and learning analytics

Learning analytics is shaped by two trends: the application of virtual learning environments in education and the expansion of data mining techniques used in the operations of organizations (Agudo-Peregrina et al 2014). The development of information technology with a variety of data collection and storage techniques has created diverse, high-speed, and large-volume data warehouses that form big data warehouses. Big data are large, complex, and diverse datasets, so they require effective data management and processing solutions.

Artificial intelligence can be defined as "computer systems that are capable of engaging in human-like processes such as learning, adapting, synthesizing, self-correcting, and using data for complex tasks. AI has many branches and sub-branches, such as (a) machine learning (ML), which includes algorithms that use educational data to identify patterns through continuous training with data; (b) deep learning, which uses large datasets to simulate and predict educational outcomes; and (c) natural language processing (NLP), which uses language recognition algorithms to extract and analyse the meaning of text. In education, AI supports and enhances learning environments by using intelligent tutoring systems, agents, and collaborative learning systems. Recently, interdisciplinary AI research has been needed to integrate several fields, including scientific computing, image processing, linguistics, psychology, and neuroscience (Salas-Pilco et al. 2022).

Research on Artificial Intelligence in Education (AIED) has developed learning analytics (LA) techniques and learner modelling in complex learning contexts (Greer & Mark, 2016). This forms the basis for building an intelligent educational system. AIED researchers have exploited educational data (EDM) to propose various learner modelling techniques (e.g., regression models, cognitive models), data analysis, and visualization mechanisms. The main purpose of this study was to identify strategies for designing better learning environments. Smith (2022) also proposed using collected data to extract comprehensive information from users interacting with an educational chatbot, which can be integrated with an

LMS and analysed across all student interactions with the chatbot (e.g., the VirtualTA platform). This includes not only dialogues but also emotional nuances through questions or messages, providing deeper insights into the emotional context of their questions and their impact on learning.

Ramteja Sajja's (2020) research has also improved with features such as Flashcard generation and quiz functionality, closely monitoring user engagement with these features, tracking variables such as time spent on each question, and total time spent on quizzes and tests. This information provides insight into students' preferred learning methods, their understanding of the subject matter, and their level of engagement with various learning activities.

However, while algorithms and machine learning provide insights into student behaviour and learning outcomes, they sometimes ignore the pedagogical context, complicating the interpretation of results and their application for educators. AI-enhanced LA integrated with virtual teaching assistants may reveal important implications for pedagogical theory and teaching practice. This calls for a solution that accounts for differences in educational settings. Efforts to monitor emotional states during learning are often rudimentary and fail to capture the complexity of the learning process.

Dawson et al.'s (2010) study of extracting data from student social networks and displaying them as structured graphs (Figure 17.2 available in the Online Appendix link https://tinyurl.com/he50Appendices) was found to aid in the interpretation of the quality of learning. Behaviour detection was used to provide a value for the extent to which a given behaviour was observed via a camera, recording the behaviour of the presenter, recording the time the presenter looked at the audience, and also viewing or listening to audio recordings, which were then analysed. Multimodal Learning Analytics (MMLA) emerged as a set of techniques that can be used to collect multiple high-frequency data sources (video, logs, audio, gestures, biosensors), synchronize and encode the data, and examine learning in a realistic, ecologically valid, social, multimedia learning environment". MMLA refers to the use of diverse communication modalities, such as text, audio, language, space, and images, to exchange information and meaning between individuals. The concept of "multimodality" in learning analytics is different from the concept of "multimedia." The MMLA process can observe three main activities: using diverse learning trace sources (multimodal data), processing and integrating these trace data (multimodal analysis and fusion), and studying human behaviour in real learning environments (learning behaviour detection and learning structure estimation). The implementation model of the MMLA, which includes four steps, is shown in Figure 17.2 (available in the Online Appendix link https://tinyurl.com/he50Appendices). First, multimedia signals were recorded from relevant participants in the learning activity. Then, these recordings were automatically processed to extract low-level multimodal data traces, which were then analysed and merged automatically or semi-automatically to produce high-level traces. These high-level traces were used to detect the occurrence of the desired behaviour and estimate the learning outcomes. Finally, the system builds an analysis engine and the resulting estimates are used to provide a tool to feed information back to the participants in the learning process.

The results of the consolidated analysis phase provide information regarding the occurrence of the identified behaviours, which can be used for computational or statistical analysis (or qualitative analysis in the case of MMLA systems) to calculate the degree, level, or intensity of the studied learning construct. However, MMLA systems may present increased uncertainty in detecting the manifestations of behaviours because the estimates of the coefficients between the raters may differ; therefore, the reliability of the coding is not high.

The visualization of the data was clear, which had an impact on the LA field. While comprehensive data collection and analysis are the foundation of any analytics tool (Sit et al., 2021), these tools translate this complex data into a form that is easy to understand, supports decision making, enhances understanding, and ultimately improves experiential learning for students (Alabbad et al., 2022).

Despite its usefulness for research on MMLA and its potential as a technical and pedagogically integrated solution, most current MMLA tools have only reached the prototype stage (Xavier Ochoa, 2019). The most important of these are cost, hardware, network, software issues) and scalability (which need to be feasible to deploy the system across an entire educational institution).

AI and learning analytics on LMS

The LA tool is integrated with various LMS platforms to analyse the learning outcomes of interactive students; the main focus in the development and implementation of this tool is to convert interactions into data for meaningful analysis (Figure 17.3 – available through the Online Appendix link https://tinyurl.com/he50Appendices). The learning analytics system is designed to collect data through a series of stages - pre-processing, analysis, and secure storage - in the LA tool. To further enrich this data, smart Artificial Intelligence integration was deployed, performing sentiment analysis and learning progression.

The LA tool was introduced to integrate with various educational platforms and analyse student interactions to generate insights. This flexibility ensures compatibility between educational chatbots and LMSs. The main focus of the development and deployment of the tool is to convert interactions into data points for meaningful analysis.

The directions for developing AI solutions integrated with an LMS are as follows:

• Natural language inference: The LA tool has exploited the ability of the AI Chatbot model to query users because of its ability to understand natural language AI and recognize broader contextual complexities measuring stress, curiosity, confusion, and excitement by continuously measuring emotions over a series of interactions, tracking the emotional journey throughout the student's learning process, and detecting trends or spikes in specific sentiment scores that can indicate areas of the learning material that are particularly difficult, interesting, or frustrating for students.

Topic Analysis and Question Patterns

• Topic analysis and question patterns are two important components of the LA tool functionality. The tool analyses topics by applying AI Chatbots to each student question or interaction by identifying the topic or question and then storing and organizing this information.

Preferred Learning Methods

• To understand the learning preferences of students, tools that track whether students ask questions, create note cards, ask questions on topics, or search for summaries of specific topics allow the identification of the method used by each student.

Learning Progress

• The LA tool also incorporates a method for tracking students' learning progress. Each student's interaction with the LMS (messages and questions asked) was analyzed using Bloom's taxonomy. AI can extract cognitive level indicators from student queries, allowing changes in cognitive levels to be tracked over time.

Student Interaction Tracking and Analysis

• The LA tool also includes an extended module dedicated to tracking and analysing student interactions with the questions provided. When a student selects a test related to a specific topic, a number of parameters are recorded, allowing for the analysis of student subject preferences and potential areas of difficulty as well as the time required to complete the entire test, providing insights into student time management skills, comprehension speed, or areas that may be difficult based on extended completion times.

The implementation of the LA tool relies on a robust and synchronous technical infrastructure owing to computational demands and the need to manage the extensive datasets generated from student interactions. A key aspect of this infrastructure is the efficient data and secure storage system required to house and process the critical data streams. There is a need for a powerful database system that can manage large datasets and facilitate rapid access to data.

AI Challenges in Learning Analytics

While AI learning analytics algorithms offers many benefits, they also face some important issues and challenges. These difficulties can be due to the following reasons: Education data may be incomplete or contain many errors, leading to inaccurate analysis results. Collection and analysis of personal student data must ensure information security. Many AI algorithms operate as a "black box", making it difficult to explain how they make decisions, making it difficult to ensure reliability and transparency. Deploying learning analytics systems can require large investments in infrastructure, software, and personnel training. At the same time, it is necessary to ensure that learning analytics tools and platforms can integrate and be compatible with existing learning management systems.

While AI can show active student engagement and connections between students and instructors, it does not provide information about the quality of those interactions. At the same time, there are many ethical debates around issues including privacy, the issue of opaque 'black box' algorithms, and the risk of machine learning on datasets that can lead to biased predictions. Addressing these issues requires the development of algorithms that work closely with technology, education, administration, and policy makers to ensure that AI algorithms in education are used effectively, fairly, and responsibly.

Conclusion

AI learning analytics is not just a supporting tool, but also a key to unlocking the future of smart higher education, where learners and lecturers are empowered in a comprehensive and sustainable knowledge ecosystem. AI learning analytics is creating a new approach in smart higher education. By combining learning theory with advanced AI models, learning data can be leveraged to optimize the learning experience, personalize teaching content, and improve teaching and management efficiency.

Advances in technology such as machine learning, natural language processing, and data mining have laid the foundation for learning analytics to achieve higher accuracy and stronger predictive capabilities. However, the implementation of AI in learning analytics needs to be carefully considered in terms of data security, algorithm transparency, and human resource training to maximize the potential of the technology.

In the future, combining learning analytics with elements such as adaptive learning emotional AI promises to deliver superior learning experiences. At the same time, ethical models and humanistic approaches are also needed to ensure that AI not only improves the quality of education but also promotes equity and inclusion in learning.

18

Transforming Education 5.0: Personalized and Adaptive Learning through Artificial Intelligence (AI)[37]

Vo Thi Kim Anh[38]

Abstract

This literature review explores the transformative potential of Artificial Intelligence (AI) in shaping the future of education, with a particular focus on Education 5.0. It examines the integration of advanced AI technologies in creating personalized and adaptive learning environments, highlighting their capacity to revolutionize the educational landscape. The review discusses the benefits of AI in Education 5.0, including enhanced learning outcomes, increased accessibility, and the cultivation of essential 21st-century skills. It also addresses AI adoption challenges and ethical considerations, such as data privacy, algorithmic bias, and the digital divide. These findings emphasize the transformative potential of AI in fostering equitable and inclusive learning environments while presenting implications for policymakers, educators, and technology developers. Highlighting the importance of ethical principles, the chapter outlines some strategies to mitigate risks and ensure transparency.

---

37 All references, tables, figures, author affiliation and biography used in this chapter are available on the Online Appendix link at https://tinyurl.com/he50Appendices.

38 Corresponding author: vothikimanh1007@gmail.com

Introduction

The rapid advancement of technology has ushered in a new era of possibilities across various sectors, and education stands at the forefront of this transformation. The integration of Artificial Intelligence (AI) is driving a pedagogical revolution, promising to reshape the way we teach and learn fundamentally. Education 4.0, characterized by the incorporation of technology into traditional teaching methods, has laid the groundwork for the emergence of the more advanced Education 5.0. While Education 4.0 primarily focuses on enhancing digital literacy and connectivity, Education 5.0 represents a paradigm shift towards AI-driven personalized and adaptive learning experiences (Rane et al., 2023). This transition signifies a deeper and more profound integration of AI, evolving from its role as a supplementary tool in Education 4.0 to becoming a central element that revolutionizes the acquisition, processing, and utilization of knowledge.

The Figure 18.1 (see in the Online Appendix link https://tinyurl.com/he50Appendices) illustrates the intricate relationship between core AI technologies and their practical applications in education. It underscores how these technologies serve as the foundation for various AI-powered solutions that are transforming the educational landscape.

Education 5.0 is not merely an extension of technology integration; it signifies a fundamental reimagining of the educational landscape. AI is poised to play a pivotal role in facilitating personalized and adaptive learning experiences, catering to the unique needs and learning styles of individual students. This paradigm shift reflects a broader societal movement towards Society 5.0 and Industry 5.0, where technology is harnessed to enhance human well-being and address societal challenges (Carayannis & Morawska, 2022). In this context, Education 5.0 emerges as a crucial driver in preparing learners for the complexities and opportunities of the 21st century. This literature review delves into the transformative role of AI in Education 4.0 and 5.0, examining its potential benefits, challenges, and prospects, with a particular emphasis on the exciting possibilities that Education 5.0 holds for the future of learning.

Literature Review and Previous Studies:

The integration of AI in education has garnered significant attention from researchers and educators alike, with a growing focus on the transformative potential of Education 5.0. While earlier studies explored the benefits of AI in enhancing learning outcomes and promoting inclusivity in Education 4.0, recent research has shifted towards investigating the more profound implications of AI in the context of Education 5.0.

Studies have shown that AI-powered tutoring systems can significantly improve student academic performance compared to traditional classroom setups (Mukul & Buyukozkan, 2023). The individualized feedback and customized learning paths offered by AI systems have been identified as key factors contributing to improved student success (Rane, Choudhary, & Rane, 2023). Moreover, research has highlighted the potential of AI-driven adaptive learning platforms to address disparities in educational achievement among marginalized student groups (Cai, Ma, & Chen, 2020).

The transformative potential of AI in Education 5.0 lies in its ability to create truly personalized and adaptive learning experiences. Intelligent Tutoring Systems (ITS) can effectively emulate human tutors, offering guidance, feedback, and tailored resources based on individual student performance (Aithal & Aithal, 2023). AI-powered personalized learning platforms leverage data analytics to provide customized learning paths, content suggestions, and assessments, catering to the unique needs and preferences of each learner (Lantada, 2020).

The impact of AI in Education 5.0 extends beyond personalized learning to encompass various aspects of the educational landscape. As shown in Table 18.1 (see the Online Appendix link https://tinyurl.com/he5OAppendices), AI is being utilized to automate administrative tasks, streamline curriculum development, enhance student engagement through gamification, and enable early intervention through predictive analytics. These diverse applications of AI showcase its potential to revolutionize teaching and learning practices, making education more efficient, effective, and inclusive.

Table 18.1 (available in the Online Appendix link https://tinyurl.com/he5OAppendices) provides a concise overview of how AI is being leveraged to transform various teaching and learning activities in the context of Education 5.0.

The literature also acknowledges the challenges and ethical considerations associated with AI adoption in education. Concerns about data privacy, algorithmic bias, and the potential impact on teacher-student relationships persist (Kwon, 2023). Ensuring transparency, fairness, and accountability in AI systems remains crucial to building trust and promoting inclusivity in Education 5.0. Addressing the digital divide and providing adequate training and support for educators are also essential for the successful and equitable implementation of AI in this new era of education.

Methodology

This literature review employed a comprehensive methodology to delve into the integration of AI in Education, with a particular emphasis on the transformative potential of Education 5.0. The research process encompassed several key steps:

1. **Literature Search:** An extensive search was conducted across various electronic databases, including PubMed, IEEE Xplore, Scopus, and Google Scholar. The search strategy involved utilizing relevant keywords related to AI and education, specifically within the contexts of "Education 4.0," "Education 5.0," "personalized learning," and "adaptive learning." This approach aligns with the methodology employed in various studies examining the impact of AI in education (Chen et al., 2020). The focus on Education 5.0-related keywords ensured the retrieval of studies specifically addressing the advanced integration of AI in education.

2. **Inclusion and Exclusion Criteria:** The retrieved articles were meticulously screened based on predefined inclusion and exclusion criteria. Studies that explicitly focused on the integration of AI in Education 5.0, particularly those exploring personalized and adaptive learning environments, were given priority for inclusion. Articles that primarily focused on Education 4.0 or did not delve into the advanced AI applications characteristic of Education 5.0 were excluded, along with those not published in peer-reviewed journals. This rigorous selection process ensured the quality and relevance of the included studies, aligning with the practices emphasized in

various research methodologies (Zawacki-Richter et al., 2019).

3. **Data Extraction and Analysis:** Pertinent data from the included studies were extracted and analysed. This encompassed information on the specific AI technologies employed, their applications within educational settings, the reported benefits and challenges of AI integration, and the ethical considerations surrounding AI adoption. The data extraction and analysis process adhered to the systematic and rigorous practices commonly employed in literature reviews, ensuring the validity and reliability of the findings (Chiu et al., 2023).

4. **Synthesis and Interpretation:** The extracted data were synthesized and interpreted to identify key themes, trends, and research gaps specifically within the realm of Education 5.0. The findings were then critically evaluated and discussed in relation to the broader context of educational transformation and the potential impact of AI on personalized and adaptive learning. This step involved a comprehensive analysis of the literature to draw meaningful conclusions and identify areas for future research, as highlighted in various studies (Chen et al., 2022).

This systematic and focused approach ensured a thorough examination of the existing literature, providing a solid foundation for understanding the current landscape and future prospects of AI integration in Education 5.0. By prioritizing studies that explicitly address the advanced applications of AI in Education 5.0, this review offers valuable insights into the transformative potential of this emerging paradigm.

Analysis and Results:

The analysis of existing literature reveals that AI is being utilized in various ways to enhance personalized and adaptive learning, particularly within the framework of Education 5.0. Intelligent Tutoring Systems (ITS) have been shown to effectively emulate human tutors, offering guidance, feedback, and additional resources based on individual student performance. This real-time, personalized assistance enhances the learning experience and promotes a deeper understanding of the material (Al-Emran & Al-Sharafi, 2022). Furthermore, AI-powered personalized learning platforms leverage data analytics to provide customized learning paths, content suggestions, and assessments, catering to the unique needs and preferences of each learner (Lantada, 2020). This empowers students to take ownership of their learning and progress at their own pace.

Adaptive assessment systems, another crucial application of AI in education, utilize algorithms to administer personalized assessments that dynamically adjust to the learner's skill level and knowledge gaps (Rane, Choudhary, & Rane, 2023). This approach provides a more accurate and comprehensive evaluation of students' abilities, enabling educators to identify areas where students may need additional support or challenges.

The literature also highlights the role of AI in fostering innovation and creativity within educational settings, aligning with the goals of Education 5.0 to cultivate 21st-century skills. AI-powered tools can facilitate the development of new pedagogical approaches, support collaborative learning environments, and provide opportunities for experiential learning through simulations and gamified experiences (Aslam et al., 2020). These innovative applications of AI not only enhance student engagement and motivation but also cultivate essential skills such as critical thinking, problem-solving, and creativity.

Diagram 18.1 (available in the Online Appendix link https://tinyurl.com/he50Appendices) showcases the diverse applications of AI in both Education 4.0 and 5.0, emphasizing how these technologies contribute to achieving the goals of personalized learning, adaptive experiences, lifelong learning opportunities, and the fostering of 21st-century skills and innovation. It visually represents the interconnectedness of AI technologies and their impact on various aspects of the educational landscape.

Furthermore, AI is being leveraged to promote lifelong learning and continuous skill development, a key characteristic of Education 5.0. AI-powered learning platforms and micro-credentialing systems enable individuals to acquire new skills and knowledge beyond formal education settings, adapting to the evolving demands of the 21st-century workforce (Tavares et al., 2022). This empowers learners to stay competitive in a rapidly changing job market and pursue their personal and professional development goals.

In summary, the analysis of the literature demonstrates that AI is playing a transformative role in shaping the future of education, particularly in the context of Education 5.0. From personalized learning and adaptive assessments to intelligent tutoring systems and innovative pedagogical approaches, AI is revolutionizing the way we teach and learn. However, it is crucial to address the challenges and ethical considerations associated with AI adoption to ensure its responsible and equitable implementation in educational settings.

Opportunities and Challenges of AI in Education 5.0

The integration of AI in Education 5.0 presents a multifaceted landscape of opportunities and challenges. The potential of AI to revolutionize education is undeniable. Personalized and adaptive learning, powered by AI, has the potential to significantly enhance learning outcomes, cater to diverse learning needs, and promote inclusivity in education (Carayannis & Morawska, 2023). AI-driven tools and platforms can empower students to take control of their learning, providing them with tailored content, real-time feedback, and adaptive assessments that optimize their educational journey (Aslam et al., 2020). Furthermore, AI's ability to automate administrative tasks and streamline curriculum development can free up educators' time, allowing them to focus on more meaningful interactions with students and fostering a more supportive learning environment (Fernández-Cruz & Rodríguez Legendre, 2021).

However, the widespread adoption of AI in education is not without its challenges. Ethical considerations, particularly regarding data privacy and algorithmic bias, are paramount. Safeguarding student data and ensuring that AI systems do not perpetuate existing inequalities or discriminate against certain groups of students are critical for building trust and promoting equitable access to AI-powered educational opportunities (Qiu et al., 2023). Additionally, the digital divide, characterized by disparities in technology and internet access, poses a significant barrier to the equitable implementation of AI in education. Bridging this divide is essential to ensure that all learners, regardless of their socioeconomic backgrounds, can benefit from AI-driven educational advancements.

Transitioning from Education 4.0 to 5.0

Education 4.0, characterized by the integration of technology into traditional teaching methods, has paved the way for the emergence of Education 5.0. While Education 4.0 focuses on enhancing digital literacy and connectivity, Education 5.0 represents a paradigm shift towards AI-driven personalized and adaptive learning experiences (Rane et al., 2023). This transition signifies a deeper integration of AI, moving beyond its role as a supplementary tool in Education 4.0 to becoming a central element that fundamentally transforms how knowledge is acquired, processed, and utilized.

In Education 4.0, AI primarily aids in administrative tasks, assessments, and personalized learning recommendations based on student data. In contrast, Education 5.0 envisions AI's pervasive influence across the entire educational landscape, impacting curriculum design, content delivery, student engagement, and assessment (Rane et al., 2023). AI algorithms in Education 5.0 dynamically adjust learning paths based on individual student progress, preferences, and learning styles, resulting in highly personalized learning experiences.

Furthermore, Education 5.0 emphasizes the development of critical thinking, problem-solving, and creativity skills, with AI serving as both a facilitator and catalyst. It prioritizes interactive, hands-on learning facilitated by AI-driven virtual environments, simulations, and immersive technologies, fostering a more active and engaging learning process.

Table 18.2 (available in the Online Appendix link https://tinyurl.com/he50Appendices) provides a concise comparison between Education 4.0 and Education 5.0, highlighting the key distinctions in their focus, AI integration, pedagogical approaches, and desired learning outcomes. It emphasizes the evolution from technology-enhanced learning in Education 4.0 to a more profound integration of AI for personalized and adaptive learning in Education 5.0.

Collaborative Approaches and the Evolving Role of Educators in AI-Driven Education

The evolving role of educators in the age of AI is another crucial aspect of the discussion. As AI takes on more routine tasks and provides personalized learning experiences, educators need to adapt their roles to become facilitators, mentors, and guides in the AI-enhanced learning process (McDonnell-Naughton & Păunescu, 2022). This requires a shift in pedagogical approaches and a focus on developing students' critical thinking, creativity, and problem-solving skills, which complement the capabilities of AI.

Furthermore, the literature highlights the importance of collaboration and interdisciplinary approaches in harnessing the full potential of AI in education. Partnerships between educators, technologists, policymakers, and industry stakeholders are crucial for developing and implementing effective AI-integrated educational solutions (Lewandowska, Berniak-Woźny, & Ahmad, 2023). By working together, these stakeholders can address the challenges and ethical considerations associated with AI adoption, ensuring its responsible and beneficial use in education.

In conclusion, the integration of AI in Education 4.0 and 5.0 presents a transformative opportunity to create a more personalized, adaptive, and inclusive educational experience. However, it is essential to approach AI adoption with a balanced perspective, considering both the potential benefits and challenges.

Diagram 18.3 (available in the Online Appendix link https://tinyurl.com/he50Appendices) presents a concise overview of the potential benefits and challenges associated with integrating AI into education. It emphasizes the need to consider both aspects for successful AI implementation. A concise overview of the potential benefits and challenges associated with integrating AI into education. It emphasizes the need to consider both aspects for successful AI implementation. By addressing ethical considerations, bridging the digital divide, and fostering collaboration among stakeholders, we can harness the power of AI to shape a future of education that empowers all learners to reach their full potential.

Conclusion

In conclusion, the integration of AI in Education 5.0 heralds a transformative era in education, promising to revolutionize the learning landscape by creating personalized, adaptive, and inclusive environments that cater to the unique needs of every student. The literature underscores the potential of AI to enhance learning outcomes, increase accessibility, and foster the development of essential 21st-century skills. However, the successful realization of this potential, hinges on addressing the challenges and ethical considerations associated with AI adoption.

To fully harness the transformative power of AI in Education 5.0, several recommendations emerge:

- **Prioritize Ethical AI and Inclusivity:** The development and deployment of AI systems must adhere to principles that prioritize fairness, transparency, and accountability. It is crucial to mitigate biases in AI algorithms and safeguard student data privacy to build trust and ensure equitable access to AI-powered educational opportunities (Diaz Lantada, 2020).

- **Bridge the Digital Divide:** Addressing the disparities in technology and internet access is essential to ensure that all learners, regardless of their socioeconomic backgrounds, can benefit from AI-driven educational advancements. This necessitates initiatives to provide equitable access to AI-enabled resources and bridge the gap between those who have and those who do not have access to technology (Tavares et al., 2022).

- **Empower Educators as Facilitators:** As AI takes on more routine tasks, educators need to transition into roles of facilitators, mentors, and guides in the AI-enhanced learning process. Professional development programs should focus on equipping educators with the skills and knowledge to effectively utilize AI tools and foster a student-centered learning environment (Muzira & Bondai, 2020).

- **Foster Collaboration and Interdisciplinary Approaches:** Collaboration among educators, technologists, policymakers, and industry stakeholders is vital for developing and implementing effective AI-integrated educational solutions. By working together, these stakeholders can address the challenges and ethical considerations associated with AI adoption, ensuring its responsible and beneficial use in education (Carayannis & Morawska, 2023).

- **Promote Research and Innovation:** Continuous research and development are necessary to explore the long-term effectiveness of AI in fostering lifelong learning, skill development, and socio-emotional well-being. Additionally, investigating innovative AI applications, such as quantum computing and brain-computer interface integration, can open new avenues for enhancing personalized learning experiences and pushing the boundaries of Education 5.0 (Rane, Choudhary, & Rane, 2023).

By proactively addressing these recommendations and embracing a collaborative and human-centric approach, we can navigate the complexities of AI integration and unlock its full potential to shape a future of education that is not only technologically advanced but also equitable, empowering all learners to thrive in the 21st century.

19

Unlocking English as a Foreign Language (EFL) Teachers' potential in AI adoption: Factors Influencing Teachers' Readiness and challenges[39]

Ngo Van Giang[40] and Tran Ngoc Giang

Abstract

This chapter aims to explore personal reflection of EFL teachers' readiness and challenges regarding their adoption of AI in their teaching practices. A narrative enquiry approach is adopted to offer insights into factors influencing EFL teachers' AI adoption. In-depth interviews of 20 university teachers and document analysis of related technological policies reveal different degrees of readiness for AI adoption. Findings also show that technological literacy, resistance and ICT platforms are major hindrances against their adoption.

Introduction

The rapid integration of Artificial Intelligence (AI) into education is transforming traditional teaching practices, particularly in English as a Foreign Language (EFL) instruction. AI technologies offer tools for personalized learning, automated assessments, and enhanced classroom

---

39 All references, tables, figures, author affiliation and biography used in this chapter are available on the Online Appendix link at https://tinyurl.com/he50Appendices.

40 Corresponding author: gianghanuvn@gmail.com

management, presenting unparalleled opportunities for teachers to improve their pedagogical approaches (Nguyen & Pham, 2022). However, the effective adoption of AI among EFL teachers is contingent upon their readiness, which is influenced by various factors including technological competence, institutional support, and personal motivation.

One of the critical determinants of teachers' readiness is their familiarity and confidence in using AI tools. Teachers with a strong foundation in technological literacy are more likely to embrace AI and integrate it seamlessly into their instruction (Alam & Mohanty, 2023). Conversely, those lacking such skills may perceive AI as a daunting challenge rather than an enabler (Tran & Nguyen, 2022). Institutional factors also play a significant role, as access to robust ICT infrastructure and ongoing professional development are essential for equipping teachers with the skills needed to leverage AI effectively (Nguyen et al., 2023). Without these resources, educators may struggle to keep pace with the rapid advancements in AI technologies.

Challenges further compound these readiness issues. Teachers often cite concerns about the ethical use of AI, including data privacy and the risk of over-reliance on technology, which may hinder students' critical thinking abilities (SpringerLink, 2023). Additionally, the high costs of AI tools and the lack of tailored training programs remain significant barriers to adoption. These complexities lead to the following research questions:

1. What are the major challenges in AI adoption for EFL lecturers in teaching?

2. What are effective AI teaching practices?

3. What can higher education institutions do to prepare EFL lecturers for AI integration in teaching?

Addressing these questions is essential for unlocking the potential of EFL teachers in AI adoption. By fostering technological competence, enhancing institutional support, and mitigating barriers, stakeholders can empower educators to harness AI's transformative potential in education.

The rapid development of Artificial Intelligence (AI) is reshaping higher education, particularly in the domain of English as a Foreign Language (EFL) instruction. As AI technologies revolutionize traditional teaching methods, understanding the factors influencing EFL teachers' readiness and the challenges they face in adopting AI becomes critical. This literature review synthesizes recent research on AI integration in higher education, focusing on EFL lecturers' experiences, readiness, and the challenges that hinder adoption.

The role of AI in higher education for EFL and Technological Competence of teachers

AI technologies have the potential to enhance learning outcomes and teaching efficiency in EFL contexts. Tools such as AI-driven chatbots, virtual tutors, and personalized learning platforms offer new ways to engage students and optimize their learning experience. AI is also widely used in automating repetitive tasks like grading, lesson planning, and generating interactive content (Nguyen & Pham, 2022).

Moreover, AI provides opportunities for personalized learning. Adaptive platforms such as Grammarly and ChatGPT can analyse individual student performance and adjust lessons to meet specific needs, ensuring that students' progress at their own pace. Such tools enable teachers to focus on high-order pedagogical tasks, such as critical thinking and fostering creativity (Tran & Nguyen, 2022). Despite these advancements, the uptake of AI among EFL lecturers remains limited, partly due to varying levels of readiness and awareness.

Technological competence is one of the most significant factors influencing EFL teachers' readiness for AI adoption. Teachers proficient in basic ICT tools such as PowerPoint and Google Classroom are more likely to embrace AI tools. However, a lack of familiarity with advanced AI technologies like automated grading systems and natural language processing tools often acts as a deterrent (Nguyen et al., 2023). Studies highlight that teachers with higher technological literacy are more confident in experimenting with AI tools, whereas those without prior exposure perceive them as complex and intimidating (SpringerLink, 2023).

Training, Professional Development, Personal Motivation and Perception

Professional development programs play a crucial role in enhancing teachers' readiness for AI. Tran and Nguyen (2022) emphasize that tailored training sessions on AI tools can significantly boost teachers' confidence and ability to use AI effectively in their classrooms. However, the availability of such programs is often inconsistent. Many institutions fail to provide structured training, leaving teachers to self-learn or rely on external resources (Nguyen & Pham, 2022). Continuous professional development and access to resources for hands-on practice are thus vital in preparing teachers for AI integration (Cukurova et al., 2024).

Teachers' attitudes and motivation toward AI adoption are also pivotal. Educators who perceive AI as a tool to enhance teaching effectiveness and reduce workload are more likely to adopt it (Nguyen et al., 2023). On the contrary, concerns about losing control over the teaching process or becoming redundant may discourage adoption (Tran & Nguyen, 2022).

Challenges in AI Adoption for EFL Lecturers

Infrastructure, resource constraints and Ethical Concerns

A significant barrier to AI adoption is inadequate infrastructure. Studies reveal that many higher education institutions lack the ICT facilities required to support AI technologies, such as high-speed internet, updated hardware, and AI-compatible software (SpringerLink, 2023). Financial constraints further exacerbate the issue, as premium AI tools often require costly subscriptions, which institutions may not subsidize (Nguyen & Pham, 2022).

Ethical issues, particularly regarding data privacy and security, are prominent among EFL teachers. AI tools often require access to personal and student data, raising concerns about how this data is stored, processed, and protected. The lack of transparency in AI algorithms also adds to the apprehension, with teachers unsure of how decisions are made and whether biases might influence them (Tran & Nguyen, 2022).

Over-Reliance on AI and Lack of Clear Policies

Another challenge is the potential over-reliance on AI, which could undermine students' critical thinking and creativity. Some educators fear that students may use AI tools as shortcuts, bypassing the cognitive processes necessary for language acquisition (Nguyen & Pham, 2022). Moreover, the role of the teacher as a mentor and facilitator might be diminished if AI tools are perceived as replacements rather than supplements (Felix, 2020).

Institutional policies play a crucial role in shaping teachers' readiness for AI adoption. However, many institutions lack clear guidelines on how AI should be integrated into teaching practices. The absence of such policies often leads to inconsistent adoption rates and a lack of accountability for using AI tools (Nguyen et al., 2023).

Need for Supportive Culture

A supportive institutional culture is equally essential. Teachers are more likely to adopt AI if they perceive a collaborative and encouraging environment. Tran and Nguyen (2022) highlight that institutions promoting experimentation and providing platforms for peer learning can significantly enhance adoption rates.

Research Design

This study employs a qualitative research design, which is particularly suited for exploring complex phenomena such as the adoption of Artificial Intelligence (AI) in teaching English as a Foreign Language (EFL). The design facilitates an in-depth understanding of lecturers' perceptions, experiences, and challenges in this area. A narrative inquiry approach was adopted to delve into the personal and professional stories of EFL lecturers, capturing their unique perspectives on integrating AI into their teaching practices (Barkhuizen et al., 2013). By focusing on individual narratives, the study seeks to illuminate the nuanced ways in which technological innovations intersect with pedagogical practices in higher education.

The research was conceptually grounded in three theoretical frameworks: Diffusion of Innovations Theory (Rogers, 1981), Technology Acceptance

Model (TAM) (Davis, 1989), and Technological Pedagogical Content Knowledge (TPACK) (Mishra & Koehler, 2006). These frameworks provided a robust lens for examining the factors influencing AI adoption, the perceived challenges, and the role of institutional and individual readiness. Specifically, these theories informed the development of interview questions, data coding, and thematic analysis, ensuring a rigorous and theoretically sound approach to exploring the research questions.

Participants

The study involved 20 EFL lecturers teaching at both public and private universities in Vietnam. Participants were selected using purposive sampling, ensuring diversity in teaching experiences, institutional contexts, and levels of familiarity with AI technologies. Their teaching experiences ranged from 5 to 20 years, encompassing a variety of specializations within English language teaching, including general English, academic English, and subject-specific English for Special Purposes (ESP).

The inclusion criteria for participants required that they:

1. Be actively teaching English in higher education institutions in Vietnam.

2. Have varying levels of exposure to and familiarity with AI tools used in educational contexts.

3. Be willing to share their reflections on institutional and individual factors affecting AI adoption.

This diverse participant pool allowed the study to capture a wide spectrum of experiences, from technologically novice lecturers to those with advanced technological expertise. Their narratives offer rich insights into both shared and unique challenges encountered in the process of adopting AI in teaching.

Data Collection

The primary method of data collection was semi-structured interviews, which allowed flexibility while ensuring that all key areas of inquiry were addressed. The interview guide was meticulously designed, incorporating elements from the Diffusion of Innovations Theory, TAM, and TPACK frameworks. It covered topics such as:

- Participants' familiarity with AI tools and platforms.
- The perceived benefits and limitations of using AI in teaching.
- Institutional support and barriers to AI integration.
- Individual factors, such as motivation, confidence, and perceived competence in using AI.

Interviews were conducted in various modes, including face-to-face, online video calls, and written responses, depending on participants' preferences and availability. Each interview lasted between 45 and 60 minutes and was audio-recorded with the consent of the participants. Written transcripts were produced verbatim to ensure accuracy and completeness.

In addition to interviews, document analysis was conducted to examine institutional policies, training materials, and technological guidelines related to AI integration. This triangulation of data sources added depth and context to the findings, enabling a more comprehensive understanding of the institutional landscape.

Data Analysis

Thematic analysis, as proposed by Braun and Clarke (2006), was employed to systematically analyse the data. This method was chosen for its flexibility and rigor in identifying, analysing, and reporting patterns within qualitative data. The analysis was carried out in the following stages:

1. Data Familiarization: The interview transcripts and documents were reviewed multiple times to ensure an in-depth understanding of the content. Preliminary notes were taken to highlight recurring ideas and potential areas of interest.

2. Code Generation: A detailed coding process was conducted, wherein segments of the data were assigned descriptive labels. Coding was both inductive, emerging from the data, and deductive, informed by the theoretical frameworks and research questions.

3. **Theme Searching**: Codes were organized into broader themes that captured the essence of the data. Themes were carefully examined for their alignment with the research objectives, ensuring that they addressed the key aspects of AI adoption, challenges, and institutional preparation.

4. **Theme Reviewing**: The identified themes were rigorously reviewed for coherence, consistency, and relevance. This step involved cross-checking themes against the data to ensure that they accurately reflected participants' perspectives.

5. **Theme Definition**: Each theme was clearly defined and named, capturing its specific scope and significance. This process ensured that the themes were distinct, interconnected, and directly addressed the research questions.

6. **Thematic Report**: The final step involved the integration of the themes into a comprehensive narrative, connecting the findings to the theoretical frameworks. The report highlighted key insights into the challenges, practices, and institutional roles in AI adoption for EFL teaching.

This systematic approach ensured a robust and credible analysis, providing a rich, nuanced understanding of the phenomenon under investigation. By grounding the analysis in established theoretical frameworks, the study contributes to a deeper understanding of the interplay between technology, pedagogy, and institutional readiness in the context of AI integration.

Findings and Discussions

The analysis of interview data revealed a range of challenges that EFL lecturers face in adopting Artificial Intelligence (AI) technologies in their teaching practices. A recurring theme was the technological and skill barriers that many lecturers encounter. A significant number of participants reported limited familiarity with advanced AI tools, relying primarily on basic applications such as Google Classroom and PowerPoint. While these tools serve essential purposes, they fall short of leveraging the full potential of AI in teaching. The interviews also revealed a gap in skill development. Many lecturers expressed strong demand for structured, hands-on training programs that could help them integrate AI into lesson planning, assessment, and resource creation more effectively. The lack of confidence in using AI tools was another significant challenge, often linked to insufficient training opportunities and limited chances to practice and experiment with these technologies. These findings align with the observations of Mehdaoui (2024), who emphasize the critical role of professional development in fostering AI adoption.

Infrastructure and access-related challenges also emerged as significant barriers. Many lecturers described inadequate ICT infrastructure in their institutions, pointing to issues such as unreliable internet connectivity, outdated hardware, and the absence of AI-compatible devices. These limitations were compounded by financial constraints, as several AI tools require paid licenses. Participants frequently noted that institutions often do not subsidize such costs, making access to these tools financially prohibitive for many educators. These findings suggest that both systemic and resource-based limitations are significant hurdles to the effective adoption of AI in EFL teaching.

Institutional and policy gaps further exacerbate these challenges. The absence of clear guidelines or comprehensive frameworks for AI integration was a common concern among lecturers. While some institutions provide basic resources or sporadic training, many offer minimal assistance, leaving educators to navigate the complexities of AI adoption independently. This lack of consistent institutional support often discourages lecturers from experimenting with and fully utilizing AI technologies in their teaching.

Ethical and pedagogical concerns were also prominent in the data. Many lecturers expressed apprehension about ensuring equitable access to AI tools for students, particularly those from economically disadvantaged backgrounds. There were also concerns about over-reliance on AI, with participants highlighting the risk of students becoming overly dependent on these technologies for learning tasks, potentially at the expense of critical thinking and creativity. This sentiment was encapsulated in comments that emphasized the passive learning behaviours AI might inadvertently encourage.

Time and workload pressures were another major theme in the findings. Lecturers frequently reported that the demands of their teaching and administrative responsibilities left them with limited time to explore and practice with AI tools. The process of adapting teaching materials and methodologies to incorporate AI was described as labour-intensive and often overwhelming. Several participants noted the difficulty of balancing these additional demands with their already heavy workloads.

Resistance to change, both among peers and within individual practices, also emerged as a challenge. Some lecturers described encountering skepticism or reluctance from colleagues who questioned the reliability or relevance of AI tools in education. Furthermore, transitioning from traditional teaching approaches to AI-driven methods posed a significant challenge, particularly for those who were less familiar with digital tools.

Broader societal and technological challenges, such as the rapid pace of AI advancements and concerns about data privacy, were also highlighted. Participants noted the difficulty of staying updated with the latest AI technologies, which often evolve faster than educators can adapt their practices. There were also ethical concerns regarding the protection of student data and the transparency of AI-driven decision-making processes.

Despite these challenges, the study also identified effective practices for integrating AI into EFL teaching. Many lecturers recognized the potential of AI to enhance personalized learning through adaptive platforms that tailor exercises and feedback based on individual student progress. AI-driven content creation was another area of promise, with tools like ChatGPT and Canva being used to generate lesson plans, multimedia resources, and interactive exercises. Participants also highlighted the role of AI in automating assessment processes, providing instant feedback, and facilitating collaborative and inclusive learning environments. These practices, when combined with proper training and institutional support, could significantly enhance the teaching and learning experience.

The findings of this study reveal a spectrum of readiness and perceptions among EFL lecturers regarding the adoption of AI in their teaching practices. A striking observation is the variation in familiarity with AI tools. While some lecturers demonstrated a high level of familiarity and confidence in using tools like ChatGPT, Canva, and Grammarly, others had minimal exposure and felt hesitant to explore more advanced applications. This disparity underscores the need for targeted training and professional development programs to bridge the skill gap and build confidence among educators. For instance, one participant remarked, "I have used tools like

Google Classroom and Canva, but I am not confident about exploring more advanced AI tools" (Participant, TID04). This comment encapsulates the hesitancy that stems from limited exposure and inadequate training.

Despite these challenges, the study revealed a generally positive outlook among lecturers regarding the potential of AI to transform EFL teaching. Many participants viewed AI as a valuable resource for enhancing efficiency in lesson planning, facilitating personalized learning, and engaging students more effectively. One lecturer noted, "AI can save time and create more interactive lessons" (Participant, TID12). Such perspectives highlight the potential for AI to address some of the long-standing challenges in education, provided that the necessary support systems are in place.

However, significant barriers persist, particularly in terms of infrastructure and access. Poor ICT infrastructure, characterized by weak internet connections and outdated devices, was a recurring issue. One participant pointedly stated, "The ICT infrastructure is inadequate for seamless AI integration" (Participant, TID09). Financial constraints further compounded these challenges, as many lecturers were unable to afford premium AI tools and had to rely on free versions with limited features. These barriers not only limit the adoption of AI but also exacerbate inequalities among educators and institutions.

Time constraints were another critical challenge highlighted by participants. Lecturers described the difficulty of finding time to learn and experiment with AI tools amidst their heavy teaching schedules and administrative responsibilities. One participant explained, "Adopting AI requires time to experiment and understand its applications, which is challenging given the other responsibilities we have as teachers" (Participant, TID08). This lack of time for hands-on practice and integration efforts limits the potential impact of AI in EFL classrooms.

Ethical concerns also featured prominently in the discussions. Many lecturers expressed apprehension about data privacy and the potential for students to become overly dependent on AI for learning tasks. As one participant observed, "There is a risk of students depending too much on AI for answers" (Participant, TID20). These concerns point to the need for clear guidelines and ethical frameworks to govern the use of AI in educational contexts, ensuring that its adoption enhances rather than detracts from the quality of teaching and learning.

In summary, while AI holds significant promises for transforming EFL teaching, its adoption is hindered by a complex interplay of technological, institutional, and personal barriers. Addressing these challenges will require concerted efforts from institutions to provide the necessary training, infrastructure, and policy support. At the same time, fostering a culture of innovation and experimentation among educators will be crucial for unlocking the full potential of AI in education.

Key Challenges in AI Adoption

The findings reveal several systemic, institutional, and personal challenges that hinder EFL lecturers from fully leveraging AI in their teaching practices. Technological and skill barriers emerge as significant obstacles, with many lecturers expressing limited familiarity with advanced AI tools and a lack of confidence due to insufficient training opportunities. Furthermore, inadequate ICT infrastructure and financial constraints exacerbate the problem, leaving many educators unable to access or afford essential AI tools.

Institutional and policy gaps further compound the challenges. The absence of comprehensive guidelines and inconsistent support mechanisms force lecturers to navigate AI adoption independently, often without adequate resources. Additionally, ethical and pedagogical concerns, such as equity in access and the potential for over-reliance on AI, add layers of complexity to the adoption process. Broader societal and technological challenges, such as the rapid pace of AI advancements and concerns over data privacy, also emerge as critical barriers.

Effective AI Teaching Practices

Despite these challenges, this study identifies a range of effective AI teaching practices that can revolutionize EFL education. These include leveraging adaptive learning platforms for personalized instruction, using AI-driven tools for content creation and assessment, and employing gamification and virtual tutors to enhance engagement. Additionally, AI can support inclusive and accessible teaching by offering assistive technologies and translation tools.

The findings also emphasize the importance of promoting ethical AI use. Training students and educators in critical thinking skills to evaluate AI-generated outputs is essential to mitigate risks like misinformation and plagiarism. By integrating AI with pedagogical strategies, educators can foster dynamic, student-centered learning environments that prioritize engagement, inclusivity, and real-world applicability.

The Role of Higher Education Institutions

Higher education institutions play a pivotal role in enabling AI integration in EFL teaching. The study identifies several strategic actions that institutions can undertake to support lecturers. First, providing comprehensive training programs is critical to building lecturers' confidence and competence in using AI tools. This includes hands-on workshops, ongoing professional development opportunities, and focused skill development initiatives.

Second, institutions must prioritize improving ICT infrastructure, ensuring that lecturers have access to high-speed internet, up-to-date devices, and premium AI tools. Financial and technical support, such as subsidized licenses and dedicated IT assistance, can further alleviate barriers to adoption.

Moreover, institutions need to establish clear policies and guidelines that address ethical concerns, incentivize AI use, and promote strategic integration into teaching workflows. Fostering a supportive culture of innovation, encouraging peer collaboration, and addressing equity issues are equally vital for successful AI adoption.

Implications and Future Directions

The integration of AI into EFL teaching offers immense opportunities to enhance instructional efficiency, personalize learning, and prepare students for the demands of a technology-driven world. However, these benefits can only be realized if institutions address the systemic and contextual barriers that hinder adoption. By fostering an ecosystem that combines robust infrastructure, practical training, and a supportive institutional culture, higher education can unlock the full potential of AI in transforming EFL education.

Future research should explore longitudinal impacts of AI integration on both teaching practices and student outcomes. Investigating strategies to mitigate ethical concerns and ensuring equitable access to AI tools will also be critical areas of focus. As AI technologies continue to evolve, a sustained commitment to innovation, collaboration, and critical evaluation will be essential for harnessing their transformative potential in education.

Conclusion

AI is not merely a tool but a catalyst for reimagining EFL teaching and learning. While challenges persist, the effective practices and institutional strategies identified in this study provide a roadmap for overcoming barriers and embracing the opportunities AI presents. By addressing these challenges systematically, educators and institutions can create a future-ready learning environment where technology and pedagogy intersect to enrich the teaching and learning experience.

20

Using ChatGPT to Teach Vietnamese to non-Vietnamese Students[41]

Phạm Thị Hương Quỳnh[42] and Duc Hong Thi Phan

Abstract

The integration of artificial intelligence (AI) into higher education has become an essential driver of innovation and adaptation in the era of Education 5.0. This chapter presents an experimental study on the use of ChatGPT to support Vietnamese language learning for international students. By incorporating AI into language education, the study explores how technological advances can enhance teaching effectiveness, foster learner engagement, and contribute to cultural exchange. The experiment involved preparatory students who planned to pursue higher education in Vietnam. The experimental group was guided to use ChatGPT in their language practice, while a control group followed traditional methods. Assessment results revealed that students who integrated ChatGPT into their study routines achieved higher performance scores and expressed greater enthusiasm for learning. These findings suggest that AI-driven tools, when applied appropriately, not only improve language acquisition but also enrich the broader educational experience of international learners.

---

41 All references, tables, figures, author affiliation and biography used in this chapter are available on the Online Appendix link at https://tinyurl.com/he50Appendices.

42 Corresponding author: hqp2000@gmail.com

Introduction

Language education plays a pivotal role in promoting cross-cultural understanding and fostering international collaboration in higher education. Teaching Vietnamese to international students is not only a linguistic task but also an important contribution to the dissemination of Vietnamese culture. With the growing number of international learners choosing Vietnam as a study destination, there is an urgent need to explore innovative methods that align with the principles of Education 5.0 - personalization, digital transformation, and learner-centered approaches.

This chapter addresses two key research questions:

1. Why should ChatGPT be integrated into the teaching of Vietnamese?

2. To what extent can ChatGPT enhance the effectiveness of Vietnamese language education for foreign learners?

The significance of these questions lies in the shift from traditional teaching models to technology-enhanced learning environments. Artificial intelligence, particularly ChatGPT, enables personalized instruction, interactive practice, and immediate feedback—features that are central to Education 5.0. This chapter, therefore, presents an experimental study that investigates the role of ChatGPT in supporting Vietnamese language acquisition among international students. The study highlights how integrating AI into language pedagogy can contribute to more engaging, efficient, and culturally responsive learning experiences, positioning Vietnamese language education within the broader movement toward innovation in higher education.

The year 2025 marks a "restructuring" of language-education research under the influence of AI in general and ChatGPT in particular. A position piece in *System* argues that generative AI is reshaping core constructs in applied linguistics—from notions of input/output to classroom assessment—and calls for new research designs and professional standards for language teachers (Chapelle, 2025). Recent systematic reviews in Zhu and Wang (2025), Feng et al. (2025) document a clear shift in the field: AI is most frequently used for writing, vocabulary, and assessment, while ethical concerns, equity, and AI literacy remain underexamined. For less commonly taught languages (LCTLs) such as Vietnamese, the evidence base is still thin, and findings from English cannot be transferred uncritically (Kim, 2025).

Regarding pedagogical effectiveness, a classroom study in Abdelhalim and Alsehibany (2025) shows that integrating ChatGPT for vocabulary study and retention improves learning outcomes through interactive practice, contextrich examples, and principled repetition. This has direct implications for Vietnamese, where classifiers and reduplication patterns benefit from abundant, varied contextualization. Complementing this, a comparative study in Shi *et al.* (2025) finds that ChatGPT can provide writing feedback that rivals traditional automated writing evaluation (AWE) systems in improving text quality and strengthening learners' "ideal L2 writing self," suggesting a teacher–AI hybrid feedback model. At the same time, Saricaoglu and Bilki (2025) cautions that while GPT4 is highly accurate at flagging problems, it can be less specific on higherlevel criteria such as argument development and coherence; teacher guidance and validation therefore remain essential.

For reading input, Odo (2025) reports that AIsimplified texts can be as comprehensible as—sometimes more comprehensible than—humansimplified texts, though quality varies by task and reading criterion. This suggests that Vietnamese curricula can use ChatGPT to generate graded readers aligned with proficiency levels, while carefully checking linguistic accuracy, naturalness, and cultural nuance. In writing instruction, Lu and Zeng (2025) shows that ChatGPTgenerated model texts used as a feedback instrument led to improved learner writing and generally positive perceptions, yet students still worry about decontextualization and slightly unnatural style—issues that need tailoring for Vietnamese genres and registers. Equity also matters: Kim (2025) analyses indicate that AI may benefit some learner profiles more than others, underscoring the need for compensatory scaffolding in diverse Vietnamese classes.

Directly for teaching Vietnamese to nonnative learners, Le and Ziegler (2025) presents action research on technologymediated taskbased language teaching (TBLT) for beginners, offering task frameworks, tools, and languagedevelopment measures that Vietnamese programs can adopt. Evidence from Shin and Choi (2025) shows that AI chatbots can enhance grammar learning depending on proficiency level and task type; this can transfer to Vietnamese features such as address terms, classifier usage, and modal particles through scripted dialogue practice. Finally, Issa and HahnPowell (2025)'s research on computerassisted pronunciation training

(CAPT) highlights the value of automatic speech recognition and realtime feedback; for Vietnamese - a tonal, isolating language - combining ChatGPT (to generate dialogues and minimal pairs) with CAPT tools is promising, provided taskbased evaluation and teacher oversight mitigate model "overconfidence".

Empirical Research Design

The study adopted an empirical research design, grounded in verifiable evidence, to examine how artificial intelligence can reshape language learning in the era of Education 5.0. The process was structured to combine traditional pedagogy with AI-enhanced methods, thereby reflecting the dual focus on innovation and adaptation.

Step 1 – Introducing learning content. Students were first provided with time-related vocabulary (spring, summer, autumn, winter, hour, minute, second, hot, cold, cool, warm) and guided through grammar structures such as: *"What season is it now?"*, *"How is the weather in autumn?"*, *"What time is it?"*. This ensured a common baseline of knowledge across both groups.

Step 2 – Visual engagement. To represent the learner-centered principles of Education 5.0, the vocabulary was introduced through visual materials and interactive examples, catering to diverse learning preferences.

Step 3 – AI-assisted review. The experimental group was instructed to use ChatGPT to consolidate their vocabulary and grammar practice. By engaging with AI, students were able to access immediate feedback, generate contextualized examples, and personalize their practice routines. This represents a core principle of Education 5.0: leveraging technology to create adaptive, self-directed learning experiences.

Step 4 – Assessment of outcomes. Both groups undertook the same set of tasks designed to evaluate vocabulary retention and grammar application. The use of standardized exercises provided reliable evidence for comparison.

Step 5 – Comparative analysis. Performance between the experimental and control groups was compared to determine the added value of integrating ChatGPT into the learning process.

Step 6 – Drawing conclusions. Findings were synthesized to assess how AI tools can enhance both cognitive outcomes (knowledge acquisition) and affective outcomes (motivation, engagement).

The study employed quantitative methods, relying on measurable indicators such as test scores and performance percentages. This evidence-based approach provided a rigorous foundation for evaluating effectiveness. At the same time, the design highlighted how AI integration transforms language education from a teacher-centered process into a dynamic, technology-supported, learner-centered experience—a defining feature of Higher Education 5.0.

Empirical Research Process

The participants in this study were international students enrolled in *Vietnamese language preparatory courses* within the Vietnamese Studies Department. These courses are designed to prepare learners for academic majors at Vietnamese universities once they achieve the required language proficiency certification. The participants, aged between 18 and 22, represented a range of national and cultural backgrounds, reflecting the growing diversity and internationalization of higher education in Vietnam.

To ensure balanced comparison, the students were divided into two groups of equal size: an *experimental group* (n = 10) and a *control group* (n = 10). All participants' identities were anonymized and personal information kept strictly confidential in line with ethical research practices.

Both groups were enrolled in *A2-level courses* according to the Vietnamese proficiency framework established by the Ministry of Education and Training. Importantly, the groups were similar in terms of national distribution and overall language abilities, thereby providing a fair basis for comparison. Each group studied the same lesson content and completed the same assignments. The key difference was that the experimental group received structured guidance on integrating ChatGPT into their learning, while the control group relied solely on traditional self-reflection and review methods.

The choice of participants underscores the essence of Education 5.0, where diversity and inclusivity are central to the learning process. Bringing together learners from multiple nationalities not only enriches classroom interactions but also positions Vietnamese language education as a bridge for cross-cultural exchange and global academic mobility. Within this environment, the integration of AI tools such as ChatGPT represents a step toward personalized, adaptive learning pathways, aligning with the vision of higher education systems that are innovative, globally connected, and student-centered.

Research Design – Empirical Process

This study employed an empirical research design to examine how artificial intelligence, represented by ChatGPT, can be integrated into Vietnamese language instruction for international students. The design combined conventional pedagogical approaches with AI-enhanced methods, reflecting the dual commitment of Higher Education 5.0 to both innovation and inclusivity.

Participants and Context

The research was conducted with preparatory students enrolled in the Vietnamese Studies Department, who were preparing to pursue higher education programs in Vietnam after attaining the required language proficiency. The participants came from diverse national and cultural backgrounds, mirroring the increasing internationalization of higher education in Vietnam. Their diversity provided an ideal context for testing AI-supported learning, as it highlights the need for flexible, personalized approaches that respond to different linguistic and cultural experiences.

Empirical Research Steps

The experimental procedure was structured into six steps, ensuring both methodological rigor and alignment with the learner-centered ethos of Education 5.0:

1. *Introduction of learning content*: Students were presented with time-related vocabulary (spring, summer, autumn, winter, hour, minute, second, hot, cold, cool, warm) and grammar structures

such as: *"What season is it now?", "How is the weather in autumn?", "What time is it?"*. This created a shared baseline of linguistic knowledge.

2. *Visual engagement*: Vocabulary and grammar were introduced through visual materials, supporting multimodal and culturally inclusive learning styles. This approach encouraged students to connect abstract concepts with concrete images, reducing language barriers for learners from different backgrounds.

3. *AI-assisted practice:* The experimental group was guided to use ChatGPT as a review tool. By interacting with the AI, students were able to access instant feedback, generate context-rich examples, and customize their learning pathways. This step embodies the principles of Education 5.0 by fostering self-directed, adaptive learning that respects individual pace and style.

4. *Assessment of learning outcomes:* Both groups completed equivalent tasks designed to measure vocabulary retention and grammar application. These assessments provided quantifiable evidence of learning progress.

5. *Comparative analysis:* The results of the experimental group and the control group were compared in order to determine the effectiveness of integrating ChatGPT into the learning process.

6. *Synthesis and conclusion:* The findings were analyzed to identify not only cognitive outcomes (knowledge acquisition) but also affective dimensions, such as motivation, engagement, and learner confidence in using Vietnamese.

Methodological Considerations

The study relied on quantitative methods, using test scores and performance percentages to provide objective measures of effectiveness. At the same time, the design highlighted the qualitative impact of AI on student engagement and intercultural learning experiences. In doing so, the research reflects the broader vision of *Higher Education 5.0*: a system that combines technology and human interaction, supports global academic mobility, and creates personalized, learner-centered educational environments.

Results

Vocabulary Retention

In *Exercise 1*, which assessed vocabulary through speaking and writing, most students in both groups were able to recall and use the target words, though with notable differences. In the experimental group, only 1 out of 10 students failed to remember a given word, meaning that 90% retained all or most of the 11 new words. In contrast, the control group demonstrated lower retention rates:

- 40% forgot words such as *spring, winter, hot, cold,* and *cool*.
- 50% failed to recall *minute* and *second*.
- 30% did not remember *hot*.
- No student in the control group managed to recall all 11 words, while one experimental student (SV8) achieved full recall.

These results highlight the value of AI-assisted learning in reinforcing vocabulary. ChatGPT not only supported memorization but also encouraged repeated practice and contextual application, key principles of personalized learning emphasized in Education 5.0.

Grammar Structures

Performance also differed significantly for *Exercise 2*, which tested grammar application through speaking and writing.

- For Structure 1 (*What season is it now?*), 90% of experimental students met requirements compared with 60% of control students.
- For Structure 2 (*How is the weather in autumn?*), 90% of experimental students were successful, while only 50% of control students achieved accuracy.
- For Structure 3 (*What time is it?*), 80% of experimental students succeeded compared with just 40% of control students.

The results suggest that ChatGPT-based practice improved not only vocabulary but also syntactic mastery. Learners were able to practice sentence formation in interactive, low-pressure settings, reflecting the adaptive and student-centered methods of Higher Education 5.0.

Storytelling and Communicative Skills

In *Exercise 3*, students were asked to tell a story using at least four new words and two grammar structures. This higher-order task required both vocabulary recall and creative application. The outcomes were as follows:

- *Experimental group*: 50% scored Excellent (8–10), 40% scored Fairly Good (6–7), and 10% were Average (5).
- *Control group*: 20% scored Excellent, 40% Fairly Good, and 30% Average.

No student in either group scored below 5. The experimental group, however, demonstrated a *30% higher rate of Excellent performance* and a *20% lower rate of Average performance* compared with the control group.

This finding is particularly meaningful in the context of Education 5.0. Storytelling integrates cognitive and affective learning outcomes: knowledge of grammar and vocabulary, creativity, and confidence in communication. ChatGPT provided a scaffold for students to experiment with language in engaging contexts, helping them transform input into authentic expression.

Student Attitudes

A post-experiment survey assessed students' perceptions of ChatGPT. Results showed that:

- 70% reported positive attitudes ("liked"),
- 30% were neutral, and
- None expressed negative attitudes.

In terms of effectiveness:

- 80% rated ChatGPT as effective,
- 20% rated it as normal.

These attitudes demonstrate the motivational benefits of incorporating AI into language education. Students reported greater enjoyment and less pressure during learning, aligning with Education 5.0's vision of inclusive, engaging, and emotionally supportive learning environments.

Findings

The results of this experiment indicate that integrating ChatGPT into Vietnamese language learning:

1.Enhances knowledge acquisition – students in the experimental group achieved higher vocabulary retention and grammar accuracy.

2.Supports personalized practice – learners benefited from immediate, adaptive feedback tailored to their performance.

3.Encourages creativity and engagement – storytelling outcomes illustrate how AI tools can foster authentic language use.

4.Promotes positive attitudes – students felt more motivated and less constrained, reducing barriers to learning.

In the framework of *Higher Education 5.0*, these outcomes exemplify how AI can transform traditional teacher-centered instruction into a student-centered, technology-supported, and culturally inclusive learning experience. The findings provide evidence that AI, when carefully integrated, can serve not only as a tool for knowledge delivery but also as a catalyst for learner empowerment and intercultural exchange.

Discussion

The findings of this study underscore the transformative potential of AI in language education. The experimental group consistently outperformed the control group across vocabulary retention, grammar mastery, and storytelling tasks, while also reporting higher levels of motivation and engagement. These outcomes suggest that ChatGPT can effectively support both the cognitive dimension of learning (knowledge acquisition and skill development) and the affective dimension (confidence, creativity, and enthusiasm).

From the perspective of Higher Education 5.0, the results illustrate a shift from traditional teacher-centered instruction toward a learner-centered and technology-supported model. By providing instant feedback, adaptive examples, and opportunities for creative expression, ChatGPT enabled students to practice in ways that respected their individual learning styles and cultural backgrounds. This aligns with the broader aim of Education 5.0 to integrate personalization, inclusivity, and innovation into higher education.

Importantly, the study highlights the role of AI not as a replacement for teachers, but as a collaborative partner in the learning process. Teachers remain crucial in designing meaningful tasks, ensuring academic integrity, and contextualizing content, while AI can reduce routine workload and provide students with immediate, tailored support. This human–AI partnership represents a sustainable model for future higher education, in which technology amplifies rather than diminishes the educator's role.

The experiment also demonstrates how AI can enhance the internationalization of education. Students from diverse cultural and linguistic backgrounds were able to engage more confidently with Vietnamese, a less commonly taught language, by leveraging AI tools. This suggests that AI has the capacity to bridge linguistic gaps, expand access to underrepresented languages, and facilitate cross-cultural academic mobility—a priority for global higher education in the 21st century.

Looking ahead, the study provides evidence that AI-driven tools like ChatGPT can contribute to the future of higher education innovation. By embedding AI into language learning, universities can design more engaging curricula, support students in personalized ways, and cultivate the skills of adaptability, creativity, and digital literacy. These are the very competencies demanded by Education 5.0, where technology and human values intersect to prepare students for uncertain and dynamic futures.

Conclusion

This study explored the integration of ChatGPT into Vietnamese language instruction for international students, marking one of the first attempts to apply AI to the teaching of Vietnamese as a foreign language. The experimental results showed that students who used ChatGPT achieved higher performance in vocabulary retention, grammar application, and storytelling tasks compared with those who relied on traditional methods. Equally important, students expressed more positive attitudes toward learning, reporting higher levels of motivation, confidence, and enjoyment.

In the broader context of Higher Education 5.0, these findings illustrate how AI can enrich teaching and learning by fostering personalized, inclusive, and adaptive learning experiences. ChatGPT functioned not as a substitute for teachers but as a complementary partner, offering instant feedback, creative prompts, and opportunities for self-directed practice. For international students, particularly those navigating cross-cultural environments, AI support helped reduce learning pressure and created a more engaging entry point into Vietnamese language and culture.

The research therefore contributes to both theory and practice. It addresses a clear gap in the literature by providing empirical evidence for AI-assisted Vietnamese language education, while also suggesting practical ways to integrate AI into curricula in ways that empower students and support teachers. Looking forward, further studies with larger and more diverse cohorts are recommended, as well as continued exploration of ethical considerations, data accuracy, and culturally sensitive applications of AI in education. This experiment shows that when used with care, AI can become more than just a tool — it can serve as a partner that inspires innovation in higher education, helping us move closer to the vision of Education 5.0: collaboration between humans and technology, learning that reaches across cultures, and classrooms that truly place students at the center.

www.ingramcontent.com/pod-product-compliance
Lightning Source LLC
Chambersburg PA
CBHW071403300426
44114CB00016B/2172